Archaeology, Sexism, and Scandal

Archaeology, Sexism, and Scandal

The Long-Suppressed Story of One Woman's Discoveries
and the Man Who Stole Credit for Them

Second Edition

Alan Kaiser

Foreword by
Zofia H. Archibald

ROWMAN & LITTLEFIELD
Lanham • Boulder • New York • London

Published by Rowman & Littlefield
An imprint of The Rowman & Littlefield Publishing Group, Inc.
4501 Forbes Boulevard, Suite 200, Lanham, Maryland 20706
www.rowman.com

86-90 Paul Street, London, EC2A 4NE

British Library Cataloguing in Publication Information Available

Library of Congress Cataloging-in-Publication Data

Names: Kaiser, Alan, author.
Title: Archaeology, sexism, and scandal : the long-suppressed story of one
   woman's discoveries and the man who stole credit for them / Alan Kaiser.
   Other titles: Long-suppressed story of one woman's discoveries and the man
   who stole credit for them
Description: Second edition. | Lanham : Rowman & Littlefield, [2023] |
   Includes bibliographical references and index. | Summary: "This new
   edition provides a summary of these new archival discoveries and
   assesses their impact on our understanding of the decisions Ellingson
   and Robinson made"-- Provided by publisher.
Identifiers: LCCN 2023003326 (print) | LCCN 2023003327 (ebook) | ISBN
   9781538174968 (cloth) | ISBN 9781538174975 (paperback) | ISBN
   9781538174982 (ebook)
Subjects: LCSH: Ellingson, Mary Ross, 1908-1993. | Women
   archaeologists--United States--Biography. | Archaeologists--United
   States--Biography. | Excavations (Archaeology)--Greece--Olynthus
   (Extinct city) | Robinson, David M. (David Moore), 1880-1958. |
   Plagiarism--United States--History--20th century. | Olynthus (Extinct
   city)
Classification: LCC CC115.E45 K35 2023 (print) | LCC CC115.E45 (ebook) |
   DDC 930.1092 [B]--dc23/eng/20230126
LC record available at https://lccn.loc.gov/2023003326
LC ebook record available at https://lccn.loc.gov/2023003327

The second edition of this book is dedicated to all the invisible archaeologists: the unacknowledged who, because of their gender, religious, racial, or other identity toiled on excavations but never saw their names on the publications they helped produce. This is the story of one invisible archaeologist for whom the evidence survived, and it must stand as a proxy for all those whose names and contributions to the field we will never know.

Contents

~

Acknowledgments

I would like to thank the University of Evansville's Alumni Research and Scholarly Activity Fellowship Committee for their support of my research. Also a number of librarians have been very helpful and generous with their time: Jennifer Ford, Jeffrey Boyce, and Jessica Leming of the Special Collections, University of Mississippi Libraries; James Stimpert of the Ferdinand Hamburger Archives in the Sheridan Libraries at Johns Hopkins University; and Margaret Atwater-Singer, Kathryn Bartelt, and Laura Summers of the University of Evansville's Bower Surheinrich Library as well as interns Stephanie Marcotte, Hilary Wolkan, and Dominique DePriest who helped to organize and digitize Mary Ross Ellingson's papers and photos. I am also indebted to Barbara Petersen for sharing Ellingson's correspondence with me as well as stories about her mother. Rowman and Littlefield editors Andrea O. Kendrick and Leanne Silverman supported this project from the beginning and put me in touch with excellent peer reviewers who had much useful advice. Kendrick had such a strong belief in this project and showed such a tenacity in seeing it through that I have doubts this book would ever have been published without her. Their successor at Rowman and Littlefield, Erinn Slanina, suggested the idea for a second edition and helped to shepherd the process. Gregory Britton, editorial director at Johns Hopkins University Press is spearheading the effort to gain Mary Ellingson recognition for her work. I am also deeply appreciative of others who contacted me after the first edition of the book came out to provide me information I had not known, particularly Miriam Dyak for stories about her mother, Gladys Weinberg, and Steven Holzer, for a thorough analysis of the legal issues surrounding questions of plagiarism. Countless others, too numerous to mention by name, helped me with my research, particularly the many people at conferences and lectures who told me stories of these archaeologists and gave me ideas for new directions into which I could take my work. Finally, I must thank fellow archaeologist and my wife Christine Lovasz-Kaiser, who patiently combed through archives with me, edited drafts of my work, and offered invaluable suggestions that made this a much stronger work; her belief in this project never wavered even when mine did. Sharing a road trip to Oxford, Mississippi, with her made it the adventure of a lifetime.

~

Foreword

It is a real pleasure for me, as a co-director of the ongoing field project at ancient Olynthos (2014–2024), to write these words in warm support of this second edition of Alan Kaiser's book. Here is a detective story that deserves a wide public, an intriguing mystery that takes in a wide cast of characters from 1930s North American campuses and European heritage institutions. This highly readable account delves into the history of expanding research horizons, as universities grew their faculty and disciplines in response to demand for student places, between the 1920s and 1960s. It explores the lives of young researchers, men and women, who wanted to become archaeologists in the Mediterranean area, and needed to fulfil their fieldwork experience at ancient sites. It is also a fascinating insight into the value of personal, as well as public archives, and how the discovery of connections between personal and public records can change the ways in which we think about the recent, as well as the remote past. Readers will find that it was not the author who sought out Mary Ross Ellington, but Mary herself who seems to have found him as an eloquent advocate.

There is, indeed, a tale of sexism and academic scandal within these pages, but this exciting behind-the-scenes account of archaeology in Greece during the early 1930s, and the consequences that these experiences had for those who took part, is a bigger story than some plain facts about plagiarism. The contents of this book are far more intriguing, and revealing, than reviews of the first edition have intimated. It is impossible to consider the 'authorship question' without also taking account of the nexus of relationships that researchers found themselves in. Archaeology, like other interdisciplinary subjects, requires teamwork, cooperation, and a shared understanding of goals and the means to achieve them. The mutual codependence among archaeologists working on a project makes it hard to decide exactly who gets to publish what.

Helen Mary Magdalene Ross Ellingson was a young Canadian archaeologist who joined the excavations at Olynthos, in northern Greece, in 1931, as a graduate student. She was a remarkable woman, one of a tiny number of women who completed a PhD in those years, as well as a master's qualification. Even at the time when she returned to academic teaching, at the University of Evansville, in the 1960s, academic faculty often lacked PhDs. Mary became an undergraduate student of classics at the University of Alberta at Edmonton in 1925. In 1930, on the recommendation of her professors at Edmonton, she moved to Baltimore, and on to Johns Hopkins University to study classical archaeology. Her professor, and doctoral supervisor at Johns Hopkins, was professor of classics David Moore Robinson. Mary was one of three women graduate students, along with Gladys Davidson (later Davidson Weinberg), and Sarah Freeman, who were tasked by Robinson with supervising dozens of workmen in trenches during the 1931 season. Mary was a careful, meticulous field worker, who kept her own records of progress and of finds, as well as completing the site notebooks.

Alan Kaiser uses Mary's letters to family members, and her photographic archive, which were bequeathed by Mary's daughter to the University of Evansville, as a resource to understand better what took place at Olynthos, and how Mary responded to the research challenges that the excavations posed. Having seen the site notebooks in copies that were made for Julia Vokotopoulou, the Greek archaeologist and museum director at Thessaloniki from 1982 to 1995, it is clear to me that the data that Alan Kaiser has collected from the Evansville University archive enhances our knowledge of the first Olynthos excavations in many ways. Mary's letters and photographs offer an additional, professional, as well as personal angle on this work, as well as offering insights into the other archaeologists working at Olynthos, most of whom went on to become leading professionals in the field.

Mary married in 1939, the year in which she completed her PhD, based on her research of terracotta figurines at Olynthos. Alan Kaiser's comparison of her master's and doctoral dissertations with the published texts of Olynthos volumes VII and XIV shows that Robinson effectively published Mary's master's text under his own name in volume VII, and part of her doctoral dissertation in the first chapter of volume XIV. It is not clear why Robinson chose not to include Mary's name in either of these volumes, even though George

Mylonas published his dissertation on the Neolithic settlement as volume I of the Olynthos monograph series; James Walter Graham co-authored volume VIII, the Hellenic House, with Robinson, and Paul Clement co-authored volume IX, on the Chalcidic Mint. This was a manifest injustice to Mary, the quality of whose research was recognised by Robinson in letters to Mary (as well as by reviewers, who assumed that the work was Robinson's).

Kaiser explores the story of Mary Ellingson's career as a classical archaeologist, putting her into the context of her contemporaries. I am convinced that she deserves to have her authorship of volume VII and co-authorship of volume XIV recognised by the Library of Congress.

The closing sections of the book reflect on the role of women in classical archaeology, over the course of the twentieth century. Today, the three directors at Olynthos are all women, in a diverse field team. This gives a flavour of change over the past century. It will be up to the upcoming generation of scholars to decide what differences, if any, this has made to archaeology.

— Zofia H. Archibald, co-director of Olynthos Project, and reader, archaeology, classics, and Egyptology, University of Liverpool

~

Preface

This book was not supposed to be a big deal. I remember describing it in my original proposal to Rowman and Littlefield as my "stolen-moments project." To be honest, when they sent me a contract for the book, I was not certain what I was opening at first. What neither I nor anyone at the publishing house could have imagined was that we were creating a work that spoke to the moment. The responses in reviews were good, but the personal messages people sent me often felt overwhelming. Older women who had worked as archaeologists for years wrote about the kinship they felt with Mary Ellingson. Younger women and people of color early in their careers told me about their struggles against systemic sexism and racism. High school students have written to me and even asked for autographs explaining they planned to become the archaeologist Ellingson could never quite be. The tremendous reaction to the book's publication as well as the way the world of archaeology has changed so rapidly in this short space of time have made it clear it is time to reconsider and rework this book. It is time for a new edition.

A second edition of *Archaeology, Sexism, and Scandal* offers three opportunities to improve it that were simply not available in 2014 when it was first published: to celebrate an accomplishment, to answer unanswered questions based on new information, and to reflect on the place of Mary Ellingson and classical archaeology within the broader history of the feminist movement. Taking advantage of these opportunities, every chapter in this book has been revised, augmented, and updated to a degree that is unusual with new editions, making it a very different work from the original. To explain how and why, it is best to start with that first opportunity a new edition presents, the opportunity to celebrate.

A Time to Celebrate

When Johns Hopkins University Press published *Excavations at Olynthus VII* in the 1930s and the first chapter of *Olynthus XIV* in the 1950s, on the title page the editors listed the sole author as David Robinson. As *Archaeology, Sexism, and Scandal* shows, he did not actually write these works, instead he took the thesis and dissertation of Mary Ellingson, removed her name, and submitted the texts to the Press. Ellingson's thesis and dissertation record the "one woman's discoveries" referred to in the subtitle of this book, with Robinson, of course, being the "man who stole credit for them." There is no reason to believe anyone at Johns Hopkins knew what he was doing, especially since he signed a form claiming authorship of the works. When the Press submitted forms to the Library of Congress to copyright the works, they listed Robinson as the sole author. Johns Hopkins University Press renewed the copyright in the 1980s and so remains the copyright holder even though all fourteen volumes of the series have gone out of print and no plans exist to reprint them.

Once editors at the Press learned of Robinson's deception in 2022, they vowed to act. After extensive consultation with personnel at the university and publishing house and hearing no objections, they have submitted a change of author form to the Library of Congress for *Olynthus VII* and requested Ellingson be added as a contributor to *Olynthus XIV*. As holders of the copyright, they have every right to make this change and there seems little reason to believe the Library of Congress will deny the request. To my knowledge, the Library of Congress has never been asked to posthumously restore the name of the true author to a plagiarized work. It is only a symbolic step and one about which neither Ellingson nor Robinson will ever know since each passed away long ago, but it is the only way to offer Ellingson some degree of recognition for her work. This book, therefore, inspired a change in history. That is worth celebrating.

New Information

A second opportunity a new edition of this book presents is to include new information. So much previously unpublished documentation has emerged since the original printing that I have been forced to rewrite large portions of this book. After *Archaeology, Sexism, and Scandal* first came out, others curious about the history of archaeology and particularly the people discussed in these pages conducted their own research, uncovering primary-source material about which I had been unaware when I first wrote. Recent publications based on these materials discussing Ellingson, David Robinson, and Georg von Peschke required me to reconsider some of my conclusions since they threw details about the motivations and decisions of some of those in Ellingson's world into much sharper focus. Some of these researchers have also come across more surprising and even shocking anecdotes that illuminate the characters and times vividly. Canadian readers also encouraged me to seek books and journal articles about the historical context of Ellingson's home country, context that better explains her decision-making process. Incorporating information from these new sources has made for a much clearer narrative.

The book also inspired readers with firsthand knowledge of the events I mentioned to contact me and share details about which I could never have known. I heard from Gladys Weinberg's daughter, many of George Hanfmann's graduate students, and a retired lawyer conversant in copyright law among others. These contacts spurred me to interview some of the individuals who reached out to me or people they mentioned who were relatives, friends, or colleagues of Ellingson, Robinson, or others discussed in the book. These interviews were a great deal of fun, and I met some wonderful people. I include much of what they had to say in the pages that follow, sometimes using direct quotes to preserve the tone and spirit of our conversation.

The original publication of the book made others curious about the documents they had access to relating to Ellingson, Robinson, and the Olynthus project. People shared unpublished information from archives and other sources. In one case, a sleuth at Johns Hopkins University Press uncovered paperwork of which the Johns Hopkins archivists had been unaware when I had originally contacted them. These clever detectives pushed me to track down more historic records that I had not thought to seek when first researching the book. The most unexpected find was David Robinson's last will and testament, which revealed his acts of plagiarism were still on his mind in the month before his death. That will encouraged me to reinterpret Robinson's assessment of his own actions.

And then there were people who thought my interpretations were wrong, opinions they either told me, wrote to me, or put in print in reviews. In some cases, I had to agree. As I look back at portions of what I wrote in the first edition, some interpretations appear naïve. In other cases, their criticisms prodded me to seek new evidence to defend a claim I made and in which I still believe. Either way, the current text is stronger thanks to their challenges.

Many readers and reviewers of the first edition were quite taken with Ellingson's photographs and felt they explained details of the story in a way words cannot. This edition, therefore, contains new, never-before published images. Once the original book came out, it also became clear that some of the images were difficult to read or obscure. I have edited or replaced these to resolve these problems. Readers have delighted in pointing out or asking about details in some of the photographs, which led me to augment many captions, sharing significant, interesting, or even charming elements that I fear readers might otherwise miss when perusing them. I hope the captions as well as the discussion of images in the text will guide readers to discover other aspects of the visuals they, and I, may not have otherwise noticed.

Archaeology and Feminism

A new edition offers a third opportunity, to briefly contemplate the impact of the feminist political movement on the history of archaeology and lives of archaeologists, namely on Mary Ellingson. Some college faculty who teach upper-level courses on subjects such as women in the sciences or the history of archaeological method and theory have been struck by what a useful case study Ellingson provides, allowing them to explore their class themes through the lens of one person. Ellingson's experiences and setbacks are illustrative, but the joy she found in her life, particularly while working at Olynthus, makes hers an inspiring case study. At the request of some of these professors, I have included a final appendix in which I muse about the impact of the feminist movement on archaeology, classical archaeology, and Ellingson's life. Hopefully this appendix will make the book more useful in these classes.

For anyone who read the first edition of this book, get ready for something new. The story of Ellingson, Robinson, plagiarism, and even that painting is about to get a lot more compelling and the ending a lot more satisfying. For the reader who is new to this book, prepare to travel to a famed excavation in Greece with a charming and witty aspiring archaeologist as a guide. And follow along as mystery arises and the path to solving it takes some surprising turns.

~

Introduction

A Great Archeological Discovery

Although they rarely admit it, all archaeologists sometimes think about what their greatest discovery might be. I once helped excavate the remains of a nearly perfectly preserved human skeleton. It was incredible, but I would not call it the greatest find of my career. At a site in Spain my team found a tiny glass bead shaped to look like the face and head of the Egyptian goddess Isis made by Phoenician glass smiths in the eastern Mediterranean. That was spectacular, but still not the greatest. I worked on a project on the Caribbean island of Nevis searching for a lost eighteenth-century synagogue. At one point we had to hack our way through the rain forest with machetes, which was a great deal of fun, but we did not find the synagogue, so it was also not the greatest. I have worked on other archaeological projects in Italy, at Pompeii, in Greece, Israel, England, and several places in the United States. Despite this wide variety of possibilities, where I made my greatest discovery is the last place anyone would have expected, especially me. The moment before I made my career-defining discovery, I was not holding a trowel and sweating at a dusty site. Instead, I was holding a red pen while sitting at my desk in my university office, contemplating a pile of student papers. The stack did not seem to shrink despite my best efforts. At that moment I could not possibly have understood that I was about to make the archaeological discovery of a lifetime.

Late on that November afternoon in 2003, I drew the next paper from the stack and sighed. The name on the paper belonged to a student who usually did poor work, always waiting until the night before an assignment was due

1

to complete it. Outside rain fell and the wind blew, inside all was unusually quiet as no one seemed to be around. Standing to stretch my legs, I wandered into the suite outside my office, looking for anything to distract me. We had a storage shelf there stacked with things that probably needed to be thrown away. Doing a little housecleaning seemed more appealing than returning to the paper on my desk.

Amid the forgotten office supplies and antique computer hardware I spotted the photo album under a large envelope stuffed with yellowing papers and resting on a couple of boxes. For two years I had walked past this shelf every day and had never stopped to take a good look at what it held. A letter on top indicated this material had been gathered by Helen Madeline Mary Ross, later to become Mary Ross Ellingson after she married. The boxes were heavy and contained a surprise—a number of plaster casts of ancient Greek terracotta figurines wrapped in paper towels as well as some ancient pot shards. Most of the casts were of figurines that dated to the fifth and fourth centuries BCE. The pot shards were actual artifacts, not casts, with black decoration painted on the orange-red fabric of the clay. Picking up the album, a black-and-white photo of Ellingson fell to the floor. A young woman with a stylish 1930s bobbed hairdo stood beside a large stone grave marker (see figure I.1). I recognized the setting immediately from my own visits to Athens. She stood in the Kerameikos, an ancient cemetery of the city. Intrigued, I opened to a random page in the middle of the album. Ellingson appeared in only a couple of these photos, but again I recognized the location. The photos showed the excavations at Olynthos, or Olynthus as the Greek name of the site was transliterated in the 1930s when the photos were taken, but not a photo I had ever seen before (see figure I.2).

The excavations at Olynthus are counted among the great American-led excavations of the twentieth century. David Robinson of Johns Hopkins University directed four campaigns at Olynthus between 1928 and 1938. Archaeology in Greece had been dominated by excavations of public structures such as temples, theaters, and the buildings around the *agora*, the central square of ancient Greek cities. Robinson was one of the first archaeologists to focus his excavation almost exclusively on houses to better understand domestic life. These were the days of large-scale excavations, which are simply no longer financially feasible today. Robinson used a workforce of hundreds of local laborers each season to uncover enormous portions of the site. While such large-scale excavation precluded careful supervision by enough properly trained staff, Robinson still excavated more houses at Olynthus than had or have since been excavated at any other site in Greece. All modern studies of the ancient Greek house still begin with the Olynthus excavations. When

Figure I.1. Mary Ross Ellingson in the Kerameikos cemetery, Athens, June 1931.
Photo courtesy of the University of Evansville Archives

I was a graduate student, I was required to read one of the fourteen volumes of the *Excavations at Olynthus* series for class but had read the rest on my own because I found them so interesting and useful for my own research on ancient urbanism. The thoroughness with which Robinson published was also quite remarkable for his day in that he announced the intention to publish all artifacts he felt were important, not just the most attractive pieces.[1] While modern archaeologists see gaps in his excavation methods and the materials Robinson chose to publish, he set a new standard for his day about which materials warranted recording and publication.[2] The pace with which Robinson published these volumes as well as numerous articles in scholarly journals about the excavation is quite impressive, even dizzying. Some archaeologists are notorious for the slow rate at which they publish their data; Robinson was definitely not one of these.

Olynthus was the perfect place to study Greek domestic structures. Located in northeastern Greece on the Chalcidic peninsula (see figure I.3), citizens of the city became embroiled in the conflicts between Athens, Sparta, and Macedonia in the fifth and fourth centuries BCE. Fearing the people of Olynthus were plotting against him, Philip II of Macedonia, the one-eyed father of Alexander the Great, laid siege to the city in 349 BCE. In three speeches still preserved today, the *Olynthiacs*, one of the great orators of ancient Greece, Demosthenes, urged his fellow Athenians to aid the people of Olynthus and to defy Philip. Despite his warnings, Athens and the other

Figure I.2. Overview of Block A VI at Olynthus looking northeast as it appeared on June 4, 1931; House A VI 6 is in the foreground, Mary Ross Ellingson is on the left.
Photo courtesy of the University of Evansville Archives

Greek city-states were slow to realize that the conquest of Olynthus was only one phase in Philip's larger and eventually successful plan of mastering all of Greece; they chose to send no troops to help the beleaguered city. Philip eventually took Olynthus by treachery in 348 BCE, ordering the city to be looted and destroyed and the survivors of the siege to be sold into slavery. Olynthus was never rebuilt. Although subsequent generations used the site as a quarry, reducing the ruins of the buildings to their foundations, a great deal of evidence survived illustrating life in the city before and during the siege.[3] Indeed, Robinson's team even found six arrowheads and about a dozen lead sling bullets with Philip's name on them amid the ruins of the city, dramatic testimony to the city's final days.[4]

Ellingson had clearly worked on this excavation. The photos in the album were all carefully pasted to stiff black paper pages and labeled underneath in neat white letters. Accompanying the album was a stack of letters and news clippings as well as the boxes of figurine casts and pot shards. She had been a graduate student at Johns Hopkins University studying classical archaeology and had excavated with Robinson at Olynthus in 1931. Ellingson had

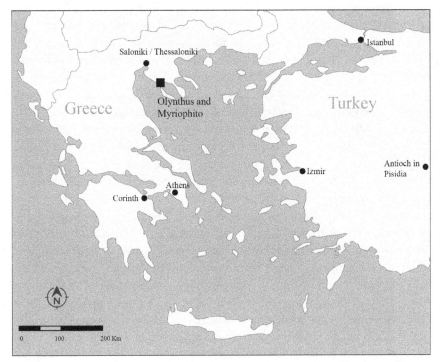

Figure I.3.   Map of Greece showing the location of places mentioned in the text. Adapted from Wikimedia Commons, Aegean Sea Map, https://upload.wikimedia.org/wikipedia/commons/8/8d/Aegean_Sea_map_ku.png

penned the letters to her family to tell them about her experiences abroad. After Ellingson's death in 1993, her daughter donated the album to the University of Evansville where Ellingson had taught Latin and English courses in her later years. Someone had placed all this material on the shelf long before the university had hired me.

The importance of this find slowly dawned on me. Ellingson had participated in an excavation significant in archaeological history and had written about it in a candid and often humorous way as it was happening. I knew of no other behind-the-scenes record like this of the Olynthus excavations. I took the photo album and letters back to my office and sat down to read. Over the next several hours I forgot about student papers and the gathering gloom outside. The ghost of Mary Ross Ellingson came alive, telling me in her own words about her experiences excavating at Olynthus and showing me what she saw through her numerous photographs. Her stories were unique to that time and place. I had known some of the names she mentioned of her fellow excavators only from their later archaeological publications and their highly respected reputations. In her letters they became real people to me. Robinson was witty, flirtatious, and stingy. Gladys Davidson Weinberg, an authority on ancient glass, was a kind, generous, and supportive friend. George Mylonas, who would go on to direct excavations at Mycenae, the Bronze Age site of the legendary Agamemnon's palace, was stiff and formal, never lapsing from the most proper decorum. J. Walter Graham, later to become an authority on the Minonan architecture of Crete, was an energetic supervisor with a large appetite at mealtimes who was always happy to help Ellingson with her work. Sarah Freeman, who would eventually be a recognized expert on ancient coins and medals, came to dislike Ellingson, a feeling that was apparently mutual. Long after they shared their season at Olynthus, some of her fellow excavators became professors, museum curators, and respected excavators. One would be wounded aiding the Greek opposition to the Italian invasion at the beginning of World War II, another is rumored to have joined the American intelligence effort against the Nazis, many years later two would be awarded the Archaeological Institute of America's Gold Medal in recognition of their contribution to the field, and one would die in a gruesome murder fifty years after working at Olynthus. Yet here in her letters they all were young, unknown graduate students excited by their first field experience, playing bridge, swimming in the clear blue water of the Gulf of Cassandra, and enjoying a night of dining and dancing. Virtually no candid snapshots or personal written accounts of the excavations at Olynthus survive making Ellingson's letters and photos a rare archive of a significant pre–World War II excavation.

While the details of her stories are unique to Olynthus in 1931, the themes are universal to all excavations and in them I recognized echoes of my own experiences in the field. Everyone who has worked on an excavation has felt the excitement of being the first person in centuries to lift an artifact from the dirt, has established lifelong friendships with fellow excavators, has complained about the food rations, and has delighted in discovering the modern culture of the place they are working. In articulate and artful language, she captured all aspects of life in the field in a way few others have.

Some scholars have noted that Robinson made some crucial changes to his goals and techniques over the years that he excavated at Olynthus. Ellingson unknowingly captured glimpses of those changes and their consequences in her letters and photographs proving that 1931 was a critical year in the development of the project. Robinson is celebrated for being one of the first archaeologists to focus a research project solely on Greek domestic structures but that was not his original intent. During his first season at Olynthus in 1928, he sought to find temples and civic structures, as was usually done at classical sites at the time. Ellingson's letters show that Robinson only really began to focus on houses as *the* unit of study in earnest in 1931. The shift in focus required a radical revamping of his excavation and recording procedures to allow him to gather the data he needed. The 1931 season is when these new techniques made their debut.

It was also during that season that Robinson first engaged in an experiment to see if women could oversee trench work for an entire season. During the excavations he had directed earlier in his career, Robinson had always relied on men to supervise the field work. During the 1931 season at Olynthus, he planned from the beginning to have the three women—Ellingson, Weinberg, and Freeman—work in the trenches and supervise Greek workmen instead of having them primarily wash, mend, and inventory finds in the dig house, tasks he had assigned the female graduate students who joined his earlier projects. Robinson helped create a new generation of women archaeologists. Ellingson, Weinberg, and Freeman were part of the so-called second generation of women in archaeology. Unfortunately, this new generation was appearing at a time when opportunities for women were contracting. A complex array of evolving economic and social factors developed that limited their opportunities to participate in archaeology and academia and would make their work less conspicuous than that of their contemporary male counterparts. The lack of women's visibility has led to the muting or elimination of their contributions from written accounts of the history of classical archaeology; Ellingson's archive helps add the voices of women back into the history of the discipline.

The three women were not the only people whose career trajectories developed or changed as a result of the 1931 excavation season—the same was true for several of the men. Graham and a fellow graduate student, Alexander Schulz, decided during that season that they would use the material from Olynthus for their thesis and dissertation respectively, the most important decision any graduate student has to make. Another man, Arthur Parsons, made the opposite decision after spending the season with Robinson and sought a dissertation topic elsewhere. This decision changed the course of his career and even his life quite radically. The 1931 season at Olynthus did not simply launch careers, however, it also saved one. Robinson, an aging archaeologist who seemed unaware of the many developments in archaeological techniques that had taken place around him, was panned for the poor quality of his work at Olynthus in 1928. There were veiled suggestions that his excavation permit should be revoked. The shift in focus and techniques he followed in 1931 saved his reputation as well as his career and helped establish him as one of the great American classical archaeologists. Much changed in 1931 at Olynthus and even in classical archaeology and I could see it all unfolding in real time through Ellingson's eyes. The place in history of both the archaeology and archaeologists of the 1931 season at Olynthus, therefore, is the focus of the first of three parts of this book.

Engrossed in my discovery, I did not realize that Ellingson's ghost was telling me something else, the final reason the 1931 season at Olynthus was significant. I was soon to uncover a clue she had intentionally left behind that would lead me to expose one of the most shocking plagiarism scandals yet publicly recorded in the history of the discipline. Robinson himself left a second clue, a message hidden within a painting currently on display at the University of Mississippi, which would confirm the scandal and make a blunt statement that only Ellingson could have fully understood. As the significance of the photo album and letters slowly came into focus over the weeks that followed, I found myself telling friends stories about discoveries that sounded more like they came from a mystery novel than the halls of academe. The scandal, therefore, is the focus of the second part of this book.

The third and final part of the book relays one more unexpected twist; some archaeologists knew Robinson and Ellingson's secret, but they did not want others to know. For years I would strive to publish the truth only to see my efforts at publication thwarted. Some members of the older generation of American archaeologists even chastised me for discussing the scandal. They worried about the damage it would cause to the reputation of the American individuals and institutions based in Greece. At the same time they asked me to be silent, they would tell me even more scandalous tales about Robinson that helped give context to his treatment of Ellingson, tales they told me should not be in print. A plucky junior editor would prove the key to getting this story published. And the calls of reviewers and readers would move the current copyright holder of Robinson's work, Johns Hopkins University Press, to petition the Library of Congress to right the wrong Robinson committed. In an unprecedented and historic move, Mary Ellingson's name will soon be reunited with her work.

Notes

1. Cf. David M. Robinson, *Excavations at Olynthus XIV: Terracottas, Lamps, and Coins Found in 1934 and 1938* (Baltimore, MD: Johns Hopkins University Press, 1952), v–vi.

2. For a recent assessment of the advancements and shortfalls represented by the Olynthus excavations see Nicholas Cahill, *Household and City Organization at Olynthus* (New Haven, CT: Yale University Press, 2002), 61ff.

3. Cahill, *Household*, 24–25.

4. Cahill, *Household*, 46.

PART I

~

MARY ROSS ELLINGSON'S ARCHAEOLOGICAL ADVENTURE

Figure P.1. Mary Ross Ellingson at the Greek site of either Tiryns or Mycenae in June 1931
Photo courtesy of the University of Evansville Archives

CHAPTER ONE

~

Journey to Olynthus

The earliest letter in Ellingson's box is dated March 10, 1931. In it, Ellingson describes setting sail from New York for Europe on the first leg of her journey to Olynthus. She shared a third-class cabin with her two Johns Hopkins classmates, Sarah Freeman and Gladys Davidson (later Davidson Weinberg). In the first letter, Ellingson introduces her family to them. While Ellingson describes the desire of the three women to learn the methods of archaeologists, she shows they had another goal during their season at Olynthus. Being part of the second generation of women in archaeology, each had to define where she belonged within the discipline. Arriving in Greece, they were met by J. Walter Graham, Alexander Schulz, and Arthur Parsons, fellow archaeology graduate students at Johns Hopkins. The "boys," as Ellingson calls them, were all looking for dissertation topics at Olynthus, a decision that would have enormous implications for their future career options. Together, all five traveled to Thessaloniki, where they joined David and Helen Robinson. Like his graduate students, Robinson had a career goal during the 1931 season at Olynthus. Recently his field techniques had come under heavy criticism, so he was looking to regain his reputation as a field archaeologist. Picking up the equipment they needed, Robinson and his students drove the final leg to Olynthus. The last members of the team arrived after them, Greek archaeologist George Mylonas, a Greek photographer named Euripides Melanides, and a peripatetic artist named Georg von Peschke. Mylonas had recently completed his dissertation and was on the hunt for permanent employment, an elusive quest during the Depression in Greece. Melanides eagerly photographed whatever Robinson wanted, even if it required him to try something risky. Von Peschke wanted desperately to create a new identity for himself among the archaeologists, hiding his past. Ellingson had something to say about each of them. First, though, it is worth introducing Ellingson herself.

Mary Ross Ellingson

Helen Mary Magdalene Ross, Ellingson's name at birth, was born in Edmonton, Canada, on September 21, 1908.[1] She spent her childhood in the city and attended Edmonton's University of Alberta from 1925 to 1931.[2] Classical archaeologist Margriet Haagsma, inspired by the first edition of this book, published research on Ellingson's early years arguing the atmosphere of that city and that university at that time significantly influenced who Ellingson grew to become. A boomtown, Edmonton brimmed with opportunities, energy, and new ideas. Ellingson's grandparents and parents settled in Edmonton in the 1890s with other pioneering families. Her father's family

Figure 1.1. Mary Ross Ellingson, age twelve, prepares for a horseback ride while on a family vacation in the mining town of Cadomin, Alberta. Note the kitten in her arms.
Photo courtesy of the University of Evansville Archives

descended from Scottish immigrants[3] while her mother came from an old royalist family that had left the United States for Canada after the American Revolution. Her maternal grandparents established a farm on the outskirts of town because farming was, according to her grandfather Edward Dean, "the only thing worth doing."[4] Her family was solidly upper-middle class as her father built his own real estate and insurance firm that allowed the family to live in a comfortable home near the provincial capital building.[5] The year her paternal grandparents settled in Edmonton, 1897, the town's population was 1,638.[6] With the creation of the province of Alberta in 1905 and Edmonton's designation as the provincial capital, the city experienced tremendous growth. By the year of Ellingson's birth, the city's population clocked in at 18,500. A provincial capital needed a university, so that same year, 1908, the University of Alberta opened its doors. By the time she graduated from that institution in 1931, the city's population stood at 79,059.[7] Despite living in a city experiencing an exponential increase in population, her family never forgot their rural roots. They took vacations in the more rugged parts of Canada, during which Ellingson developed an enduring love for hiking and the outdoors (see figure 1.1). These excursions prepared her well for the rigors and privations of archaeological fieldwork.

Ellingson entered the University of Alberta shortly before her seventeenth birthday determined to study law but soon discovered an aptitude for, and love of, classical languages and cultures.[8] A reporter describes Ellingson as "popular" in an article for the university's newspaper, *The Gateway*, which discusses her post-graduate plans.[9] While classical languages were her primary focus, she also cultivated an interest in journalism, working as an editor for *The Gateway* and contributing articles to the off-campus newspaper, the *Edmonton Bulletin*, one of which was among her letters. She eventually joined the staff at the *Bulletin* as an assistant editor.[10] Her journalistic training later helped her keenly observe the excavation, Greek cultures, and people at Olynthus and write about them in her letters in a clear and insightful way. While at the university she studied French and at some point, either during or before her time as an undergraduate, learned German well enough to at least read scholarly articles.[11] In the spring of 1930, Ellingson graduated with honors (figure 1.2).

Haagsma suggests that while the vitality of a nascent Edmonton was the first influence on Ellingson's views of the world's possibilities, two faculty members in the Department of Classics at the University of Alberta were the second. William Hardy Alexander, affectionally known as "Doc Alik" on campus, chaired the department. A graduate of the University of Toronto, he received his MA and PhD in classics, specializing in Latin, from the University of California in 1900 and 1906, respectively. Alexander became one of four founding members of the University of Alberta in the year of Ellingson's birth. As the university and department grew, Alexander hired Geneva

Figure 1.2.   A twenty-one-year-old Mary Ross Ellingson in her college graduation photo taken in the spring of 1930.
Photo courtesy of Barbara Petersen

Misener in 1913. After graduating from Queen's University in Kingston, Ontario, she completed her PhD at the University of Chicago with a focus on ancient Greek in 1903. She held various teaching posts over the next decade and traveled to Italy and Greece to study archaeology.[12] In what must have been an unforgettable trip, she toured Greek sites with Wilhelm Dörpfeld,[13] famed as Heinrich Schliemann's successor directing the project at Troy and the man who brought order to the chaotic excavation and recording methods Schliemann had initiated at the site.[14] As the only two classicists at the university at the time, Ellingson took many classes with each professor. She and Alexander grew close while she completed directed reading courses with him in Greek archaeology and Greek private life.[15] He took on the role of her mentor, helping at key points as her career developed in the years during and after she left the university.

Under the guidance of Alexander and Misener, Ellingson cultivated a deep passion for classical Greek culture and an unshakable belief in the superiority of the ancient Greeks. As she dreamed en route of seeing Athens for the first time, she effuses in a March 20 letter,

> Oh, I don't want to sound like a guide-book or a circular sent out by the Chamber of Commerce of Athens but you can't imagine the wonderful feeling it gives me to think that tomorrow I shall see [Athens] as it remains to the world today. In the fourth & fifth centuries B.C. Athens reached a perfection in art that never will be equaled again. And I think it a great privilege to be going to gaze upon the relics of the perfection. Oh the more I say the more it sounds like the publicity department but at least it's the way I feel.

During the first half of the twentieth century, many of those who studied classical cultures saw themselves as the guardians of ancient Greek art, architecture, poetry, and democracy.[16] This legacy needed protection. The impressionistic movement in art and modernism in architecture, poetry, and literature all represented a rejection of the ideals of the classical Greeks. Along with all these changes, in 1931 the world was still grappling with the mechanized killing unleashed during World War I and the ever-present threat from Communist revolution and invasion after the beginning of the Russian Revolution in 1917; democracy and humanism seemed under attack. Ellingson had joined a field that was a bulwark of conservatism. Indeed, her own conservatism in art was uncompromising. While reflecting on her visit to the archaeological museum in Naples, Italy, one stop during their long journey to Greece, she tells her family in a March 19 letter, "[T]hey have a few beautiful original Greek statues but an awful mob of hideous Roman ones & Renaissance paintings, which I hate." While Alexander and Misener fed Ellingson's hunger to learn about ancient Greece, they likely shared with her another conviction they both held, that gender should not define one's opportunities. What has come to be known as the "first wave" of the feminist movement was cresting during Ellingson's childhood and early adulthood. Women in the United States were able to vote for the first time in 1920, the achievement for which many had fought for nearly a century as the first feminist wave increased in momentum. In Canada, women gained the right to vote in a piecemeal fashion with those of different provinces and different ethnicities achieving the right in different years before and after 1920.[17] In Ellingson's home province, the Alberta parliament granted women who were not of Indigenous or Asian ancestry the right to vote in 1916.[18] Alexander and Misener had been active in the suffrage movement and their activism continued unabated after the victory in 1916, indeed earning the vote for the women of Alberta seems to have accelerated their desire for women's equality. Misener was the first female faculty member at the University of Alberta.[19] Alexander likely played a significant role in her hiring as he was the chair of the department. "Doc Alik" actively advocated for university admission to be open to all regardless of gender or religious affiliation, a radical notion at a time when bans and quotas on women and adherents to certain faiths were common. Misener took on the role of advisor to the *Wauneita* club, a club for female students founded by women who vowed never to marry so they could pursue a career without distraction. The *Wauneita* club automatically enrolled incoming female students, so Ellingson was a member although it is not clear how much she participated in the club's activities. Misener never married but did raise two nieces as her own. She also caused a stir on campus more than once during presentations in which she called for equal pay for equal work regardless of gender and argued that marriage and a career should not be mutually exclusive goals for women.[20] The sweeping success of the first wave of feminism as well as the milieu at the University of Alberta and especially in the Department of Classics must have normalized progressive gender ideals for the young Ellingson and made it seem like she could do anything.

After she completed her undergraduate studies, Ellingson moved to Baltimore to begin studying classical archaeology at Johns Hopkins University having received a scholarship to support her studies.[21] Johns Hopkins was an unusual university in the educational landscape of the 1920s and 1930s United States. At that time many American colleges and universities had at best a mixed, at worst a negative, attitude toward allowing women to study. Stanford University epitomized the negative attitude when it implemented a quota on undergraduate women in 1904; for every one woman there had to be three men accepted, a policy that remained in effect until 1933.[22] Although the first women had not entered the graduate programs in arts and sciences at Johns Hopkins until 1908,[23] the institution would rapidly become one of the American universities most welcoming to women and would be one of the universities to grant the highest number of doctorates to women in the country prior to World War II.[24] This liberal policy toward women extended to the classics department where the graduate program in archaeology was one of the few in North America to accept women.[25] With ideals so in line with those at the University of Alberta, Ellingson certainly felt at home there.

It was not just the openness of Johns Hopkins that must have attracted Ellingson to study there; Robinson already had an established reputation in the world of classical art and archaeology when Ellingson was applying to the program. It seems highly likely that Ellingson had read some of his work as an undergraduate as Misener and Alexander had connections to him. Misener completed her PhD at the University of Chicago a year before Robinson completed his at the same institution.[26] Whether they knew each other personally or not, Misener had to have been aware of his work. It is clear from the tone of the letters between Alexander, Robinson, and Ellingson, now in the archives of both the University of Evansville and the University of Mississippi, that Alexander and Robinson were old friends. Alexander and Misener must have mentioned Robinson and Johns Hopkins to Ellingson when she began thinking about graduate school. More than that, however, Robinson and his department were supported by other highly respected professors. W. F. Albright, one of the greatest Biblical archaeologists of his day, was teaching there when Ellingson arrived. Tenney Frank was working on his monumental multivolume work *An Economic Survey of Ancient Rome*, one of the first and most thorough works to address the topic. Ellingson took classes with all three of these professors. Within a few weeks of their first meeting, Robinson was so impressed with Ellingson that he asked the new graduate student to join him on the staff at Olynthus. "I am really awfully enthusiastic about being an archaeologist," Ellingson wrote to her family in an undated letter. Her eager anticipation of fieldwork is equally visible in an undated photo that was most likely taken shortly prior to her departure for Greece (figure 1.3).

Figure 1.3 portrays well who Ellingson was as she departed for Olynthus: a person not afraid to get her hands dirty, one who insisted on a sense of feminine propriety and style, someone confident in her own abilities, and a woman with a sense of humor. Traits like these helped make her a good

Figure 1.3. Mary Ross Ellingson (left) elegantly dressed but ready to dig with her life-long friend Helen Boyle. The date and location are also unknown, but it is likely this photo was taken at her home in Edmonton in late 1930 or early 1931.

field archaeologist. Although she is so nicely attired in figure 1.3, she did not hesitate to pick up a shovel with dirt clinging to it. Through her childhood experiences in no-frills accommodations in the wilderness during vacations, she held no fear of tough living conditions nor of having to pitch in when manual work needed to be done. This does not mean she grew up a tomboy, quite the opposite; Ellingson would maintain the importance of a proper appearance throughout her life. She wears a fur coat in figure 1.3 and sports her signature hairdo. As she departed for the wilds of rural Greece, she maintained an immensely popular hairstyle, that of the biggest starlets in Hollywood movies and Parisian cabarets. In the photo, Ellingson stares into the camera unafraid, absolutely certain of herself. She retained the sense of confidence that she had developed at the University of Alberta and the be-lief that her gender did not define her. It is a quality that made for a strong and efficient excavator, but it left her little patience for anyone who under-estimated her, particularly because of her gender and fashionable appearance. While still traveling to Olynthus, she complains in a March 20 letter of the Greek hospitality workers:

> There is an automatic Elevator in the hotel which we would like to run but, oh no, they must do it for us. And as for us opening the front door ourselves, oh mercy me, how degrading!

Figure 1.3 demonstrates one final personality trait essential for a good archaeologist, one that indicates flexibility and an ability to get along with others: a sense of humor. In the photo, she surely intended the juxtaposition of the dirt encrusted-shovel with her fur coat and finger-wave hairdo as a joke. Her letters show an ability to find amusement in the situations around her as they are filled with quips such as this from her initial March 10 letter:

> Oh I forgot to mention that we have several celebrities on board. Ripley (you know, believe it or not Ripley) but of course he's up in 1st class so we haven't had a look at him, and the late Al Capone (you know Scarface Al Capone of Chicago-fame)'s body-guard (being deported) but they are down in steerage so we haven't had a look at them either.

This was the woman who boarded the passenger ship the *Roma* in March 1931 bound for Greece.

Gladys Davidson Weinberg
and Sarah Freeman

Somewhere on the Atlantic
Tuesday, March 10 [1931]
Dear Family,

Thanks so much for the wire. It was quite exciting getting it. I got it soon after I got on board, & then I got another just a few minutes before we sailed (from the girls in the stacks at Hopkins). Jean & 2 of her friends came down to see me off, & of course there were Sally's family, & a lot of Gladys' friends.

We [Ellingson, Weinberg, and Freeman] stayed up to see the harbor. It was really beautiful—all the way from uptown down the river past the Statue of Liberty, black night and twinkling lights shining forth from the many million sky-scrapers that make New York the only city of its kind. The Statue of Liberty, we decided, must be impressionistic art, at night, as only its torch was lit, & we could barely see its outline against the black of the Jersey shore. And then-out to sea.

Ellingson's classmate in the classical archaeology program at Johns Hopkins and her cabinmate onboard the *Roma*, Gladys Rachel Davidson, who would later add Weinberg to her name after she married, was born December 27, 1909 (figure 1.4).[27] Although her father, Israel Davidson, was a scholar of Hebrew literature, Weinberg became interested in the ancient Greek language and classical cultures in high school. She attended McGill University in Montreal but graduated with a BA from New York University in 1930 and, like Ellingson, had just started at Johns Hopkins when Robinson asked her to go to Olynthus.[28] Unlike many of his colleagues, Robinson cared little about Weinberg's Jewish heritage. Antisemitism was rife in American higher education at the time;[29] Princeton, Harvard, Yale, Columbia, Cornell, even the University of Virginia were a few of the many institutions that adopted explicit antisemitic admissions policies.[30] Discrimination existed in hiring as well; by 1940 only 2 percent of the faculty in American colleges and universities were Jewish. One historian was unable to locate a single Jewish faculty member teaching in the humanities in any American institution of higher learning prior to 1940 despite a thorough search of university records. She dubbed Jewish women like Weinberg, who entered academia prior to World War II, the "lone voyagers," indicating how rare they were.[31] The liberal admissions policy of Johns Hopkins and Robinson's welcoming attitude surely attracted Weinberg to attend graduate school there.

Weinberg was popular and likeable, as Ellingson indicates in the quote above mentioning the large number of friends who came to see Weinberg

Figure 1.4. Gladys Davidson Weinberg taking notes with her feet in a cistern on the South Hill at Olynthus. She sits on an ancient floor paved with pebbles.
Photo courtesy of the University of Evansville Archives

off when the trio set sail from New York. Ellingson expresses warm feelings toward Weinberg repeatedly in her letters. Even though she was over a year older than Weinberg, she seemed unaware her friend was only twenty-one when they watched the Statue of Liberty disappear from the deck of the *Roma.* Ellingson states in an April 9 letter, "I am the youngest on the party [(]I think Gladys is about the same age but she seems older)," which is an unintended commentary on Weinberg's maturity.

"Gladys Davidson [Weinberg], of course I am very fond of. We are very good friends. Sally Freemen & I aren't so thick but we get along O.K. I don't care much for her," Ellingson states in a letter dated April 9. Sarah "Sally" Elizabeth Freeman was a year older than Ellingson having been born in 1907[32] in Blairstown, New Jersey[33] (figure 1.5). A graduate of Mount Holyoke College in 1928, she had started at Johns Hopkins before Ellingson. While a graduate student she was a champion tennis player.[34] The competitive personality required for succeeding at tennis may have been one of the traits that rubbed Ellingson the wrong way. Regardless of what it was that annoyed Ellingson, it is clear the two women had very different personalities. While it is dangerous to read too much into such things, it is perhaps telling that in nearly every photo in which Freeman appears from Olynthus she is wearing pants (figure 1.5). Ellingson, on the other hand, is always wearing a skirt or dress in photos. Their choice of field attire speaks to two different approaches women of their generation took to working in archaeology. Wearing male clothing was a direct approach showing a woman was able to do what a man could while wearing female clothing spoke to a softer approach, reassuring men that a woman was not trying to usurp their roles.[35]

Despite their differences, all three women had an adventurous and plucky nature. In a letter dated March 16, Ellingson shows their more mischievous side:

> [We] had quite a lark the other night, after the Captain's Dinner Party. We broke the wire on the lock keeping us from 2nd class & crawled under the canvas. I was in the lead, & when I rose up from ungraceful position on hands & knees (from crawling under the canvas partition) I was face to face with one of the ship's officers. Nothing daunt[ed] . . . I waited till Sally & Gladys got thru, & we marched up to the top deck. The officer evidently decided we were harmless. After making ourselves at home in 2nd class, we watched our chances & got thru the 1st class gate, which was much easier, we didn't have to crawl under any canvas. We finally got to the top deck of 1st class, which is really beautifully fixed up. Then we decided we wanted to play shuffle board but it was too dark on 1st, so we went back to 2nd but there the things you play with were all put away & of course we couldn't ask for them. So then what [did] we do but go back to 1st (carefully avoiding all officers, deckhands & stewards) & carry enough poles & quoits or whatever they are, back to 2nd & started to play. We played until a nosey deck-hand came around, & then went off to report us, then we gracefully retired under the canvas again, so that when an officer came to put us off, we weren't there. Fooled him.

Classical Archaeology and Women Archaeologists in 1931

Ellingson was clear that she wanted to be an archaeologist working in Greece and she seems to have believed her two classmates shared her career goal; Ellingson labeled a photograph of herself, Weinberg, and Freeman taken at Johns Hopkins, "The three archaeologists" (see figure 5.1). Excavating classical sites is a vocation, not a job. The program at Johns Hopkins prepared students to be college professors and, if an academic position was not available, museum curators. None of "the three archaeologists" could have understood the full magnitude of the challenges that would face them as they pursued their vocation and careers. Foreigners like the trio sharing a cabin on the *Roma* found it difficult to pursue fieldwork in Greece because the Greek antiquities authority controlled access to excavations quite tightly. In addition, women were not encouraged to join in fieldwork, an activity commonly seen as a masculine occupation. While a few strong-willed women of the previous generation had made a place for themselves in Greek archaeology, doing so

Figure 1.5. Sarah "Sally" Freeman on-site at Olynthus. The large basin in front of her is part of an olive mill.

Photo courtesy of the David M. Robinson Collection, Special Collections, University of Mississippi Libraries

had required constant struggle. Finding a post, particularly in academia, was also challenging, although there had been recent signs that more opportunities were opening for women. The novelty of Ellingson, Weinberg, and Freeman heading out to join an archaeological excavation was still unusual enough in 1931 to warrant an article in the *New York Times* with the title "Four College Girls Join Olynthus Quest."[36]

All American archaeology in Greece was, and remains, controlled by the American School of Classical Studies at Athens. The purpose of the American School is to offer an education in classical languages, literature, history, and archaeology to students who live in the School's facilities in Athens. While attending classes at the School, students also visit museums and archaeological sites around Athens and throughout Greece. Spending a year studying at the American School is an important step toward a career in classics and classical archaeology. The American School was the first American research center abroad when it opened its doors in 1882.[37] Almost from its inception, any American who wanted to direct an excavation in Greece collaborated with the American School, which then supported his or her application for an excavation permit from the Greek government. For all intents and purposes, an American excavation director like Robinson needed the blessing of the American School to get a permit. This remains true today. This power makes the School the center of American archaeological research in Greece.[38] The advantage to this system is that the directors of the American School can insist on the highest levels of excellence when it comes to excavation technique, denying permits to those who fail to meet their standards. In this way the American School developed the first cadre of professional American classical archaeologists by the time World War I broke out.[39] The disadvantages to this monopoly on the permitting process are two-fold: it can become politically charged and new ideas can be discouraged by conservative American School directors.[40] Indeed, the conservatism of the American School is well represented by the classical echoes in the style of architecture directors adopted for the School's buildings. In a 1927 photo of the newly built addition to the School, the Gennadius Library (figure 1.6), the conservative classical Greek influences are literally set in stone.

The American School runs two of its own excavations, one at the ancient port city of Corinth and the other in the commercial, political, and social center of ancient Athens, an area known as the Agora. Excavations at the latter site began in 1896 and at the former site in 1931, at the same time Ellingson and her colleagues were at work at Olynthus.[41] Although there have been a few significant interruptions, especially during wars, these excavations have continued nearly every year up to the present. Both sites are central

Figure 1.6. The recently-constructed Gennadius Library of the American School of Classical Studies in Athens as it appeared in 1927. The façade was intended to evoke an ancient Greek temple.

Photo courtesy of the Wilhelmina Van Ingen Elarth Papers, Ms1969-004, Special Collections and University Archives, Virginia Tech, Blacksburg, Va.

training grounds; more American classical archaeologists have been trained at Corinth than at any other single site in the Mediterranean basin.[42]

From its foundation, women were eager to study at the American School. The first woman to attend a regular session at the School was Annie S. Peck, a professor of Latin at Purdue University, who arrived in 1885.[43] Directors at the School did not necessarily oppose having women there, they were simply wary about the number of women overwhelming that of men. While they were willing to have women participate as students at the School, early directors opposed women participating in excavations. It was not until 1908 that the first woman was allowed to excavate at Corinth.[44]

Despite this opposition, a first generation of American women came to Greece and participated in excavations. After spending time at the American School and being denied access to the Corinth excavations, Harriet Boyd Hawes left the oversight of the American School directors in Athens for the wild and distant island of Crete to survey for sites. Beginning in 1900, she undertook excavations at several Bronze Age sites on the island including her most famous project at the Minonan palace of Gournia. Boyd Hawes and her assistant, Edith Hall Dohan, were the first women of any nationality to direct and publish the excavation of an archaeological site in Greece.[45] They were followed by Hetty Goldman and Alice Leslie Walker who became the first women to excavate and publish a site on the Greek mainland, uncovering over 280 graves in a necropolis at the site of Halae. Goldman and Walker continued to work in Greece before and after World War I as well as in Turkey after the war.[46]

These pioneers of the first generation of American female archaeologists have been called the "radicals."[47] Ellingson, Weinberg, and Freeman were the beginning of the second generation. While some excavation directors in the United States and Britain encouraged women of this generation to participate in fieldwork,[48] those in Greece depended on a technique for dealing with the growing number of women who wanted to dig in order to avoid their radicalization: containment by segregation.[49] Many project directors chose to put women to work in the dig house cataloging finds rather than out in the field excavating with the men, a division of labor used to restrict the activities of some women of the first generation as well.[50] William Henry Fox, director of the Brooklyn Museum, explained the ideological justification for the segregation of women when he was interviewed for an article in 1933 titled "Exploring the Museum Field," published in the magazine *Independent Woman*. As Fox put it, "Women are especially suited to museum work by their love of the beautiful, their adaptability and their patience in detail work."[51] Working at the excavation homebase limited opportunities for women to publish and many wound up writing catalogs of "small finds," the coins, small figurines, or bits of metal and glass that turn up at every excavation; it was left to the men to publish grand syntheses explaining the full history of a site and all its features.[52] While cataloging finds may not be as glamorous or heroic as excavating, it is by all means a necessary component of fieldwork without which there would be no grand syntheses. Cataloguers, however, do not find their names on the covers of publications. This model for the gendered division of labor prevailed for the most part at the American-led excavations at Corinth and in the Athenian Agora.[53] Of the three future archaeologists aboard the *Roma*, Ellingson makes it clear in her letters that while she looked forward to cataloging, she also wanted to dig, an intention that may have gone unfulfilled if she had worked at a site in Greece other than Olynthus. Ellingson does not comment on Weinberg or Freeman's goals besides labeling a photo of the trio (figure 5.1) "the three archaeologists."

Although obstacles existed, there were still a few signs in the 1920s and 1930s Ellingson may have noticed that suggested the field was opening to female participation. The number of women in the field saw a slow but nonetheless significant increase in those years.[54] Although it was three years before she arrived at Johns Hopkins, Ellingson still may have heard that Goldman had taught at the university as a visiting lecturer, a clear demonstration that a woman could make it in the field of classical archaeology.[55] The first American woman had earned her PhD in classical archaeology as early as 1908,[56] and in 1933 a contemporary of Ellingson opened the field of anthropological archaeology to women by earning the first PhD in prehistoric archaeology.[57] The year after Ellingson's season at Olynthus, Mary Hamilton Swindler was appointed editor of one of the flagship scholarly journals in classical archaeology, the *American Journal of Archaeology*. Swindler had an immediate and highly visible impact on the journal, overhauling the format and setting a new standard of scholarly excellence for the journal's articles. She held the longest tenure of any editor at the *American Journal of Archaeology* remaining from 1932 until 1946.[58] Robinson had served on Swindler's dissertation committee.[59] As one known to brag about his own and his students' accomplishments, Robinson no doubt pointed out the exciting changes at the journal to his graduate students including Ellingson, Weinberg, and Freeman. The prospects for women in the field of archaeology were not good in 1931, but if Ellingson and her fellow female graduate students looked closely enough, they would have seen many signs of hope that the situation was changing in their favor.

Whether Ellingson and her cabinmates knew it or not, opportunities for women to be employed in academia also increased during and after World War I. The women's suffrage movement had helped improve the numbers of women teaching at universities as had the labor shortage during the war, a shortage that allowed women to get out of the house and work. The percentage of women faculty in American institutions of higher learning rose from 19.8 during the 1899–1900 academic year to 27.6 in 1929–1930.[60] As Ellingson entered the University of Alberta to begin her undergraduate studies, in the United States the American Association of University Professors' Committee W was examining the gender inequities in faculty employment and pay and was seeking remedies. Committee W published data that, while demonstrating encouraging trends, illuminated serious problems for women who wanted to become professors. According to a 1922 report, an average of only 4 percent of full professors at coeducational institutions were women and 23.6 percent of instructor positions were held by women. Instructors had higher teaching loads and therefore less time for research and publication, which was the primary avenue for professional advancement.[61] Any woman entering graduate school in 1930, as Ellingson and Weinberg did, would have hope for advancement in the field and in a career but must have understood that it would be difficult. Ellingson's suffrage-supporting university of Alberta professors Alexander and Misener may have also encouraged Ellingson to see these affirmative signs.

J. Walter Graham, Alexander Schulz, and Arthur and Gladys Parsons

The *Roma* docked in her home port of Rome.[62] To get to Greece, Ellingson, Weinberg, and Freeman had to cross Italy by train to the Adriatic port of Brindisi, stopping to see some of the sites along the way, and then boarded another ship for Greece. They arrived in Athens on March 20 as Ellingson wrote to her family:

> We got in today at 4. The boys, Alex Schulz (from Hopkins, who came over about 5 weeks ago, very nice boy) & Walter Graham (the Canadian who was at Hopkins last year & won a scholarship at the American School here) met us at the boat, & they had a man to arrange all our luggage etc.

The fellow Canadian, James Walter Graham (figure 1.7), was twenty-four years old when he met Ellingson on the docks in the port of Athens. Graham came to Johns Hopkins from Acadia University in Wolfville, Nova Scotia, where he had received his BA in 1927 and MA in 1928.[63] Graham may have been the first Canadian to become a Fellow in Archaeology at the School.[64] He took advantage of his time there to learn the craft of archaeology by attending lectures of, and by talking informally to, prominent archaeologists working in Greece and by participating in the School's Corinth excavation. Graham had received excellent training before joining the Olynthus staff. In 1931 he spent the first of two field seasons at Olynthus. Ellingson clearly liked Graham. In an April 9 letter from Olynthus she writes,

> Walter Graham is a very nice chap, & awfully helpful about showing one how to write reports, etc, & he has loaned me his cane, which is sure a help. They are convenient to lean on, & also convenient when there are dogs around.

Graham also lent Ellingson his typewriter. She used it to type some of her letters as well as her field reports.

The other person who welcomed Ellingson, Weinberg, and Freeman to Athens the day they arrived was Alexander Heinrich Gottfried Schulz (figure 1.8). In the same letter quoted above, Ellingson wrote of him,

Figure 1.7. J. Walter Graham illustrates his hypothesis that houses at Olynthus had second stories reached by wooden staircases, the first step of which was made from stone.

Photo courtesy of the University of Evansville Archives

Figure 1.8. Alexander Schulz demonstrating the use of a sitting ceramic bathtub found at Olynthus while smoking his pipe for comic effect. This photo was probably taken when the Olynthus excavators visited the archaeological museum in Salonica (modern Thessaloniki) in June 1931.
Photo courtesy of the University of Evansville Archives

> Alex Schulz is very nice, too. He is the life of the party type, always, I mean
> often, not always, making everybody laugh. He is Dutch & German descent.
> His father is a prof[essor] at the U[niversity] of Illinois.

Schulz was just a year older than Ellingson and had completed his undergraduate degree at the University of Illinois in Urbana where Ellingson
relates his father taught physics. His family appears to have been fairly
wealthy; Schulz is the only person in Ellingson's photos holding a pipe and
wearing a smoking jacket. He is also the only graduate student among the
Olynthus staff in 1931 who did not type his thesis himself as he could afford
to hire a typist. Schulz seems to have had a romantic-adventurous streak.
Ellingson reports in a May 20 letter that upon leaving Olynthus he intended
to rent a motorcycle with a friend and tour Europe.

After a day seeing the sights in Athens, the party of five took the train to
Saloniki, which Ellingson also spells as Salonique, and Salonica. Saloniki,
modern Thessaloniki, is one of Greece's major cities and offered the last
chance for the group to enjoy the comforts of civilization before heading into

the Greek back country. Ellingson was impressed with their accommodations as her March 22 letter makes clear:

> The Mediterranean Palace [see figure 1.9], the resort of the idle rich, the pleasure haunt of millionaires, the playground of the wealthy! A room to myself. Davey got us a 70% reduction on the rooms so we decided to stay here, as it is really a lovely hotel, & only about 80 drachmas, or 96¢ a day.

"Davey" may have been trying to compensate in advance for the living conditions he knew he would be subjecting his crew to once they were on site. He had said of the women joining the excavation, "they will have to rough it with the rest of us. I am afraid it will not prove so dramatic as they think."[65]

Ellingson describes their train journey from Athens to Saloniki in the March 22 letter:

> We came right on to Salonica last night instead of stopping off at Larissa as we had intended. It was raining when we got there so we decided that another 3 hours on the train wouldn't kill us, & we can see the Vale of Tempe on the way back. . . . We had a lot of fun on the train. The 2 boys are both very nice, and a lot of fun, so I think we shall get along o.k. Mr. & Mrs. Parsons have arrived also & Mr. & Mrs. Robinson get in this morning.

Figure 1.9. Photo of the elegant Mediterranean Palace Hotel in Saloniki (modern Thessaloniki) in June 1931.
Photo courtesy of the University of Evansville Archives

Figure 1.10. Arthur and Gladys Parsons from a group photo taken at Myriophito.
Photo courtesy of the University of Evansville
Archives

Figure 1.11. David Robinson standing in one of the houses at Olynthus. Note the pith helmet in his left hand.
Photo courtesy of the David M. Robinson Collection, Special Collections, University of Mississippi Libraries

Arthur Parsons came to Johns Hopkins from California to study classical archaeology. His father was the Protestant Episcopal bishop of his home state.[66] Recently married, he and his wife Gladys joined the staff at Olynthus together in 1931 (figure 1.10). Ellingson liked Arthur but was slow to warm up to Gladys. Nonetheless Gladys Parsons took a motherly interest in the young Ellingson. In the April 9 letter to her family in which she describes her colleagues, she writes of the couple,

> Mrs. Parsons (Gladys) is always seeing that I have a flashlight (I had to borrow one of their's permanently). Arthur Parsons is very nice. The Parsons are an awfully nice couple. They are very much in love with each other (married a year). . . . She is quite a bit older than Arthur. She is awfully interesting. Knows all sorts of interesting people, and has traveled a lot. I didn't like her at all when I first met her but I think she is a peach now.

David and Helen Robinson

The day after Ellingson and the others arrived in Saloniki they met with
David Robinson and his wife, Helen. Robinson was born on September 21,
1880, in Auburn, New York, and so was fifty years old at the time he met his
graduate-student staff members in Saloniki (figure 1.11).[67] Robinson's father
was a Baptist minister who became the pastor of a church in Brooklyn. The
young Robinson showed a powerful talent for languages, mastering Latin and
Greek as a teen and later French and German. When only thirteen years old
he began his course of study at the University of Chicago and by 1898 had
completed his bachelor's degree in Greek.[68] Promptly entering the graduate program at Chicago he supplemented his American studies with stints
abroad in Germany at Halle, Bonn, and Berlin.[69] At that time the German
universities offered the best education in classics. The German approach was
known as *Altertumswissenschaft*, literally "the scientific study of antiquity,"
and put equal weight on all aspects of ancient culture, encouraging students
to study the art history, languages, history, and archaeology of the Greeks
and Romans.[70] Robinson's career shows he embraced the German approach;
while he is known today for his archaeological research he also published
works on classical history, epigraphy, literature, philology as well as verse
translations of both Latin and Greek poets, particularly his favorite, Sappho.[71] An avid collector of ancient artifacts, he published three volumes on
vases in his own personal collection in the international multivolume catalog of Greek vases, the *Corpus Vasorum Antiquorum*.[72] As would be expected,
Robinson went to Athens to study at the American School and gained his
first taste of fieldwork in 1902 and 1903 at Corinth. He used material from
these experiences as the basis for his dissertation, which earned him his PhD
at the University of Chicago in 1904.[73]

The next year he became the first archaeologist Johns Hopkins University hired on a full-time basis for its Department of Art and Archaeology;
he would remain there as the department head for more than forty years.[74]
Temporary faculty had already turned Johns Hopkins into a major force in
the discipline of classical archaeology within the United States. In fact,
classics was the first graduate program established at Johns Hopkins after
the foundation of the university in 1876. Robinson augmented that growing
reputation and established the university as one of the preeminent places to
study the classical cultures of the ancient Mediterranean. Although professors like Frank and Albright helped, Robinson taught most of the courses
his students took.[75] He was a tremendously popular teacher throughout his
career and his undergraduate courses were always fully enrolled.[76] Awarding

MAs and PhDs is another measure of the accomplishments of a professor and a graduate school and by this standard Robinson and the archaeology program were highly successful. The Johns Hopkins Department of Art and Archaeology has been called "an academic factory" for the high number of graduate degrees it granted, especially under Robinson's leadership.[77]

While at Johns Hopkins, Robinson showed leadership in the field in other ways as well. To name just a few of his more outstanding accomplishments, he edited journals and popular magazines such as *Classical Weekly*, *American Journal of Philology*, and *Art and Archaeology*, the latter being the forerunner to the current *Archaeology* magazine. After founding the *Art Bulletin*, he was its first editor. Robinson served as president of the College Art Association and held several posts, including president, of the main umbrella group for archaeologists in North America, the Archaeological Institute of America. He also continued fieldwork in what is now Turkey excavating at the Greco-Roman cities of Sardis in 1910 and Antioch in Pisidia in 1924 (see figure I.3). His leadership of this last excavation came about purely by chance. In May 1924 Francis Kelsey was unexpectedly unable to lead the University of Michigan's excavations at the site.[78] Kelsey asked Robinson to take over at the last minute, no doubt partly because of the formidable reputation he had within the archaeological field.[79]

Robinson's most recent project was the excavation at Olynthus. He had first visited the site in 1902 and picked up shards of ancient black- and red-figured pottery as well as the heads of some small terracotta figurines on the ground surface, all of which indicated the presence of an important site.[80] The first season at the site, in 1928, did not go well. Robinson had failed to keep up with developments in excavation technique and so was digging in a manner several years outdated. One of his graduate student staff members in 1928, Wilhelmina van Ingen, wrote about her experiences in a series of letters to her mother. These letters now reside in the archives at Virginia Tech. The central task Robinson gave to van Ingen and her friend and fellow graduate student Eunice Couch née Stebbins was the inventorying of finds. Robinson brought the pair out of the dig house to help supervise the excavation trenches only a few times during the months they were at Olynthus. Even though she was a graduate student working on her first excavation, van Ingen recognized immediately specific problems with Robinson's techniques, which she catalogs in a letter dated April 11, 1928. In this quote she refers to Couch by the nickname Nike, the name of the Greek goddess of victory:

> Nike and I went up to the dig to watch trenches today—a great relief after having been cooped up in the house constantly doing close work. I hope Davy

[Robinson] lets us go out more—certainly we are needed for there are so many workmen and trenches that it is impossible to keep close enough watch over things. . . . I have been watching one trench—there were 131 workmen in it today, in an area of about thirty square yards, and it is impossible to keep an adequate record of what is found—and as soon as I get some little orderly plan worked out, Davy comes along and changes everything, so it's all rather futile.

The chief value of this experience to me will be that I shall have formed some ideas of what NOT to do, and shall have had some opportunity to observe the various sorts of objects which are turned up—if I can remember them until sometime when they can be explained AND dated by someone who knows some archaeology.[81]

In an earlier letter dated March 21 she states, "Things are not developing as easily as they might, and it is possible that the time will come when I will not care to add my presence at this dig to my list of credentials." Rumors drifted back to the American School in Athens that Robinson's techniques of recording the context in which artifacts were found were seriously lacking, causing deep concern.[82]

Upon completion of the 1928 season, Robinson began to publish articles as well as books on his findings at Olynthus with unbelievable speed. The first volume in the *Excavations at Olynthus* series appeared in 1929 and was the only one for which Robinson's name does not appear on the cover page. It was a publication of the dissertation written by his student George Mylonas on a Neolithic settlement at the site. Robinson wrote and published the second volume on the architecture at the site in 1930 less than two years after his initial field season. The following year he managed to complete and publish no less than two additional volumes, *Olynthus III* on the coins found in the 1928 season and *Olynthus IV* on the small terracotta figurines he had uncovered. Few archaeologists have ever produced so many publications in such a short amount of time.

Reviews of these volumes were mixed. Some classicists were impressed with his arguments for having found the site of Olynthus mentioned by Demosthenes in the *Olynthiacs*, while both numismatists and art historians appreciated the new evidence of well-dated pieces he had found to inform their fields.[83] The archaeologists who reviewed his work were not impressed at all, however, echoing van Ingen's criticisms. Dohan, writing about the terracotta figurines published in *Olynthus IV*, complained about a lack of contextual information stating there was little point in publishing figurines from an excavation if Robinson could not explain specifically where within the site of Olynthus they were found; naturally it matters a great deal for understanding how a terracotta figurine was used if it is found in a temple, or house, or even in the public or private rooms within a house.[84] Alan Wace, director of the British School at Athens and excavator at sites across Greece,[85] made a similar complaint lamenting the lack of information not only about the horizontal but also the vertical find spot of each lamp.[86] Another reviewer made an even more stinging charge:

> In these days when the standard of excavation is already high, and the technique becoming yearly more perfect, there is no excuse for an ill-conducted excavation. Archaeologists make it a matter of principle not to employ large numbers of workmen without the most expert and careful supervision, or to confuse evidence by overhasty search for results. Nor do the Archaeological Schools usually entrust a site, whether large or small, to anyone who has not had adequate training. The methods adopted at Olynthus were, therefore, a shock to those who saw or heard of them, nor will their reputation be retrieved by the volume under discussion.[87]

Another criticism of the 1928 season was about the failure to find fine sculptures, Greek inscriptions, or public architecture. At that time, these were the primary prizes classical archaeologists sought when digging. Van Ingen neatly sums up what all were thinking during that season in a letter dated March 16, 1928: "So far they haven't found much that's exciting—lots of private houses, terracotta, vase fragments, coins, etc. but no public buildings or inscriptions."[88] Van Ingen expressed her opinion privately in a letter but others expressed their disappointment in Robinson's finds publicly in print, adding to his humiliation.[89] Robinson came to his second season at Olynthus in 1931 looking for redemption.

Ellingson gives no indication that she was aware of these pressures on Robinson; she clearly had a deep respect and affection for the man. Although she was less than half Robinson's age, Ellingson's letters show they had a friendly, even flirtatious relationship. She repeatedly refers to him as "Davey" in her letters and, presumably, in person. Admittedly, she was not the only young woman to be so informal with him; van Ingen, referred to him repeatedly as "Davy" in her letters as well.[90] Nonetheless, in the April 9 letter to her mother quoted above Ellingson writes,

> The other night I asked him [Robinson] where the men were going to be paid, & he said "would you like to pay them? You're the prettiest girl here, you can be Miss Olynthus, & pay the men." And the other day when my hand was swollen from a flea bite, he said, "You have a pretty neck, I hope it doesn't swell up." And on rainy days, he tells me I don't need to go to the dig at all. (I mean on days when it is threatening to rain, we don't go at all on rainy days.)

It seems unlikely that their relationship ever went beyond flirtation. Mentioning the compliments Robinson made to her in a letter to her mother hardly seems the actions of a woman engaged in an adulterous affair. Ellingson also describes the protective attitude Mrs. Robinson had toward the younger woman and Ellingson never mentions anything Mrs. Robinson said or did that indicated she felt jealous. Quite the contrary, Mrs. Robinson did not hesitate to take trips to Saloniki while her husband remained at Olynthus working with Ellingson. Also in the same letter quoted above to her mother Ellingson writes, "Mrs. R[obinson], is awfully nice to me too, & she calls me 'Little One' just like you do . . . & [she] loans me her own shoes etc."[91] Nonetheless others on the crew must have noticed the pairs' flirtations.

Ellingson's affection for Robinson was not shared by all who worked with him. Van Ingen had carefully contemplated going with Robinson to Olynthus while she was still studying at the American School and as a result anticipated the coming season with trepidation. In a letter sent from Athens dated February 24, 1928, she writes, "The two months in Olynthus may not be unalloyed pleasure—Davy is exceedingly difficult to get along with and not always entirely to be commended in his actions."[92] A few months later on April 2 writing from Olynthus she sums up her feelings about Robinson: "In brief he is a poor scholar, ungentlemanly, and not always honest."[93] Her letters record fights and tears and the constant strain of dealing with a man she and her fellow graduate students found to be controlling, egotistical, and vindictive. In a fairly typical letter dated April 11 van Ingen writes,

> Davy is more or less on his good behavior, though he's always sticking sly little digs into the conversation that Nike and I know are meant for us. Also, there is a constant nervous strain trying to keep one's temper and not get wrought up over things, and seeing the dig carried on in such a careless way, and not being able to do anything about it.[94]

In early May van Ingen and her two fellow graduate student colleagues finally decided to depart the excavation ten days before they were scheduled to leave, their flight precipitated by a tremendous fight with Robinson.[95] Van Ingen finally did transfer to Harvard and successfully pursued her graduate studies without Robinson.[96] It is quite telling that of all the staff members from Johns Hopkins or the American School who joined Robinson for the initial season at Olynthus in 1928, only one, George Mylonas, returned for additional seasons at the site.

Conundrum is the best word to describe Robinson, however. While he may have been controlling of his graduate students, he also went far out of his way to take care of Ellingson and his other students by making certain they received what they needed to be successful. He helped them find grants and scholarships to support their studies and travels.[97] The American School offered fellowships to students who scored well on the School's exams in ancient Greek and history and either literature or archaeology, exams which candidates took at their home institution at the time they were applying to attend the American School. By 1934 the director of the American School, Richard Stillwell, was unhappy about the large number of Johns Hopkins students at the American School, a back-handed compliment to Robinson's efforts.[98]

Robinson was willing to do whatever it took to get his students a fellowship at the American School, perhaps even if it was not ethical. In late 1932 a graduate student at Johns Hopkins tipped off the American School's Fellowship Committee that a certain professor was feeding information to his students about specific questions and topics on the exams. An investigation ensued, during which members of the committee discreetly referred to the accused teacher as "Professor Blank," never actually giving his name. The committee made changes to the manner in which they gave the exam to thwart any future attempts to cheat. Incidental clues in the correspondence over the matter have led one historian of the American School to suggest that Robinson was "Professor Blank."[99]

Robinson also held a deeply engrained sense of meritocracy. This led him to intervene when he felt it necessary to make certain worthy students did not lose opportunities to develop their natural abilities and further their studies because of identity-focused prejudices. Among the letters of Edward Capps, the chairman of the Fellowship Committee now archived at the American School, were some from committee members objecting to giving one of Robinson's students, Marian Welker, a fellowship because of her gender and because she was "very deaf."[100] Letters from Robinson defend her fiercely, describing her as "one of the best students I have ever had, in all fields of archaeology."[101] In another instance, Robinson was asked his opinion about offering a fellowship to a student from Columbia University, Israel Walker, who had outscored the other candidates on the exams by quite a bit, but to whom some on the Fellowship Committee objected because of his Jewish identity. Robinson's response is preserved in Yale University's Manuscripts and Archives: "Personality is an important thing and I hate the Jews with a few exceptions, but these fellowships are given for scholarship and ability to do research work and not merely on the grounds of personality."[102] One has to wonder if such a slur was performative, a crude attempt to gain the confidence of the antisemitic members of the committee, or came from actual racist conviction. The latter seems unlikely as Robinson promoted the careers of several Jewish scholars. In the end, both students received the fellowships.

Whether or not Robinson really helped his students cheat on the exam, there was clearly tension between him and the leadership of the American School. During the 1920s and 1930s, faculty from Princeton University were moving into the leadership positions of the American School and a rivalry developed with students and faculty from other universities, especially Johns Hopkins.[103] Van Ingen's letters show the pleasure she and the other Johns Hopkins students took with Robinson in sharing embarrassing gossip about the Princeton students.[104] Robinson's opponents could be equally petty. Francis Henry Bacon, an architect and interior designer at the American School, snapped a photo of Robinson. On the back he labeled it "Musso-lini."[105] This rivalry had consequences for Robinson that went far beyond mere rumor spreading. In 1928 the Greek government attempted to take the power to issue permits for American-led excavations in Greece away from the American School through legislation making the government the sole entity to decide who received them. Leaders at the American School fought to have their right to decide which American projects should be recommended for permits to the Greek antiquities authorities. By the end of 1928 the American School had won the dispute and retains the right to this day. At the beginning of 1928, however, before the American School had secured this right and as the dispute with the Greek government was developing, officials at the School asserted that Robinson had to go through them before he sought a permit from the Greek government for his first season of excavation at Olynthus.[106] Robinson had been trying to establish the Olynthus excavation independent of the American School, a battle he lost. As a prerequisite for their blessing for the permit, Capps and the American School's Managing Committee defined four conditions Robinson and all subsequent American excavation directors would need to follow, nicknamed the "Olynthus Conditions." The four conditions included that the project have proper equipment and trained staff, including American School members; the project had to be completed and the site not left partially excavated; the excavator had to bear the full cost of the excavation; and publication had to happen within three years of the project's completion. Robinson was very timely with his publications of the Olynthus material, otherwise after he agreed to these conditions, he ignored the other three whenever they got in his way. As for the first condition, student members of the American School would suffice.[107] The first three student-representatives Robinson and School officials agreed upon in 1928 were from Johns Hopkins: van Ingen, Stebbins Couch, and Herbert Couch.[108] It is not clear how Robinson reacted to this assertion of power, especially when the person behind it was Capps from Princeton. It is easy, though, to imagine the strain that must have existed, especially since all the excavations Robinson had directed prior to this were outside of Greece in places where Robinson had a great deal more autonomy. In 1931 Robinson had to have known that officials from the American School would be watching his second season closely after his poor performance during the first season and would be deciding whether to allow him to have a third season in the future.

Robinson's tempestuous personality led him to bitter conflicts throughout his life. He was at his most vengeful, however, when he believed his intellectual property rights had been violated. While working on the material from his Antioch excavation in 1924, he became embroiled in a dispute with Sir James Ramsey over who had the right to publish, and therefore have the claim to have discovered, an important inscription found at the site. The inscription was a copy of the *Res Gestae Augusti*, a document the first Roman emperor Augustus wrote at the beginning of the first century CE detailing his accomplishments and justifying his position as the first emperor. Augustus was, without a doubt, one of the most influential of all the Roman emperors and the discovery of portions of his own assessment of his reign was something quite extraordinary. Pieces of the inscription had been found at other sites but having another copy with portions of hitherto unknown text made the find a huge coup. Ramsey had been supervising the area where the inscription was found, but when Robinson had agreed at the last minute to lead the excavation in Kelsey's stead, part of the agreement was that he would be allowed to publish everything that had been found there, especially the inscriptions.[109] When Ramsey published news of the discovery and his transcription of the inscription, Robinson labeled Ramsey's publication "illegal."[110] The dispute between them spread across the pages of several scholarly journals.[111] Robinson added personal insult to his legalistic invectives against Ramsey. He claimed that he had found additional pieces of the inscription in Ramsey's back-dirt pile, implying Ramsey had missed portions of this major discovery during excavation. Such a charge is the ultimate insult one archaeologist can level against another. Robinson did not stop there—he even claimed to have purchased pieces of the inscription from nearby villagers who had fished them out of Ramsey's back-dirt pile.[112] By relating the story, Robinson obliquely suggested rural farmers with no formal training in archaeology were better able to spot important finds than Ramsey.

In 1910 Robinson married Helen Haskell (figure 1.12), who was his constant companion during the Olynthus excavations.[113] Stepdaughter of the Protestant Episcopal Bishop of Maryland, she was a graduate of Bennett

Figure 1.12. Photograph by Mary Ross Ellingson taken in Saloniki on the morning of March 25, 1931, as Robinson and his crew prepared to depart for Olynthus. From left to right, George Mylanos, Helen Robinson, David Robinson, an unidentified man, Arthur Parsons, Sarah Freeman, Alexander Schulz, and Gladys Davidson Weinberg. Note the upside down wheelbarrow in the truck behind them.
Photo courtesy of the University of Evansville Archives

College, a women's college in Millbrook, New York.[114] Robinson said of his wife that she was "amply provided for by her own fortune," wealth she presumably inherited from her parents.[115] Ellingson really liked Mrs. Robinson and spoke fondly of her years after their shared experience in the field.[116] George Mylonas writes of her,

> His many students will cherish forever the picture of Mrs. Robinson as the graceful hostess who brightened so many of their days, and those who were privileged to participate in the excavations of Olynthus will never forget her kindness, her efficiency and cheerfulness in the midst of adverse conditions, and her understanding of the failings of human nature.[117]

His comments are rather cryptic, perhaps intentionally. Does he suggest that Mrs. Robinson forgave the students' human failings while at Olynthus or that she helped them forgive those of her husband?

Figure 1.13. George Mylonas excavating at Olynthus. The heavy clothing he and the workmen wear indicate this photo was taken in March or April.

Photo courtesy of the David M. Robinson Collection, Special Collections, University of Mississippi Libraries

George and Lela Mylonas

The last couple to join the expedition in Saloniki was George Emmanuel Mylonas (figure 1.13) and his wife, Lela. Mylonas was one of the Greek-speaking
natives of the western portion of Asia Minor known as Ionia, having been
born in 1898 in Smyrna, or modern Izmir. When he was seventeen years old,
Mylonas went to Athens to study classics at the University of Athens and during World War I joined the Greek army to fight against the Ottoman Empire
and its ally, Germany. He was taken prisoner and almost did not survive his
imprisonment. When he was finally released in 1923, he went to Greece at a
time of great turmoil. Greece had just concluded a disastrous war with Turkey,
which ended with an exchange of ethnic Greeks from Turkey for Turks from
Greece. Mylonas met another refugee from Turkey, Lela Papazoglu, and the
two were married in 1925. He found employment working at the American
School in Athens as a bursar and translator.[118] In 1927 the University of
Athens awarded Mylonas a PhD after he completed his dissertation on the
Neolithic period in Greece. The following year he came to Johns Hopkins
to complete a second PhD in only one year.[119] Robinson made Mylonas's
Hopkins dissertation the inaugural volume in the *Olynthus* series and gave
him the unique honor of allowing Mylonas's name alone to appear as the
author of the *Excavations at Olynthus I*.[120] In the introduction to *Excavations
at Olynthus I*, Robinson expresses his great pride in seeing Mylonas's dissertation published in the *Excavations at Olynthus* series.

When Ellingson met Mylonas at Saloniki, he was thirty-two years old
and already a distinguished archaeologist. In 1931 while he worked at the
Olynthus excavation, Mylonas was caught between two separate worlds and
lifestyles, one in Greece and the other in the United States. After arriving at
Johns Hopkins, he remained and seemed to have been hoping to emigrate but
needed a job, preferably a tenure-track position at a university. At that point
he did not know if he would be able to make the move permanently or would
have to remain in Greece. Ellingson rarely mentions him in her letters. In the
April 9 letter where she describes her fellow staff members, she merely says of
Mylonas and his wife that they were very formal, always addressing everyone
by their surnames preceded by "Mr." and "Miss." Ellingson seems to have found
them to be rather aloof.

The Final Road, the Photographer,
and the Artist

Driving the approximately sixty miles from Saloniki to Myriophito, the near-
est town to the site of Olynthus, took the better part of a day in 1931. Prior to

the team's departure in two cars and a truck on March 25, Ellingson snapped a photograph of the group (figure 1.12). All are smiling and appear to be in good spirits, a mood that would not last. In a letter to her family dated March 26, she writes of the challenges of the journey for the car in which she was riding, "We had to drive right thru a river. One sight we saw was a wall of water coming down a dry river-bed, however we got in OK." The Parsons, Weinberg, and Freeman in the other car and the truck that accompanied them did not have as easy a journey. Of them she writes in a March 29 letter,

> As I started to tell, the other car had a terrible time getting out here. We didn't start until about 1, as we had been waiting for the truck. As Wednesday was a national holiday, there were a whole lot of parades etc., so they were held up, and then they had a flat tire. As there wasn't any spare, they had to go back and get another car. The man drove back on the rim, lickety split, over rough cobblestone roads. They got another car, and finally got out of Salonica at 3.15. They caught up to the truck, which had had a flat tire when we passed it, and when they passed it, it had its wheel off and was stuck in the mud. The rain was all over by the time they came along, so they had to get out in the mud and push while the sun was shining, which was infinitely better than getting out in the rain, I suppose. Finally it got dark, and they came to the river which they had to cross, and not being able to see the road, they went right thru instead of going a little further up as we had. And of course when they got in the middle of it, they got stuck and Gladys and Sally and Arthur had to get out in the water and push. Maybe I was glad I wasn't with them. Finally they got to Modania, where Mr. Mylonas had gone to meet them, about 9.30, and they went to the inn there, which isn't so hot, I guess. They got over [to Myriophito] about noon.

When Ellingson snapped a photo of the group preparing to leave Saloniki (figure 1.12) everyone was very nicely dressed for traveling. Little did Parsons, Freeman, and Weinberg realize that in a few hours their clothes would be filthy from pushing a truck out of the mud and a car out of a river. They were not the only people who had ever had to push stuck vehicles out of a river in the area, however. In 1928 van Ingen snapped a photo of a Model T in a river near Olynthus clearly demonstrating that the rivers in the area could be quite treacherous (figure 1.14).

Once she had settled into her accommodations in Myriophito and began work, Ellingson met the final members of the Olynthus staff. Euripides Melanides was a professional photographer with a studio in Saloniki. Although photography was a costly medium at the time, Robinson understood its value in recording and publishing archaeological data and so spared no expense in getting the shots he wanted. While he took some of the photos himself, he also employed Melanides (pictured in figure 2.9) who took superb photos using a large-format camera.[121] Ellingson and Melanides struck up a friendship; she photographed him outside his studio in Saloniki and he gave her copies of photos he had taken for Robinson in which she appeared. He clearly had a great deal of affection for Ellingson and wrote enthusiastically of her, "the little girl with the bobbed hair was a queen among women."[122]

Georg von Peschke served as the expedition's artist. A member of a Habsburg noble family, von Peschke grew up dividing his time between his divorced parents, his father living in rural Croatia and mother in urbane Vienna. Only eight years older than Ellingson, he had already lived an eventful life by the time they met, seeing his wealth evaporate and titles become meaningless in the aftermath of World War I while aspiring unsuccessfully to become an artist. Disillusioned, he left a wife and two children in Croatia to bicycle across the Balkans, photographing and drawing along the way. Greece enchanted him and he settled there permanently in 1925, keeping knowledge of his Croatian family secret from his new circle of friends.[123] Von Peschke married a Greek woman from the Island of Skyros with whom he was deeply in love for the rest of his life. In Greece, von Peschke established a reputation for his Greek Modernist paintings, prints, and drawings, exhibiting them in Athens, Paris, and Vienna. It is not clear how Robinson and von Peschke met, but in 1931 the archaeologist convinced the artist to make architectural drawings for him at Olynthus as well as detailed and highly accurate illustrations of some of the mosaics and artifacts.[124] The painstaking care with which von Peschke carried out his work is well illustrated by his watercolor of a 1.3-meter diameter black and white pebble mosaic depicting Bellerophon astride the Pegasus slaying the Chimera. Von Peschke's painting reproduces the mosaic at a one to one scale, depicting every single stone exactly as each appears. The painting has become synonymous with Robinson's Olynthus excavations. Participating in Robinson's expedition was von Peschke's first experience illustrating archaeological materials and working with an excavation crew. He clearly liked the work and both he and his wife enjoyed being around the excavators. Von Peschke saw the opportunity to continue to evolve his new identity, adding archaeological illustrator to his persona as Modernist artist. Ellingson charmed von Peschke. He had her pose for sketches that he intended to use in a painting of the crucified Christ and, according to a letter Ellingson penned on May 27, wanted to use her image for Mary Magdalene. In the completed painting, Ellingson/Mary Magdalene kneels, grasping the base of the cross with chin upturned, her eyes closed. Von Peschke twists the faces of the other figures in the painting to depict their anguish at the scene, but Mary Magdalene appears serene and stoic.[125] Von Peschke must have seen Ellingson exhibit these qualities in the way she reacted to both the chaos of trenches at the site and the belligerent way Robinson led his crew.

From Archaeologists to Archaeology

A knock on my open door jolted me from my revery, transporting me back from the excavation in 1931 to the university in the present. The student apologized; she could see I was engrossed in something. She wanted to know when I thought I would finish grading those papers. I sighed.

Once she was gone, I looked at my desk. The stack of papers had been pushed off to the side to make room for the letters, newspaper clippings, and photos that now covered it. Which should I look at next? Student papers. Ellingson's letters. Papers. Letters.

The letters won. Having a moment to think about what I had read so far, questions had crept into my consciousness. Learning about Ellingson and all her friends was interesting, but what about the archaeology? Was Robinson really going to let the women excavate without male supervision? Would

Figure 1.14.   A Model T stuck in a river near Myriophito in the spring of 1928.
Photo courtesy of the Wilhelmina Van Ingen Elarth Papers, Ms1969-004, Special Collections and University Archives, Virginia Tech, Blacksburg, Va.

Greek workmen allow Ellingson to direct their digging? Did Ellingson work on any of the houses for which Olynthus was to become so famous? What was the significance of the box filled with plaster casts of ancient figurines? Were they souvenirs or did they have a more serious purpose? Student papers could wait.

Notes

1. This information is contained in a form in Ellingson's personnel file dated September 11, 1973, now in the archives at the University of Evansville. The form is difficult to read leading me to originally interpret the final digit in her birth year to be a 6. When she saw I had listed Ellingson's birth year as 1906, her daughter Barbara Petersen corrected my mistake. Unfortunately, by that point, the book was already in print. I am grateful for the opportunity to correct the error in this new edition.

2. Margriet Haagsma, "Historiography and Theory," *Journal of Greek Archaeology* 5 (2020): 631.

3. Haagsma, "Historiography and Theory," 631.

4. "Pioneer Residents of Edmonton to Mark 67th Wedding Day," *The Edmonton Bulletin*, December 31, 1940.

5. Barbara Petersen, interview with the author on December 11, 2013; Haagsma, "Historiography and Theory," 631.

6. City of Edmonton Development, "Edmonton Population, Historical," 2008, http://webdocs.edmonton.ca/InfraPlan/demographic/Edmonton%20Population%20Historical.pdf, accessed June 29, 2022.

7. City of Edmonton Development, "Edmonton Population, Historical."

8. "Excavations in Old Greece Are Recounted," *The Evansville Courier and Press*, March 3, 1940, 4.

9. Unfortunately, when Ellingson clipped this article, she failed to keep the date or the name of the reporter.

10. "Wins Degree," *The Edmonton Bulletin*, June 12, 1939.

11. Barbara Petersen, interview with the author on December 11, 2013; Haagsma, "Historiography and Theory," 633.

12. Haagsma, "Historiography and Theory," 634–35.

13. *The Alberta Women's Memory Project*, "Profiles of Alberta Women: Geneva Misener," http://awmp.athabascau.ca/profiles/gmisener/, accessed June 29, 2022.

14. Linda M. Medwid, *The Makers of Classical Archaeology* (New York: Humanity Books, 2000), 93–95.

15. Haagsma, "Historiography and Theory," 633.

16. Stephen L. Dyson, *Ancient Marbles to American Shores: Classical Archaeology in the United States* (Philadelphia: University of Pennsylvania Press, 1998), 158–59. For a contemporary view that passionately expresses the alarm felt by those who loved, and feared the loss of, Greek culture, see Eva Palmer-Sikelianos, *Upward Panic—The Autobiography of Eva Palmer-Sikelianos*. Translated by John P. Anton. (Philadelphia: Harwood Academic Publishers, 1993), 175–80.

17. See Appendix II for more detail and Kathleen A. Laughlin, Julie Gallagher, Dorothy Sue Cobble, Eileen Boris, Premiila Nadasen, Stephanie Gilmore, and Leandra Zarnow, "Is It Time to Jump Ship? Historians Rethink the Waves Metaphor," *Feminist Formations* 22, no. 1 (2010): 76.

18. *The Canadian Encyclopedia*, "Timeline, Women's Suffrage," https://www.thecanadianencyclopedia.ca/en/timeline/womens-suffrage, accessed June 30, 2022.

19. Haagsma, "Historiography and Theory," 635.

20. Ibid., 634–36.

21. Helen M. M. Ross, "The Terra Cotta Industry at Olynthus" (MA thesis, Johns Hopkins University, 1932), 69.

22. Mariam K. Chamberlain, *Women in Academe- Progress and Prospects* (New York: Russell Sage Foundation, 1988), 5.

23. Julia B. Morgan, *Women at the Johns Hopkins University: A History* (Baltimore: Johns Hopkins University, 1986), 20.

24. Margaret W. Rossiter, *Women Scientists in America: Struggles and Strategies to 1940* (Baltimore: Johns Hopkins University Press, 1982), 206.

25. Dyson, *Ancient Marbles*, 193.

26. Haagsma, "Historiography and Theory," 634–35.

27. Paul N. Perrot. "Gladys Davidson Weinberg (1909–2002)," *Journal of Glass Studies* 44 (2002): 211.

28. Aleisa Fishman, "Gladys Davidson Weinberg 1909–2002," in *Jewish Women in America: An Historical Encyclopedia*, edited by E. Paula Hyman and Debora D. Moore (New York: Routledge, 1997), 1462; Pierre de Miroschedji, Obituary for Gladys Davidson Weinberg, *Israel Exploration Journal* 52, no. 2 (2002): 97.

29. Harriet Pass Freidenreich, "Joining the Faculty Club: Jewish Women Academics in the United States," *Nashim: A Journal of Jewish Women's Studies and Gender Issues* 13 (2007): 72. See also Dyson, *Ancient Marbles*, 224.

30. David O. Levine, *The American College and the Culture of Aspiration, 1915–1940* (Ithaca, NY: Cornell University Press, 1986), 147–50.

31. Freidenreich, "Joining the Faculty Club," 93.

32. "In Memoriam: Sarah Elizabeth Freeman 1907–1986," *Ákoue*, Spring 1986, 12.

33. "Four College Girls Join Olynthus Quest," *New York Times*, February 15, 1931, 33.

34. "Students to Assist in Greek Excavation," *Baltimore Evening Sun*, February 14, 1931.

35. Lydia C. Carr, *Tessa Verney Wheeler: Women and Archaeology before World War II* (Oxford: Oxford University Press, 2012), 15 and 249.

36. "Four College Girls," 33. The fourth woman mentioned in the title, Dorothy Hill, chose at the last minute not to go to Olynthus. A year earlier the *Daily Mail* in London printed a similar article title about a British excavation: "Girl Excavators." For a discussion of this title and the fascination the press has had with women working in the field, see Carr, *Tessa Verney Wheeler*, 200–203.

37. Dyson, *Ancient Marbles*, 53.

38. Ibid., 173.

39. Ibid., 102 and 159.

40. Ibid., 86.

41. Louis E. Lord, A History of the American School of Classical Studies at Athens 1882–1942 (Cambridge, MA: Harvard University Press, 1947), 89 and 231.

42. Dyson, Ancient Marbles, 86.

43. Lord, History of the American School, 15.

44. Dyson, Ancient Marbles, 88.

45. See their biographies: Mary Allsebrook, Born to Rebel: The Life of Harriet Boyd Hawes (Oxford: Oxbow Books, 1992); Vasso Fotou and Ann Brown, "Harriet Boyd Hawes, 1871–1945," in Breaking Ground: Pioneering Women Archaeologists, edited by Getzel M. Cohen and Martha S. Joukowsky (Ann Arbor: University of Michigan Press, 2004), 198–273; Diane L. Bolger, "Ladies of the Expedition: Harriet Boyd Hawes and Edith Hall at Work in Mediterranean Archaeology," in Women in Archaeology, edited by Cheryl Claassen (Philadelphia: University of Pennsylvania Press, 1994), 41–50.

46. See her biography: Machteld J. Mellink and Kathleen M. Quinn, "Hetty Goldman 1881–1972," in Breaking Ground: Pioneering Women Archaeologists, edited by Getzel M. Cohen and Martha S. Joukowsky (Ann Arbor: University of Michigan Press, 2004), 298–350.

47. Margaret C. Root, "Introduction: Women of the Field, Defining the Gendered Experience," in Breaking Ground: Pioneering Women Archaeologists, edited by Getzel M. Cohen and Martha S. Joukowsky (Ann Arbor: University of Michigan Press, 2004), 19.

48. For example, Mortimer and Tessa Wheeler; see Carr, Tessa Verney Wheeler, 16. Aileen Fox was managing her own trench and directing two workmen during excavations at the site of Richborough in 1929, even before she met her husband, the archaeologist Cyril Fox; see her autobiography, Aileen Fox, Aileen: A Pioneering Archaeologist (Leominster, Herefordshire, UK: Gracewing, 2000), 48.

49. The concept of "containment" as a way to deal with women seeking to enter science and academia was first articulated by Margaret W. Rossiter, Women Scientists in America, 216.

50. Lydia C. Carr, Tessa Verney Wheeler, 8, 55, 167, and 201. My thanks to an anonymous reviewer from Rowman and Littlefield who pointed me to an early example of the strategy of putting women in charge of "small finds," thus keeping them out of the field. The example comes from the Roman site in Britain of Lydney Park, excavated in the early nineteenth century by William H. Bathurst. Bathurst put his daughter, Charlotte Bathurst, in charge of cataloging the coins. See William H. Bathurst, Roman Antiquities at Lydney Park, Gloucestershire (London: Longmans, Green, and Co., 1879). The text is available online at https://archive.org/details/romanantiquitie00bathgoog.

The practice of assigning women to the excavation lab instead of the field has been noted by those in the generations following Ellingson's. For two examples from Central American archaeology, see D. Z. Chase, "Archaeology, the Academy, and

Women: Finding One's Own Path," *Heritage* 4 (2021): 1729 and Hattula Moholy-Hagy, "Archaeology in a Gilded Age: The University of Pennsylvania Museum's Tikal Project: 1956–1970," *Codex* 29 (2021): 8.

51. Quoted in Mary Ann Levine, "Creating Their Own Niches: Career Styles among Women in Americanist Archaeology between the Wars," in *Women in Archaeology*, edited Cheryl Claassen (Philadelphia: University of Pennsylvania Press, 1994), 17. This article is a reworked and improved version of a paper the author presented at a conference and then published in the conference proceedings, Mary Ann Levine, "Presenting the Past: A Review of Research on Women in Archaeology," in *Equity Issues for Women in Archaeology*, edited by Margaret C. Nelson, Sarah M. Nelson, and Alison Wylie. Archaeological Papers of the American Anthropological Association Number 5 (Arlington, VA: American Anthropological Association, 1994).

52. Root, "Introduction," 12.

53. Dyson, *Ancient Marbles*, 182–84.

54. Cynthia Irwin-Williams, "Women in the Field: The Role of Women in Archaeology before 1960," in *Women of Science: Righting the Record*, edited by G. Kass-Simon and Patricia Farnes (Bloomington: University of Indiana Press, 1990), 14.

55. Mellink and Quinn, "Hetty Goldman 1881–1972," 317.

56. Edith Hall, Boyd Hawes's collaborator, earned her PhD at Bryn Mawr; see Dyson, *Ancient Marbles*, 100.

57. Frederica de Laguna received her PhD from Columbia University, see Levine, "Creating Their Own Niches," 12.

58. Dyson, *Ancient Marbles*, 191, and Richard Stillwell, "Mary Hamilton Swindler (1884–1967)," *American Journal of Archaeology* 71, no. 2 (1967): 115.

59. George Mylonas, *Studies Presented to David Moore Robinson on His Seventieth Birthday*. Vol. 1, edited by George Mylonas (St. Louis: Washington University, 1951), xxi.

60. Judith G. Touchton and Lynn Davis, *Fact Book on Women in Higher Education* (New York: Macmillan, 1991), 2. For a decade-by-decade breakdown of these figures along with related statistics on women in higher education, see chapter 5.

61. Rossiter, *Women Scientists in America*, 164.

62. The *Roma* was to have a very curious afterlife, being transformed into Italy's first aircraft carrier. With the outbreak of World War II, the Italians rebuilt the ship for its new purpose, renaming it the *Aquila*. The transformation was nearly complete when Italy signed the armistice with the Allies; the crew damaged the ship to make certain the Germans could not use it. The *Aquila* was scrapped in the 1950s. David Brown, *Aircraft Carriers* (New York: Arco Publishing, 1977), 11–12.

63. Joseph W. Shaw, "James Walter Graham 1906–1991," *American Journal of Archaeology* 96, no. 2 (1992): 325; "Miss Annie C. Hare Is Married in London to Dr. J. Walter Graham, Archaeologist," *New York Times*, July 26, 1934, 16.

64. Shaw, "James Walter Graham," 325.

65. "Four College Girls," 33.

66. "Students to Assist."

67. Mylonas, "Biographical Sketch," vii.

68. "Dr. Robinson Dies; Archaeologist, 77," *New York Times*, January 3, 1958, 21.
69. Mylonas, "Biographical Sketch," vii.
70. Dyson, *Ancient Marbles*, 28 and 102.
71. Mylonas, "Biographical Sketch," viii.
72. Dyson, *Ancient Marbles*, 193.
73. Mylonas, "Biographical Sketch," vii.
74. Ibid.
75. Dyson, *Ancient Marbles*, 96–98.
76. Jennifer K. West, "Observations on Selected Papers of David Moore Robinson from the University of Mississippi Archives" (MA thesis, University of Mississippi, 1995), 128.
77. Dyson, *Ancient Marbles*, 193.
78. For a complete list of Robinson's professional accomplishments, see George Mylonas, "Biographical Sketch."
79. David M. Robinson, "Greek and Latin Inscriptions from Asia Minor," *Transactions and Proceedings of the American Philological Association* 57 (1926): 195, n. 1.
80. David M. Robinson, foreword to *Excavations at Olynthus I: The Neolithic Settlement*, by George Mylonas (Baltimore, MD: Johns Hopkins University Press, 1929), vii.
81. Quoted with permission from the Wilhelmina Van Ingen Elarth Papers, Ms1969-004, Special Collections and University Archives, Virginia Tech, Blacksburg, VA.
82. Raymond Dessy, *Exile from Olynthus: Women in Archaeology.com. Mentoring and Networking in Greece, 1927–1928* (2005): http://scholar.lib.vt.edu/faculty_archives/dessy/T_HOME-PAGE.htm, 36–38, 41, accessed August 13, 2010.
83. For example, A. Philip McMahon, "Review of *Excavations at Olynthus, Part III: The Coins Found at Olynthus in 1928* by David M. Robinson," *Parnassus* 3, no. 8 (1931): 34; Franklin P. Johnson, "Review of *Excavations at Olynthus, Part III: The Coins Found at Olynthus in 1928* by David M. Robinson and *Excavations at Olynthus, Part IV: The Terra-cottas of Olynthus, Found in 1928* by David M. Robinson," *Classical Philology* 26, no. 3 (1931): 339–40.
84. Edith H. Dohan, "Review of *Excavations at Olynthus, Part IV: The Terra-cottas of Olynthus, Found in 1928* by David M. Robinson," *American Journal of Archaeology* 36, no. 2 (1932): 207–8. One peer reviewer from Rowman and Littlefield who read an earlier version of this book made the interesting suggestion that having women like Dohan critique his work may have made Robinson more open to trust the ability of women as fieldworkers. This could explain his differential treatment of van Ingen and Couch in 1928 and Ellingson, Weinberg, and Freeman in 1931; the former pair spent most of their season cataloging in the dig house while the latter trio spent their season in the trenches. Naturally such a suggestion cannot be proven.
85. M. Medwid, *The Makers of Classical Archaeology*, 301–3.
86. Alan Wace, "Review of *Excavations at Olynthus. Part II: Architecture and Sculpture: Houses and Other Buildings* by David M. Robinson," *Classical Review* 45, no. 2 (1931): 87.

87. Winifred Lamb, "Review of *Excavations at Olynthus. Part II: Architecture and Sculpture* by David M. Robinson," *Journal of Hellenic Studies* 51 (1931): 114–15.

88. Quoted in Raymond Dessy, *Exile from Olynthus*, 34.

89. For example, Carl W. Blegen, "Review of *Excavations at Olynthus, Part II: Architecture and Sculpture: Houses and Other Buildings* by David M. Robinson," *American Journal of Archaeology* 36, no. 3 (1932): 368–69; Lord, *A History of the American School*, 251.

90. Dessy, *Exile from Olynthus, passim*.

91. While I have come across no evidence that Robinson ever participated in an extramarital affair with Ellingson or anyone else, his wife may have been fully aware of his flirtatious behavior. For a similar but much more extreme case, see the relationship between British archaeologist Mortimer Wheeler, who had serial affairs, and his wife, Tessa, who was known to console the young ladies Wheeler abandoned when he found a new love interest; Carr, *Tessa Verney Wheeler*, 182.

92. Quoted in Dessy, *Exile from Olynthus*, 33. Quoted with permission from the Wilhelmina Van Ingen Elarth Papers, Ms1969-004, Special Collections and University Archives, Virginia Tech, Blacksburg, VA.

93. Quoted in Dessy, *Exile from Olynthus*, 36. Quoted with permission from the Wilhelmina Van Ingen Elarth Papers, Ms1969-004, Special Collections and University Archives, Virginia Tech, Blacksburg, VA.

94. Quoted with permission from the Wilhelmina Van Ingen Elarth Papers, Ms1969-004, Special Collections and University Archives, Virginia Tech, Blacksburg, VA.

95. Dessy, *Exile from Olynthus*, 42 and 46.

96. Ibid., 45.

97. There are numerous references among Robinson's, Ellingson's, and van Ingen's correspondence to grants, fellowships, and scholarships for which Robinson pushed his students to apply and helped them to obtain.

98. Natalia Vogeikoff-Brogan, "The Modern Greek Exam, 'Professor Blank's' Method, and Other Stories from the 1930s," *From the Archivist's Notebook* (October 1, 2013): http://nataliavogeikoff.com/category/women-studies/, accessed June 28, 2022.

99. Vogeikoff-Brogan, "The Modern Greek Exam, 'Professor Blank's' Method, and Other Stories from the 1930s."

100. Ibid.

101. Ibid.

102. Vogeikoff-Brogan, "The Modern Greek Exam, 'Professor Blank's' Method, and Other Stories from the 1930s." The quote comes from a post in the comments section of Vogeikoff-Brogan's blog posted by Barbara McManus.

103. Dyson, *Ancient Marbles*, 193.

104. Dessy, *Exile from Olynthus*, 28.

105. Natalia Vogeikoff-Brogan, "Tales of Olynthus: Spoken and Unspoken," *From the Archivist's Notebook* (October 1, 2015): https://nataliavogeikoff.com/2015/10/01/tales-of-olynthus-spoken-and-unspoken/, accessed June 30, 2022.

106. Lord, *A History of the American School*, 204.

107. Vogeikoff-Brogan, "Tales of Olynthus: Spoken and Unspoken."

108. Dessy, *Exile from Olynthus*, 3.

109. Robinson, "Greek and Latin Inscriptions," 195, n. 1.

110. Ibid.

111. The dispute is documented in Jennifer K. West, "Observations on Selected Papers," 121.

112. David M. Robinson, "The *Res Gestae Divi Augusti* as Recorded on the Monumentum Antiochenum," *American Journal of Philology* 47, no. 1 (1926): 3.

113. Mylonas, "Biographical Sketch," ix.

114. "Mrs. Robinson's Rites Tomorrow," *Baltimore Evening Sun*, May 16, 1960.

115. Robinson wrote this description of his wife in Item 11 of his will, dated November 26, 1957. The will is on file with the Chancery Clerk in the Lafayette County Courthouse, Oxford, Mississippi.

116. Barbara Petersen, interview with the author on December 11, 2013.

117. Mylonas, "Biographical Sketch," ix–x.

118. Lord, *A History of the American School*, 176; Spyros Iakovidis, "George Emmanuel Mylonas, 1898–1988," *American Journal of Archaeology* 93 (1989): 235.

119. David M. Robinson, foreword to *Excavations at Olynthus I*, ix; Medwid, *The Makers of Classical Archaeology*, 211; Spyros Iakovidis, "George Emmanuel Mylonas," 235.

120. George E. Mylonas, *Excavations at Olynthus I: The Neolithic Settlement. Johns Hopkins University Studies in Archaeology* 6 (Baltimore: Johns Hopkins University Press, 1929).

121. David M. Robinson, forward to *Excavations at Olynthus I: The Neolithic Settlement*, by George Mylonas (Baltimore: Johns Hopkins University Press, 1929), viii. Some of Melindes's photographs are in the David M. Robinson Collection, Special Collections, University of Mississippi Libraries. While all his photos hold useful information, some show an artist's eye as well.

122. Letter Melanides to Ellingson, October 30, 1931, now in the University of Evansville Archives.

123. Kostis Kourelis, "Flights of Archaeology: Peschke's Acrocorinth." *Hesperia* 86 no. 4 (2017): 729.

124. Kostis Kourelis, "Byzantium and the Avant-Garde: Excavations at Corinth 1920s–1930s," *Hesperia* 76 (2007): 423–24.

125. The painting is now in a private collection. Kostis Kourelis, November 18, 2013, personal communication.

CHAPTER TWO

~

The Daily Routine

I have written a few excavation site reports and have read hundreds, maybe thousands. Even though archaeology is my chosen field of study, I often find site reports difficult to slog through. Every time I read one, I am struck by what is missing. Having worked on excavations, I know that some of the best parts of the experience are not deemed worthy of inclusion in the final published report. These works never mention the friendships that grow from a shared, intense experience. They neglect to mention the food and accommodations, frequent topics of conversation. Site reports gloss over the personnel and logistical challenges excavation teams need to overcome. Readers remain unaware of when or why an archaeologist developed an interpretation or changed his or her mind, abandoning one idea in favor of another. In site reports, the disagreements and messiness disappear and everything appears to have been carefully planned and to follow a linear path of development without any bumps along the way even though that is never the way it really works. Excavation final reports do not capture the thrill of discovery, reducing the moment when excavators realize the artifact that they are holding is unique, to dry scientific descriptions in a catalog entry. Excavation reports are divorced from the realities of excavation, making them not quite accurate representations of the entirety of a field project.

The fourteen volumes of the *Excavations at Olynthus* final report present the project in the objective and scientific terms that are still standard for the field. Ellingson's letters do not. She describes the daily routine mixed with unexpected disruptions to that routine. Coupling her descriptions of the process of archaeology at Olynthus with the results reported in the final publication makes a thorough and, in my view, more honest picture of an excavation rarely available at any other site. What must have seemed like mundane details to her are particularly striking today as the style of massive horizontal excavation she describes is no longer practiced. The archaeology of Olynthus in 1931 belongs to a world that has passed. She also offers clues to two major changes in Robinson's thinking that occurred between the 1928 and 1931 seasons. The first change was his decision to allow women to work in the field supervising trenches for the entire season, not just a few days. How much of this decision had to do with the abilities of the three women cabinmates and how much of it was because of his need of supervisors will never be clear. The second change was his decision that the ancient Greek house was a unit worthy of study. During the previous season his main purpose had been to find public buildings, the traditional focus of classical archaeology at the time, and he was deeply frustrated to uncover only private structures. In 1931 he saw an opportunity in what he had considered to be of minimal value three years earlier. Both changes were to have a profound impact on Robinson and archaeology in Greece in ways he could never have envisioned nor ever intended. As I read her description of the daily routine's seemingly mundane details, I realized Ellingson was offering me a front-row seat to a landmark moment in the history of Greek archaeology, a moment she describes with the breathless enthusiasm of someone discovering fieldwork for the first time and the keen eye of someone trained as a reporter.

Starting the Day

Olynthus, March 27[, 1931].

Dear Family,

Well, here we are settled, real archaeologists. And would you guess what happened? Last night it started to snow, and boy was it cold or was it cold? We three girls and the Parsons had the top floor of a house, and we had those canvas cots. We each had three blankets and lots of sheets. All night long we lay there and wished for it to be 6.30 which was the appointed hour to get up, and of course when the alarm did go off we didn't want to get up. But as there is quite a bit of snow on the ground, we are not working today. We are over in the other house, and have a nice fireplace. [See figure 2.1.]

Robinson chose to begin his excavation in late March and to end it in early June before it became too warm.[1] The clothing fashions of the 1930s did not allow excavators to wear the shorts, t-shirts, and tank tops ubiquitous on sites today, therefore excavating while properly attired in the heat of a

Figure 2.1. **The main dig house in Myriophito where the entire team ate and worked and where the Robinsons slept. Notice no electrical wires reach the house; Myriophito lacked electricity.**
Photo courtesy of the University of Evansville Archives

Greek summer was out of the question. The current widespread availability of air conditioning also helps to cool crew members during breaks as well as during the night, but this luxury was obviously not available in rural Greece in 1931. Digging in the spring helped Robinson and his team avoid the heat but they still had to cope with the cold and rain.

As Ellingson mentions, she, Freeman, Weinberg, and the Parsons shared the upper story of a house while the bottom story was still occupied by a local family. Among Ellingson's papers is an undated news clipping from an unidentified source with the byline Thelma Atkinson.[2] Atkinson writes,

> Miss Ross writes that she found it exceedingly difficult to accustom herself to the morning invasion of the lower portions of the house by chickens, sheep and even pigs, warned by their hunger that breakfast time was near. Up at six, work commenced at seven.

The five would take their breakfast at the dig house with the Mylonas and the Robinsons. Afterward they would walk to the site wading through, or crossing via steppingstones over, the Resetnikia River and climbing a steep hill, a hike requiring some twenty to thirty minutes as Ellingson states in the same letter quoted above. In an April 8 letter, she explains further to her father:

Figure 2.2. A Greek workman carries David Robinson across the Resetnikia River with the village of Myriophito in the background.
Photo courtesy of the University of Evansville Archives

> The Retsinikia [sic], the river we have to cross to go to work, is probably impassable by now, as yesterday it was getting pretty high, and it has rained nearly all day, and heavily. When we first arrived here, we crossed the river piggy-back, on the workmen [see figure 2.2] but lately it has been so deep we have had to cross in an ox-cart, and if tomorrow weren't a holiday, I am sure we should have to swim. These Greek rivers are a howl. Half the time they are perfectly dry, and then a rain comes along, and they are raging torrents.

Once they had made it safely to the site the entire team could turn to their various work assignments.

Women Excavators Working on Site

Although Robinson had been criticized for employing such a large workforce in 1928, he insisted on having an equally large number of paid Greek workmen in 1931 to make certain he could uncover large sections of the site. Sample entries in the daily log for the 1931 season give the specific numbers for each day:

Saturday April 11, 1931—Resumed excavations with 215 men; short-handed on account of [Easter] holiday season.
Friday, May 1st, Continued excavation with 350 men.[3]

Today it is inconceivable to employ such a large workforce because labor costs are much higher and the expected ratio of workers to supervisors is much smaller. Yet even in 1931 this was an unusually large number of workers. Robinson expected the workers to move a great deal of earth quickly. He utilized Decauville railroad cars, visible in figure 2.3, to move the large volume of soil the workers excavated; these cars were originally designed for use in mining, agriculture, and industry, which suggests the scale at which Robinson conceived of his project. Workers could quickly and easily lay the narrow-gauge track on the ground, moving it to a new location when necessary. The cars' buckets swung, making them easy to empty on the back-dirt pile. The chaotic excavation conditions created by using so many men at once are well illustrated by a photo of one of the trenches the excavation's photographer Melanides snapped from atop a ladder (figure 2.4). Twenty-one men are at work in the trench surrounding Robinson, who is issuing orders to the supervisor. Each of the workers is busy in his own part of the trench.

Robinson needed as many graduate student supervisors as he could get to manage all these workers. Putting Ellingson, Weinberg, and Freeman in charge of their own trenches to work as equals with the male graduate student supervisors was probably a decision born of necessity rather than from some nascent desire for gender equality in archaeology. The fact that in his interim report on the 1931 season Robinson states after mentioning Mylonas's help that, "Mr. Graham and Mr. Schulz also assisted in excavating certain sections" without mentioning any of the women would seem to support the conclusion that Robinson had no equity intentions in mind when he put the women to work in the trenches.[4] Ellingson was both eager to meet the challenge and excited about the opportunities that would open to her with some field experience. Robinson started Ellingson out managing eight workmen but by the end of the season she was supervising sixty men at a time. In a letter of recommendation dated March 15, 1939, Robinson wrote of Ellingson, "[S]he showed remarkable executive ability and was able to superintend the Greek workmen in a very efficient way, a thing that is very unusual for a woman and which quite surprised the Greeks themselves." He added, "she is an excellent field archaeologist." The Canadian Ellingson brushed aside compliments about her archaeological and supervisory skills stating in an interview in the newspaper The Albertan published on September 18, 1931, that the reason the Greek workmen followed the directions of a woman was

Figure 2.3. Mary Ross Ellingson's team of Greek workmen excavating and depositing the dirt in the Decauville railroad cars in the background.
Photo courtesy of the University of Evansville Archives

simply because "they considered us Americans, and they have peculiar ideas about Americans." Nonetheless the fact that a reporter would ask her such a question shows that while it may not have been unprecedented, it was very unusual for a woman to fill a supervisory role on an excavation at the time.[5]

Ellingson describes what it was like to be a trench supervisor in a letter dated April 1:

> Gee it is exciting when you find something. The men all holler, "Madam, anticha!" If they find anything valuable, we give them a slip of paper with the date, our initials, and the amount of money they get for it, varying from one to four drachmas. The first man that found something for me, I gave a slip of paper, and all the others gathered round to look at it, and they all chuckled in great glee, at the epigraphy, as they call it. I have about 14 men, four with picks, 4 with shovels, three with wheelbarrows, and two with baskets. Then there is the foreman too.

Figure 2.4. David Robinson (center with left arm extended) issuing orders to a trench supervisor amid the chaos of a crowded trench. Just outside the trench in the center, right of the photo, portions of two columns are visible.
Photo courtesy of the David M. Robinson Collection, Special Collections, University of Mississippi Libraries

In another letter, dated March 27, she elaborates a bit more on how she worked with her crew:

> None of the men can speak English, except one man I have who seems to know a little bit, and I tell him what to tell the others, and then there is the foreman, who really has some archaeological instincts, and knows what it's all about. And of course Dr. R[obinson] and Dr. Mylonas come around periodically and give instructions.

Ellingson notes some of the difficulties she had managing so many men who had so little experience in archaeology and who were working with such speed. A March 27 letter shows her exasperation:

> I had one man who was a terrible trial. He thought that the more pieces he gave me the better pleased I would be, and he was tearing up perfectly good terracotta drain pipes, instead of excavating around them. However I have finally got him partly trained, if he doesn't go and forget it all by tomorrow.

There were other reasons she had to watch the men, as she explains in this May 20 letter:

> Well, such excitement as we have had around Section M, which is my dig. A week or so ago, what came up but a hoard of 63 silver coins, four of them being tetradrachms (large coins, very valuable). Well, we could hardly believe our eyes. The tetradrachms are worth about $800 each, and the smaller coins vary in price. Well, I ask you, was that a find, or was it not a find? Well, not to just stop at one hoard, what did one of my houses (I have 5 just now) produce but a hoard of 33 tetradrachms (worth about $800 each,—figure it out for yourself.) One of the workmen stole two of them. He must have shuffled them into his shoes (they all wear big shoes) and then walked off in the bushes as if he were going to the toilet, and then hid them under a stone. One of the other work-men found them there later, and reported it. So we have had to be very careful, and watch the place where they come from.

Excavating Houses

When Robinson began excavating in 1928, he was hoping to find public architecture. As the hoped-for temples and civic buildings failed to turn up, he widened the horizontal extent of his trenches in the vain hope of finding them nearby. To Robinson's frustration each shovel full of earth seemed to uncover yet another house instead and he was slow to understand that houses might be considered a significant find as well; few had yet studied houses and the daily life of the Greeks and no one had yet made this the sole focus of an excavation project.[6] Of the three volumes he published based on the finds from 1928, only one, the second, covered architecture. Less than half of this volume's text discussed the houses, a topic he saved for the third chapter after one on the excavation of a road and a second on a large, difficult-to-identify public building. Robinson was very much a product of his time in seeking public architecture. From the Renaissance through the nineteenth and early twentieth centuries, the focus of nearly all studies of ancient Greek architecture was on the public portions of cities and sanctuaries; the structures found there were considered to be the most aesthetically pleasing and worthy of imitation in contemporary architecture. At Corinth, where the American School of Classical Studies at Athens established the flagship American excavation in Greece, archaeologists had little understanding of, or interest in, the city's houses or the quotidian aspects of the lives of the city's citizens despite over three decades of digging by the time Robinson began his project.[7] In addition, in 1931 the American School was just beginning to excavate the Athenian Agora, the city's public center, where the obsession with public architecture continued. Nonetheless, a few reviewers of the early volumes of *Excavations at Olynthus* saw the potential for exploring this subject in Greek archaeology and praised Robinson for having excavated and published the domestic structures.[8] Robinson is known to have sought reviews of his work and so it seems reasonable to assume these reviews helped open his eyes to the potential of excavating houses and influenced his planning for his second season at Olynthus.[9]

Robinson's shift in focus required a shift in methodology and recording techniques. Either at Robinson's suggestion or simply with his assent, Graham devised and implemented a new system for recording the context of artifacts.[10] In 1928 Robinson had opened large horizontal trenches that uncovered several houses at once. He had recorded from which trench particular artifacts came but not which house, room, or street, making it difficult to draw conclusions about where and how the artifacts were used in antiquity.[11] To address this problem, Graham assigned every house, every room within each house, and each section of street an identifying label and had the trench supervisors record the specific location where they found each artifact. This change in recording technique answered the criticisms of the previous season's work and vastly improved the quality of the information the team was recovering. Ellingson describes the more rigorous technique in an article she wrote for the *Edmonton Bulletin* on October 19, 1931:

> When anything of value came to light, the staff members would take a knife, a tooth-brush, a piece of straw from a whisk, and dig out the object, taking care not to mar it in any way. Then the place of finding has to be measured, special attention being given to the level, as a difference of a foot or even less may mean a difference of a hundred or more years. Each find has to be recorded carefully in the daily diary, with all details. Notes have to be made on the nature of the "fill" (earth in the part being excavated). The exact position (whether right side up, sideways, etc.) has to be noted. All these facts are of the greatest importance in making records of the excavation.

Ellingson mentions that the depth of an artifact was a significant piece of information, but it is a little more complicated than she lets on. Archaeologists document the stratigraphy of a site, which is the record of the different strata of soil and the order in which they appear. Graham had the crew note in which strata they discovered artifacts in order to know the relative dates of all material. Robinson reported finding no stratigraphy during the 1928 season, a claim that was met with skepticism from at least one archaeologist who reviewed his publications.[12] Graham was able to teach the excavators to recognize and distinguish the different layers of soil and debris and to show them what to anticipate in the stratigraphy. They began digging the most recent layer of soil on the surface, which had formed as plants decayed and the wind blew dust across the plain around Olynthus. Directly below that they found the collapsed house roofs and mud brick walls dating to the sack of the city in 348 BCE. The individual mud bricks, originally baked in the sun to become hard, had dissolved over the years to form a stratigraphic layer in which the roof tiles were embedded. Surprisingly little dirt had formed over the ruins in the millennia since the town was abandoned and many years of plowing had loosened some of the topsoil that had formed, allowing rains to erode and wash it away. The remains of Olynthus, therefore, were just a few centimeters below the surface. Once the excavators had removed the debris from the collapsed buildings, they found the floors of the various rooms with their associated artifacts that had to date to 348 BCE and before (see figure 1.4 where Weinberg sits on one of these ancient floors).[13] Thanks to the inclusion of these more detailed field data that Graham taught the team to document, the records of the 1931 excavation are much more extensive than those from 1928. In addition to the notes kept by each trench supervisor, Graham wrote a log summarizing what happened each day on site. Robinson had completed that task in 1928. Graham's log is three times longer than Robinson's and contains only information about the archaeology with none of the social commentary of Robinson's log listing the archaeologists and socialites who visited the site as well as Robinson's grievances against the kitchen staff.[14] Robinson's running commentary on daily life at the site in 1928 is vivid, even entertaining, and it makes for an unusual record of an excavation of that time, but his comments crowd out the recording of some basic archaeological data necessary for publication. The lack of this basic data in the daily log helps explain the missing contextual data in the first volumes Robinson published about the site after the 1928 season that reviewers noted with dismay.

While Graham's recording technique represents a vast improvement over that employed in the 1928 excavation, Ellingson's letters reveal that gaps in the application of those techniques persisted. She states the careful recording technique was only used for "anything of value." Artifacts lacking value in Robinson's or Graham's mind included items such as iron nails, ground stone tools, ceramic vessels for cooking, and undecorated ceramics. The amount of ceramics recorded in the Olynthus excavations is well below that found at other sites suggesting the team kept little of the ceramics they excavated.[15] Those working in the cemeteries had a more difficult time recognizing different soil layers as the stratigraphy was much more subtle than among the

Figure 2.5. The moment of discovery: an amphora used as a grave, Grave 114, East Cemetery, Hill R, 0.4 m below the surface.

Photo courtesy of the University of Evansville Archives

houses, and figure 2.5 shows there was no attempt to dig stratigraphically there. The workmen were digging from the side when they came across the amphora in the photograph, not from the top. In this way they mixed the top soil with the earth underneath. They also mixed the soil from the grave with that of the surrounding area. Missing these nuances made it difficult to see later disturbances, common in cemeteries, and thereby to solidly date finds.

These criticisms notwithstanding, Robinson's decision to excavate as many houses as he could in order to study domestic life almost exclusively was something fairly new in 1931. Figure 2.6 is a plan of one of the houses Ellingson excavated, a house with the rather unromantic label of A vii 2.[16] Figure 2.7 is a photograph of the same house from the south so that the room closest to the camera when Ellingson snapped the picture is Room G. The North Hill where she was working was the location of a neighborhood newly planned in 432

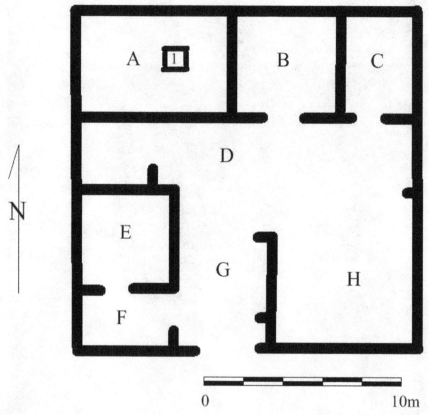

Figure 2.6. Simplified plan of House A vii 2. Compare to figure 2.7, a photo of the same house, in which Room G is closest to the viewer.

after David M. Robinson and J. Walter Graham, Excavations at Olynthus VIII, plate 99

Figure 2.7. Mary Ross Ellingson's photo of House A vii 2 looking north.
Photo courtesy of the University of Evansville Archives

BCE. Ancient surveyors had laid out the neighborhood in a grid with streets that met at right angles, following the best theory in urban design of the time. Each block was a square allowing there to be exactly ten houses of identical size on each block arranged in two rows of five with the entrances to half facing north and half south. The Greeks attributed the creation of the grid system of urban planning to one man, Hippodamus from the city of Miletus in western Asia Minor. This attribution is almost certainly incorrect; archaeologists have uncovered urban grids at Greek sites that predate Hippodamus.

Regardless of who invented it, the technique of a gridded urban layout became popular for the foundation of new colonies, the expansion of existing cities, and the rebuilding of destroyed neighborhoods. The original city of Olynthus on the south hill had an irregular layout that grew organically over time. The neighborhood on the northern hill, the location of house A vii 2, was laid out on virgin soil toward the end of the fifth century in a grid fashion, making it one of the earliest examples of this form of urban planning in Europe. According to the main source about him, book II of Aristotle's *Politics*, Hippodamus had very specific ideas about how urban planning could help create a well-functioning city. He had a strong belief in democracy and the political equality of people from different classes. Robinson's discovery of houses of identical size at Olynthus was surprising as it was the first site where Hippodamus's social views appear to have been built into the urban layout. Greeks in other cities utilized the idea of a grid layout but had little interest in Hippodamus's social ideals, building houses whose sizes varied based on wealth and social status.[17]

Figure 2.8. One of the bathtubs Mary Ross Ellingson uncovered possibly in Room G of House A vi 8.
Photo courtesy of the University of Evansville Archives

Although they shared certain elements, the internal arrangement of those elements within each house differed. All faced inward with probably few windows opening out onto the street. As with the example illustrated in figures 2.6 and 2.7, one would enter a paved courtyard from the street (G). Beyond the courtyard was a long, wide hallway/room that Robinson dubbed the *pastas* (D). Several rooms opened off of the courtyard and the *pastas*. Ellingson discovered that all evidence for at least one of the internal walls of Room H, the one at the northwestern corner of the room, had been destroyed without a trace by later plowing, therefore she was unable to determine whether entrance to this room was gained from the courtyard or the *pastas* and the wall is not represented on figure 2.6. It is difficult to assign a specific use to most rooms but features in several offer clues. One room in each house often had a raised platform along the walls on which wooden couches would have been placed. This was the *andron*, or men's dining room (E). Men and respectable women did not dine together in ancient Greece; when the men had a formal dinner party, they would recline on couches in this room. The anteroom one had to pass through in order to enter the *andron* in this particular house (F) ensured the men some privacy from prying eyes, separating the *andron* from the rest of the house. A hearth (1) in A indicates this room was a kitchen; again because of later destruction Ellingson was not able to determine where the door giving access to this room

Figure 2.9. From left to right, David Robinson, Commander Kazakos of the Greek Aeroplane Service, and photographer Euripides Melanides. Note the mount for a machine gun in the seat behind the pilot and the lack of a mount for a camera.

was located and so no doorway is represented on the plan. Attached to the kitchens of many houses were often small rooms with paved floors into which bathtubs were set (figure 2.8 and compare to figure 1.8), although House A vii 2 lacked such a feature. Putting the bathroom near the kitchen probably facilitated hot baths as the water could be heated on a hearth or brazier and quickly transported to the tub. The walls of the houses had been made of mud brick set on top of a stone foundation that, when it dissolved after the collapse of the houses, formed a layer of earth over the house foundations, floors, and the artifacts that rested on them, helping to preserve them. Ellingson uncovered bits of red-painted stucco in room C of house A vii 2, and a white-painted baseboard, evidence that at least one room had decorated walls. A vii 2 also probably had a second story, like most houses at Olynthus, but little can be said of the arrangement of space on that floor as no evidence survived the collapse of the mud brick walls.

At the end of the season architects drew the house plans and a photographer took pictures of them from the top of a tall ladder. Robinson had Melanides experiment with aerial photography, at the time a cutting-edge technology. Unlike the rest of Melanides's work, the aerial photos are of poor quality as they were snapped when the camera was pointing at wildly differing oblique angles rather than at a consistent 90-degree angle to the ground as standard aerial photography requires.[18] As a result, major parts of the photos are out of focus. It appears that Melanides did not have access to a specially designed mount for his camera as none appears on the airplane in figure 2.9. He must have been leaning over the side of the plane, gripping the camera, to take his shots. Robinson never published any of these photos nor mentioned them in print. Nonetheless, the parts of the photos that are in focus remain a valuable record of the site's architecture at the moment of excavation and may yet yield new information, especially if analyzed using modern computer techniques.

Afternoon and Evening

Lunch at noon broke up the workday. Ellingson jokingly labels one of her pictures "Lunch at a depth of .80 m. in the House of the Comic Actor" (see figure 2.10). The quantity and quality of food the crew receives is always a topic of discussion on any excavation. Olynthus was no exception. Ellingson frequently mentions what she is eating, as she does in this April 27 letter:

> Andoni the cook, has become our friend for life. We usually get 2 sandwiches, 1 hard boiled egg, 1 orange for lunch when we have it on the hill. (At the

Figure 2.10. **Members of the Olynthus staff on a lunch break in Room C of the House of the Comic Actor. Front, left to right: Mary Ross Ellingson, Alexander Schulz, George Mylonas, Gladys Davidson Weinberg. Behind wall, J. Walter Graham.**

Photo courtesy of the University of Evansville Archives

house they have more but I don't like a large lunch). On the first day Mrs. R[obinson] was in Salonica, he gave us 3 sandwiches + egg + orange. That night we told him the lunch was "poly oreia," very good. The next day we had 3 sandwiches + 3 meat croquettes + egg + orange. We told him it was poly poly oreia, very very good. The next day we got 3 sandwiches + egg + orange + huge piece of chocolate. Mrs. Robinson has since come home. Last night they were talking about how much Walter Graham ate, & how he had a "bottomless pit," & Mrs. Robinson said "next thing we know you'll be wanting 3 sandwiches for lunch." Gee we howled inwardly & praised Andoni. Not that Mrs. R[obinson] would mind us having 3 sandwiches but Davey is always talking about how much it costs to have lunch up on the hill, at 2 sandwiches per person.

According to the article by Thelma Atkinson, the crew worked until 5:30 or 6:00 p.m. Ellingson states in her March 26 letter that upon returning to the dig house at Myriophito they enjoyed "tea, crackers or bread, & the best cherry jam or peanut butter." But their workday was not complete at that point. "From then till dinner we work on our daily reports, and do any cataloging, until dinner, and then finish," she writes in an April 1 letter. The reports she refers to are daily records of where they dug and what they found, complete with the contextual information required by Graham's recording method.

The artifact cataloging had another significance for each graduate student. Robinson chose who would catalog each category of artifact assigning Graham all the lamps and loom-weights they found. The Parsons looked after the coins.[19] All bronze artifacts were the provenance of Schulz.[20] Weinberg was in charge of the pottery.[21] Each of Robinson's graduate students knew that they had to make a serious decision about the artifacts they were cataloging. They all needed topics for their theses or dissertations, and each had to determine if the material from Olynthus provided them what they needed to write the defining document of their scholarly careers. This would be a question they would not be able to answer until the end of the season. They would also have to assess how well they could work with Robinson and determine if he was the kind of person with whom they could collaborate closely in order to complete a thesis or dissertation. Cataloging, therefore, was more than just another duty.

Robinson selected Ellingson to catalog terracotta figurines. Because of their potential artistic merit, terracottas were a prized category of artifact and Robinson had noted from the beginning the potential for the site to produce them. It is another testament to Robinson and Ellingson's relationship that he gave her the pick of the artifacts to catalogue. In a pair of undated letters, she writes of her enthusiasm for her assignment:

> I have been busy, because we have discovered a most marvelous cache of ter-racottas, in what we think is the cemetery. They are simply the most marvelous things I have ever seen, and it gives me a big thrill to be the one to look after them. We got two dancers that are absolutely the most beautiful things I have ever seen. We have about 70 figurines already, and we are sure of lots more. I have given up my house on the North Hill, and have been transferred to the trench where the terracottas are, so I can see 'em come out of the ground.
>
> I sure got the pick of the inventories. I'd hate to be doing vases or loom weights or something like that. So far I have cataloged 220 terracottas.

Robinson required Ellingson, and each of his staff, to write a description of each of their artifacts in a specific, standardized way. She described the process in her October 19 article in the *Edmonton Bulletin*, "These [terracotta figurines] had to be measured at all points, and carefully described in regard to color, texture of the clay, pose of the figure, drapery, etc." Ellingson also kept her own personal inventory, however, as she had decided these terra-cotta figurines would be the subject of her master's thesis. Using Graham's typewriter, she typed her own catalog for her professional use once she got back to Johns Hopkins.[22] Ellingson threw herself into this project with great enthusiasm.

Another part of the cataloguing process involved creating a visual record of the more spectacular artifacts. One particularly significant piece Ellingson discovered came from a grave in the East Cemetery. As Ellingson lifted it

Figure 2.11. Mary Ross Ellingson took this photograph of some of the terracotta figurines she found at Olynthus while she was cataloguing them in Saloniki. The painted dancer figurine is on the far left.
Photo courtesy of the University of Evansville Archives

out of the ground and brushed off the remaining dirt, she must have noticed immediately that the paint on this particular figurine of a dancer holding a tambourine still remained. Paint rarely survives on terracotta figurines, making the lines decorating the woman's cap and the laurel wreath painted in white on the tambourine welcome discoveries. It is likely this dancer was one of the two Ellingson described in the letter above as "the most marvelous things I have ever seen." Ellingson assisted Melanides in photographing this and other artifacts, keeping a log so they would know which artifact appeared in each photograph. Again, Ellingson went beyond this taking her own personal research photographs (figure 2.11) and making a dozen plaster casts, which are now in the possession of the Department of Archaeology at the University of Evansville, to help her study them in more depth once she returned to the United States. Since only black and white photography was widely and inexpensively available in 1931, Robinson had von Peschke paint a watercolor of the figurine, again a process with which Ellingson most likely helped (figure 2.12).

Dinner was at 8:00 or 8:30 p.m. and Ellingson happily relates how much she liked the food in a letter from April 9:

> You would be amazed if you could see me eating SPINACH. Andoni, the cook, cooks it marvelously, so that it doesn't taste like spinach, we always have oranges or apples for dessert at lunch. Lovely oranges too. Andoni makes lovely desserts too. His caramel custard is lovely.

Bed followed dinner fairly quickly, as she explains in this April 1 letter:

> We go to bed around 9.30. The three of us girls are in a nice big room, the second story of a house not far from here, and the Parsons have the other room. We have a nice fireplace, and have a fire every night while getting undressed.

Figure 2.12. Georg von Peschke's water color painting of the terracotta figuring representing a dancer that Mary Ross Ellingson found in the East Cemetery at Olynthus. Note the same figurine appears in figure 2.11.

Robinson, David Moore. Excavations at Olynthus: Part VII: The Terracottas of Olynthus found in 1931. pp. Frontispiece. © 1933 Johns Hopkins University Press. Reprinted with permission of Johns Hopkins University Press.

In a May 20 letter, she elaborates on their accommodations and gives further insight into her relationship with Weinberg and Freeman:

> Gladys has a fever but she isn't ill at all. When Gladys got the fever, Sally moved out of our room into the hall, and it makes it ever so much nicer in our room. Before we had three cots side by each in the room, and it always looked so crowded and messy but now there is lots of room for Gladys and me, and we can keep it looking respectable. I have a very comfortable bed, in fact one of the best there are around here, I think.

The Archaeologist as Anthropologist

At this point, it was dark outside, and I really should have been preparing to go home, but I was quite enjoying perusing her letters. Ellingson made my reading of the *Excavations at Olynthus* series as a graduate student complete. She turned the standardized, sterile descriptions of artifacts, features, and architecture in those volumes into a real human experience of hard work and discovery. I felt I had come to understand the Olynthus project and its excavators as if I had been digging there beside them.

Certain details from her daily life she mentioned lingered in my mind, however. She described the food. Their cook Andoni seemed to be making Greek food and was not trying to cater to American tastes. Eating the cuisine is one part of archaeology I enjoy as it is a unique way to participate in the local culture. Ellingson also mentioned how she, her two roommates, and the newlyweds Arthur and Gladys Parsons were sharing the upper story of a house. A local family seemed to be living in the bottom floor. This bit of minutia got me wondering how much she interacted with the people in Myriophito. I believe an archaeologist can become an anthropologist as well as a tourist in the field. Did Ellingson share this view and embrace the opportunities to learn about the people and places around Olynthus and in Europe? If so, what were Myriophito, Greece, and the Continent like in 1931? I should have been preparing to go home. Instead, I turned on my desk lamp and shuffled through the letters and photos for answers.

Notes

1. "Students to Assist in Greek Excavation," *Baltimore Evening Sun*, February 14, 1931.

2. According to a news clipping among Ellingson's papers at the University of Evansville Thelma Atkinson was the maid of honor at Ellingson's wedding, so presumably they were old friends and she had read Ellingson's letters and spoken with

her about her time at Olynthus. The clipping about the wedding is titled "Mary Ross Is Married Quietly at Family Residence, Saturday" and, unfortunately, lacks a masthead or any indication of in which paper it was originally published.

3. J. Walter Graham, "Excavations at Olynthus Second Campaign 1931," Box 37, David M. Robinson Collection, Special Collections, University of Mississippi Libraries.

4. David M. Robinson, "Mosaics from Olynthus," *American Journal of Archaeology* 36, no. 1 (1932): 16.

5. For details on a few other women who directed crews of local workmen at foreign and domestic sites see Lydia C. Carr, *Tessa Verney Wheeler: Women and Archaeology before World War II* (Oxford: Oxford University Press), 11.

6. German and French archaeologists had done more work on Greek houses than American archaeologists prior to the commencement of Robinson's excavations at Olynthus, see Theodor Wiegand and Hans Schrader, *Priene: Ergebnisse der Ausgrabungen und Untersuchungen in den Jahren 1895–1898* (Berlin: G. Reimer, 1904); Joseph Chamonard, *Exploration archéologique de Délos. Fascicule viii. Le Quartier du Théâtre* (Paris: E. de Boccard, 1924); Hetty Goldman, "Excavations of the Fogg Museum at Colophon," paper presented at the fourteenth annual meeting of the Archaeological Institute of America, Washington, DC, December 29, 1922. *American Journal of Archaeology* 27 (1923): 67–68. In 1933, after Robinson had completed two seasons at Olynthus, Chamonard would publish another important addition to the corpus of household studies: *Exploration archéologique de Délos. Fascicule xiv: Les mosaïques de la Maison des Masques* (Paris: E. de Boccard, 1933).

7. Stephen L. Dyson, *Ancient Marbles to American Shores: Classical Archaeology in the United States* (Philadelphia: University of Pennsylvania Press, 1998), 86–87.

8. For example, Franklin P. Johnson, "Review of *Excavations at Olynthus, Part II: Architecture and Sculpture: Houses and Other Buildings* by David M. Robinson," *Art Bulletin* 12, no. 4 (1930): 421–22; and Alfred Merlin, "Review of *Excavations at Olynthus, Part II: Architecture and Sculpture: Houses and Other Buildings* by David M. Robinson," *Revue Historique* 165, no. 2 (1930): 348–50.

9. Jennifer K. West, "Observations on Selected Papers of David Moore Robinson from the University of Mississippi Archives" (MA thesis, University of Mississippi, 1995), 126.

10. Nicholas Cahill, *Household and City Organization at Olynthus* (New Haven, CT: Yale University Press, 2002), 63; Dyson, *Ancient Marbles* 194–95.

11. Cahill, *Household*, 63.

12. Alan Wace, "Review of *Excavations at Olynthus. Part I:. Architecture and Sculpture: Houses and Other Buildings* by David M. Robinson," *Classical Review* 45, no. 2 (1931): 87.

13. Cahill, *Household*, 61–63.

14. Both logs are preserved in Box 37, David M. Robinson Collection, Special Collections, University of Mississippi Libraries.

15. Cahill, *Household*, 62–63.

16. For a full description of this house and its architecture, see David M. Robinson and J. Walter Graham, *Excavations at Olynthus VIII: The Hellenic House; a Study of the Houses Found at Olynthus with a Detailed Account of Those Excavated in 1931 and 1934, Johns Hopkins University Studies in Archaeology* 25 (Baltimore, MD: Johns Hopkins University Press, 1938), 117–18.

17. For more on Hippodamus of Miletus and the origins of urban planning, see Richard E. Wycherly, *How the Greeks Built Cities* (London: Macmillan, 1949), chapter 2. Although it is a bit dated now, Wycherly provides a highly readable account of the development of Greek city planning.

18. These photos are in Box 42, David M. Robinson Collection, Special Collections, University of Mississippi Libraries.

19. David M. Robinson, "Mosaics from Olynthus," *American Journal of Archaeology* 36, no. 1 (1932): 16, no. 2.

20. David M. Robinson, *Excavations at Olynthus XI: Necrolynthia, a Study of Greek Burial Customs and Anthropology, Johns Hopkins University Studies in Archaeology* 32 (Baltimore, MD: Johns Hopkins University Press, 1942), vii.

21. David M. Robinson, *Excavations at Olynthus V: Mosaics, Vases, and Lamps of Olynthus Found in 1928 and 1931* (Baltimore, MD: Johns Hopkins University Press, 1933), xi.

22. David M. Robinson, *Excavations at Olynthus VII: The Terra-Cottas of Olynthus Found in 1931* (Baltimore, MD: Johns Hopkins University Press, 1933), viii.

CHAPTER THREE

~

Travel in Greece and Europe in 1931

The formal definition of archaeology is the study of the human past through material culture. No archaeologist who goes into the field, however, is interested only in the people of the past; all are interested in the living as well. I always love talking to anyone from the local area. On one crew I joined in Spain, only I and one other person were non-Spaniards, and we both had great fun perfecting our language skills and comparing cultural experiences with our hosts. Even when excavation teams are majority Americans working abroad, they interact with the people who own and run the hotels and restaurants on which they rely. Sometimes archaeologists get lucky and make friends. I have had people invite me to their homes for a meal and have happened to be somewhere during a local festival in which I was able to participate. And of course, wherever I go, I must see the local sights.

As I read more of Ellingson's letters, memories of my own travels and excavations in Greece and Europe came back to me. As with the excavation process, Ellingson captured this cultural side of archaeology that never makes it into the final site reports, the joy of immersion into another society and traveling in a foreign world. Her tales were sometimes poignant, sometimes funny, but always showed a deep empathy for the people she was meeting and enthusiasm to fully experience the place she was visiting. Her story, and the story of the excavation of Olynthus, is hardly complete without understanding the broader sense of place.[1]

Ethnicity in Myriophito

April 1, 1931

If you could ever see the men [see figure 3.1]. A lot of them are Turks, some are refugees, and some native Greeks. They have come from all around the countryside to work, and we have about 190 I think, altogether. And the outfits they wear. Especially their shoes. A lot of their shoes are made from old tires, bound around with pieces of heavy cloth. Some of them wear wool-len [sic] scarves tied around their head, and some the queerest trousers you ever did see. The village of Myriophito [see figures 3.2 and 3.3] where we live is simply priceless. It is really out in the country, everything is genuine, and no fakes. The peasant costumes are some of them awfully pretty, and some of them comical. They have picturesque old wells. The houses are all very cleanly whitewashed. They have all sorts of animals. In our front yard is a sheep corral, and every morning when we emerge from the door, there is a swarm of chick-ens, who run immediately [when] they see us. There are all sorts of donkeys.

Figure 3.1. One of Mary Ross Ellingson's work crews. Several wear the type of sandal-shoe made from the rubber of old tires Ellingson mentions.
Photo courtesy of the University of Evansville Archives

Myriophito had a population of only about five hundred people when Ellingson was there, although many more lived scattered around the sur-rounding countryside.[2] Most of the local inhabitants worked small farms, herded sheep, and raised silkworms while living in small, one-room mud

Figure 3.2. View of Myriophito from the site of Olynthus.
Photo courtesy of the University of Evansville Archives

brick homes (see figure 3.4).[3] Photos like figure 3.4 suggest many were eking out an existence. Despite the small local population there was still strong ethnic diversity. Ellingson elaborates on the refugees to whom she refers in an article that appeared in the *Edmonton Bulletin* on October 19, 1931:

> These men were, for the most part, Greeks, whose forefathers had lived in Asia Minor for generations, until they had become Turks in everything but descent, and were then rudely deported from Turkish soil to their homeland, which was in no condition to receive them. They drag out a meager existence from a small plot of land donated by the Greek government, hail with great joy the "coming of the Americans," for that means that many of them will earn a few drachmas a day. [See figure 3.5.]

As the Ottoman Empire slowly atomized into nation states during the late nineteenth and early twentieth centuries, the resulting territorial wars led to the migration of people from one nascent country in the Balkans to another. The most devastating of these wars was the result of a failed attempt by Greece to capture a major portion of western Asia Minor in the 1920s, a culturally mixed region where Greek-speaking people had resided for millennia. In what came to be known in Greece as "The Catastrophe," the Turkish military routed the invading Greek forces. The low point in the debacle came when Turkish forces entered Smyrna on the coast of western Asia

Figure 3.3. A photo in front of the dig house in Myriophito, from left to right: Andoni (the cook), the vase-mender Apostolos Kontogeorgis, Argerol (a maid), Smaro (a maid), Gladys Weinberg, Mary Ross Ellingson, Arthur Parsons, Gladys Parsons, J. Walter Graham, Helen Robinson, Sally Freeman, Alexander Schulz, and the mayor of Myriophto, Praedros.

Photo courtesy of the University of Evansville Archives

Figure 3.4. Unidentified woman and children in front of their home.

Photo courtesy of the University of Evansville Archives

Minor (see figure I.3), set fire to much of the city, and massacred many of the Greek-Christian residents. This disaster ensured that George Mylonas, Ellingson's colleague in the excavations, could never return to his hometown. In the subsequent Treaty of Lausanne, Greece ceded claims to the region, and Greece and Turkey were required to exchange populations. Greeks, defined as Christians, had to leave Turkey for Greece; and Turks, defined as Muslims, had to leave Greece for Turkey.[4] The Greek government settled about half of the more than one million refugees in one of the least populated parts of the country, a region that included Myriophito (figure 3.6).[5] The newcomers had few possessions to bring with them to their new homeland.[6]

Two factors that motivated Robinson to excavate at Olynthus when he did were the fact that the refugees were starting farms in the area and were thus destroying portions of the site through plowing (the thin topsoil offered little protection to the lightly buried ancient remains underneath), and the fact that the refugees provided a workforce that was very inexpensive to hire as they had few other job prospects in the area.[7]

Of course, there were people living in the area at the time the refugees arrived. Greek- and Turkish-speaking farmers had lived in Myriophito for centuries. In addition to these groups there was an ethnic minority known as the Vlachs. Vlachs speak a language descended from Latin and they inhabited the Balkans from Greece to Romania in 1931. Ellingson mentions two types of Vlachs that she encountered in and around Myriophito. One group was made of sedentary farmers living a life similar to that of their Greek- and

Figure 3.5. The workmen gathering to be paid. The main dig house for the excavation is in the background on the right.
Photo courtesy of the University of Evansville Archives

Figure 3.6. Ellingson identifies this woman and child in front of a house in Myriophito as Greek refugees from Turkey. The woman spins wool in a manner little changed for millennia with a spindle in her right hand and distaff in her left.

Photo courtesy of the University of Evansville Archives

Turkish-speaking neighbors. The other type of Vlachs were nomads who wandered among the Balkan countries making a living tending their herds of sheep and horses, trading wool, cheese, and live animals with the villagers along the way. Over the course of the last century, Vlach culture has been disappearing. A hardening of borders among the countries that emerged from the collapse of the Ottoman Empire after World War I curtailed their nomadic lifestyle as did the fighting across the Balkans during World War II and the subsequent Greek Civil War. The Vlachs Ellingson saw were in transition even in 1931 as the nomads were settling with their cousins in the villages of Greece and neighboring countries to the north. In less than a decade Vlach caravans like the ones she saw and photographed would never again be seen in Greece (figure 3.7). After World War II, the settled Vlachs migrated from the rural villages to become assimilated into mainstream Greek culture in the cities. Although an estimate in 1987 predicted that the Vlach language would disappear from Greece in the early twenty-first century,[8] cultural organizations have slowed but not ceased the decline by encouraging some children to learn the language.[9] In 1931 the nomadic Vlach mode of life had changed little from earlier centuries. Ellingson took photos of one of these groups of Vlach nomads passing through Myriophito (see figure 3.7). This group was still transporting their tents, clothes, and

Figure 3.7. Group of nomadic Vlachs passing through Myriophito.
Photo courtesy of the University of Evansville Archives

other belongings on the backs of horses and ponies. The children wrapped in furs in figure 3.7 indicate Ellingson took this photo in late March or early April when the weather was still chilly. The distinctive short, hooded jacket the woman wears made her instantly recognizable as a Vlach.

Other groups of Vlachs were more settled in the villages around Myri-ophito. By chance, Ellingson had the opportunity to participate in a local Vlach wedding procession and then observe the wedding. Two photos in the album show the wedding procession (see figures 3.8 and A.3). Her April 21, 1931, letter is one of the most extraordinary in the collection because of the detail with which she describes the event. She records her observations of a type of wedding ceremony that is fast becoming extinct. The letter also il-lustrates Ellingson's enthusiastic embrace of cultures in which she was living as well as her great good humor:

> Well such excitement as there was on Sunday! Yours truly rode in a wedding procession and right beside the bridegroom in the place of honor at that! The Greeks still have the same custom as they had in ancient days—the bridegroom sets out from his home—(this one was in Mariana, not far from Myriophyto) in his cart and horse with 2 other carts, and the father riding horseback in front, kind of a herald glorified. He drives to the home of the bride (at Cassandra, about 10 miles from Myriophyto) and she gets in one of the carts with her attendants, 3 women, 2 small girls, and her mother, and the party starts back again. Well here is where I came in . . . Davey [Robinson] and I walked over to the next village, Hagias Mamas to look at some inscriptions on stone. . . .
>
> We were walking along the road, when we heard the tramp of horses' feet and the rhythmic song of the [Vlachs] approaching. Turning around, we saw horses, carts, people, banners approaching at a great rate of speed. Much shout-ing and firing of guns and pistols. The party stopped when they got to us . . . [they] got out, they passed the cognac around and invited Davey and me to come along which we did, I being very anxious to ride in a bridal procession. The groom got out . . . so we rode in his cart, me on the front seat between the driver and one of the male attendants. Now I must explain about these carts, there is a board across the front, to sit on, but no place to put your feet or brace yourself. . . . Well off we went, me feeling very tickled the while. . . . Bump no. 1.—Mary slips back a little on the seat. Pistol shot no. 1, horses lurch forward, Mary falls back into cart, upon Davey and other members of the bridal party. After resuming my original place—on we go. Bump no. 2.—Mary slips back a little—Pistol shot no. 2.—horses lurch forward and Mary, by dint of . . . a few friendly pushes from the back retains seat. . . . Oh I forgot to say that he [one of the men riding in the back of the cart] told Dr. Robinson he would like to marry me, and thought I was very beautiful (this being my 3rd proposal dur-ing the course of the afternoon). Finally we arrived at Myriophyto, where the

whole village . . . was out to greet us. Much firing of pistols etc. . . . Andoni, the cook [see figure 3.9], was out to see it too, and when he saw Davey and me sitting up in the front cart, as large as life, and twice as natural,—well his eyes just about popped. After recovering his first surprise he made one dive for the house and shrieked at the bunch—M'sieur Robinson—Mam'selle . . . marriage! They didn't know what it was all about, and wondered if Davey and I were eloping, Mrs. R[obinson] being away in Saloniki for the week-end.[10]

The Easter Celebration

The biggest holiday the Olynthus team participated in while residing in the village was Easter, which they celebrated with a mixture of Eastern Orthodox ceremony and Greek tradition. While Ellingson had studied ancient Greek both as an undergraduate and graduate student, the Greek spoken in Myriophito had evolved a great deal and she had to start from scratch to learn it. In an April 11 letter, Ellingson shows she was trying to remember various words and phrases of the modern Greek she picked up:

Figure 3.8. The Vlach wedding procession. In the center of the cart seat Mary Ross Ellingson sits between the driver (left) and one of the groom's attendants (right). The groom stands beside the cart. David Robinson looks out from the back of the cart. Photo courtesy of the University of Evansville Archives

There are great doings around Myriophito now. Easter Time. They sure make a job of it. Last night they had a big ceremony & buried the Savior. (They had a real grave.) Early this morning, before 6, there was a long procession to the church, & the bells rang nearly all night. . . . Yesterday the lambs were all a sight, all washed nice & white, with blue ribbons around their necks. . . .

At 11 the real service started. At 12 sharp, the priest reads from the Bible the passage where it says "Christ is Risen," only in Greek it is Ὁ Χριστός Ἀνέστη—ho Christos anesti—then there is singing until 1.30, and some more service, at 2.30 they start feasting—oh I forgot to say that on Saturday am they kill a lamb in front of every house, & let the blood run over the threshold, & skin the lamb, & hang it up in the front hall. Then at 2.30 they roast it on a spit [see figure 3.9]. There is much feasting during the night, and then all day Easter Sunday, there is dancing in the village. Everybody you meet says 'ho Christos anesti.' . . . Church again at 11.30 with everybody dressed in their very best. Little babies in spotless white with great chains of Turkish coins around their necks. Mothers in bright garments, long skirts, and large hand-kerchiefs, some of them beautifully embroidered, some spotless white linen of the finest weave, and their smart little black jackets, fitted tight at the waist with leg o' mutton sleeve. The unmarried girls wear bright ribbons around their heads. They surely are a picturesque sight. Everybody carries a candle to church. The pappas (παππάς) (priest) enters the church with his lighted lamp, and all the men rush to get their candles lit from his, and the women, who have been consigned to ὑψηλα (hypsila) the gallery, come shyly around later to get their candles lit. After the ceremony, they make a long parade from

Figure 3.9. Andoni (left), the excavation team's cook, roasts the Easter lamb.
Photo courtesy of the University of Evansville Archives

Figure 3.10. Men dancing in unison in front of the dig house in Myriophito during Easter celebrations in 1928. A man provides music with his violin on the right.
Photo courtesy of the Wilhelmina Van Ingen Elarth Papers, Ms1969-004, Special Collections and University Archives, Virginia Tech, Blacksburg, Va.

the church around the village, and then they dance somewhere. Yesterday afternoon they danced right in front of our house [see figure 3.10]. It was very pretty. Many of them were regular artists. (It was funny to see our workmen trip the light fantastic gracefully, after we had been watching them sling a pick all day for 2 weeks.) One of them had had too much uzo (a kind of drink, harmless in small quantities but after that rather prone to become intoxicating) and he was a perfect scream. He danced with all the abandon of a wild Bacchante of ancient Greece, dancing in a frenzied celebration of Dionysius, the wine god. (This part of Greece is the country of Dionysius, you know.)

Free Time

Ellingson's photos show that in her free time she took an interest in daily life in the village, not just special occasions. In one photo (figure 3.11), Ellingson borrows a book from a mobile lending library in the village carried on the back of a donkey. Other photographs she took in Myriophito and in other parts of Greece during her travels after the excavation was complete show Greeks engaged in daily tasks using tools that had changed little in millennia. A woman uses a distaff and spindle to spin yarn from sheep's wool (see figure 3.6), fishermen throw a weighted net into shallow water, and a woman uses a sickle to harvest grain (figure 3.12). The distaff, net weights, and sickle blade were similar to the artifacts the team was finding on the hill at Olynthus. Ellingson may have been recording these scenes to help her better understand what she was seeing emerge from the ground.

Of course the Olynthus team did not work every day. As Ellingson wrote in a letter dated April 11, "We only have 2 kinds of days—work days and other days. The other days are either Sunday or holidays and rainy days."

Figure 3.11. Mary Ross Ellingson borrows a book from a mobile lending library.
Photo courtesy of the University of Evansville Archives

Figure 3.12.   An unidentified woman reaps grain with a sickle near Delphi.
Photo courtesy of the University of Evansville Archives

On those "other days" Ellingson could sleep a little longer since breakfast was not until 9:00 a.m. In the morning, they would catch up on their field reports or artifact inventories. Sometimes they would have a bath. Conditions at Myriophito were primitive. The village had neither electricity nor phone service, houses lacked air conditioning and the only heat came from fireplaces and stoves. Villagers had to draw water for daily use and baths

Figure 3.13.   Unidentified villagers in Myriophito drawing water from the well beside their house. As no one had running water in the village, this was a common sight in 1931 as people would have drawn water several times during the day.
Photo courtesy of the University of Evansville Archives

Figure 3.14. Mary Ross Ellingson cutting David Robinson's hair on the balcony of the dig house where the light was best.

Photo courtesy of the University of Evansville Archives

Figure 3.15. Mary Ross Ellingson has her photo taken as she enjoys a visit to a café on University Street in Athens. Curious Greek customers look on.

Photo courtesy of the University of Evansville Archives

from a well (figure 3.13). Lacking a hot water heater, water for a bath had to be warmed on the stove, making a hot bath an extravagant luxury. Without a barber in the village, Ellingson and her friends had to attend to their own grooming, as she explains in a May 4 letter:

> Yesterday we ran a barber shop. I cut Alex [Schulz]'s hair, & Gladys [Weinberg's] hair, & Gladys cut mine. None of the cuts were too positively terrible, however. That took us all morning, as we are rather slow. [See figure 3.14.]

During the afternoons on free days, Ellingson and various other members of the staff would go somewhere, usually on foot. Communication with the outside world was intermittent. Everyone was grateful for a letter from home and the occasional English-language newspaper, even if they were dated by the time they arrived. In one response Ellingson reports how pleased she is to receive a letter from her mother only seventeen days after she had mailed it from Edmonton; Ellingson thought it arrived with admirable speed. To get mail, telegrams, or newspapers, however, someone had to volunteer to walk to another, larger, nearby village on one of their free days. As Ellingson explained in an April 9 letter,

Figure 3.16. **Gladys Weinberg (left) and Sarah Freeman amusing themselves with a donkey ride on their day off.**
Photo courtesy of the University of Evansville Archives

It has been a joke around here ever since we arrived. After every meal somebody says "well who's going to Modonia today?" And we all say yes we're going.
So today Alex [Schulz] & I really went. It's 5 miles. We had had 2 rainy days,
so were good & rested. When we got there we went to the café & had uzo (I
don't know if that's how you spell it but you pronounce it ew-z-o.) which is
the Greek national drink I think [see figure 3.15]. Tastes like a combination of
licorice root and Castoria. Then we got the mail & came home, eating numerous chocolate bars by the roadside. We made it in 1 hr 40 minutes each way
& think we are pretty smart.

Without even a battery-operated radio, the Olynthus staff had to find their
own entertainment where they could. In a March 27 letter Ellingson writes,

I rode part way home on a donkey yesterday afternoon. Gee, it was fun. Mr.
Mylonas got home before the rest of us, and came back with a donkey, and let
me ride it home. When we got near home, there is a fork in the road, and I
wanted to take the one to the right but the donkey evidently thought differently, as his home is on the left, so I had to be rescued.

It certainly helped that the staff got along exceptionally well. Ellingson
makes repeated statements such as "We are having a keen time, it is heaps of
fun. And the people are all awfully congenial, we have a fine time at meals, and
working."

While they worked inside on days when it rained or snowed, jokes and
funny stories made the atmosphere bright. In an undated letter she records
some ill-informed statements from undergraduate exams and essays that were a
great source of amusement to the group. It is not clear from her letter whether
these were actual exam answers Robinson and his graduate students had seen or
whether they were reading from a magazine titled *College Humor*:

Vesuvius is a volcano, and if you climb up to the top you can look in and see
the creator smoking.
Pompeii was destroyed by an eruption of lava from the Vatican.
All Gaul is quartered into three halves [a mistake for the opening line of
Caesar's *Gallic Wars*: "All Gaul is divided into three parts"].
Pax in Bellum[11] ["peace in the midst of war"] means freedom from indigestion.
The deacon is a mass of inflammable material.
Democracy believes in God, and a republic doesn't.
The process of turning water into steam is called conversation.

The group also enjoyed the game of bridge. In an April 27 letter she reports,

We were wild & reckless on Saturday night. We stayed up until 12 o'clock,
playing cards. Usually we go to bed at 9.30 or 10 at the latest but we decided

Figure 3.17.　Georg von Peschke's caricature of Mary Ross Ellingson holding the tools of a barber.
Photo courtesy of the University of Evansville Archives

that it wouldn't kill us to stay up late one night, and it didn't. Sundays we don't have breakfast until 9. (that seems early at home but here it is late when you're used to having it at 5 to 7 every morning).

She adds in a letter dated April 1, "[W]e just had another bridge game, Canada vs. the United States, and of course Canada won." Ellingson and Graham were the two Canadians in the group.

When they could find an excuse for a party, they would take advantage of it as this May 27 letter shows:

The Sun[day] before we left Myriophito was Mrs. R[obinson]'s birthday so we had a surprise party for her. We got Andoni to make a cake (it was the first one we'd had) & we got wine, & the artist [von Peschke] drew cute caricatures of

Figure 3.18. **From left to right Gladys Davidson Weinberg, Alexander Schulz, J. Walter Graham, and Mary Ross Ellingson out for a swim in the Gulf of Cassandra.**
Photo courtesy of the University of Evansville Archives

everybody. I enclose mine—it is me in characteristic attitude—cutting hair. [See figure 3.17.]

The caricature she mentions became one of the souvenirs Ellingson pasted into her photo album. In a May 17 letter, Ellingson writes of another impromptu party the von Peschkes threw for the crew one Saturday night: "They brought a radio with them—so after dinner we all went over to their house, & they had the best wine we've had since Athens, & cookies & chocolate, & we danced."

Once the weather warmed as summer approached, swimming became their favorite leisure-time activity both in the nearby Resetnikia River and at the more distant beaches on the Gulf of Cassandra (see figure 3.18). Her May 11 letter relates some of their aquatic exploits:

We had the best swim today. As soon as the whistle blew we hit for the river, where the boys have made a dam. There is a place where the current flows very fast—you just lie down & boom you sail merrily down the stream about 40 mph. It isn't very deep, however, but you can dive if very careful. Then we ate our lunch & lay on the beach, lovely warm sand, until time to come back to work. It was keen fun.

But oh boy swimming in the ocean is the clean stuff tho! Yesterday I went in at Athatal, & the water was simply marvelous. Lovely & warm, & clear as crystal. You could almost see the individual grains of sand. A fish swam along not far from me, & I could see him plain as day.

Although the beaches were some distance from Myriophito, the hike to them was not necessarily unpleasant as she indicates in a May 4 letter:

Then in the af[ternoon] Gladys & Sally & Walter & Alex & I went swimming down to the beach—which was much fun. On the way home we came thru the most beautiful place—where a lot of apple trees were in bloom, a clump of tall poplars, the fields just one mass of flowers—yellow and pink and purple and red and white. Really I never saw anything like the wildflowers here. They just absolutely cover the ground. The poppies grow in the grain fields, and are just about as thick as the grain.

Return to Saloniki

The previous excerpt comes from the latter part of their time at Olynthus. At that point Ellingson and her colleagues had a little over a month until their departure for Saloniki. As the departure date neared, they had less time for leisure. Closing down an excavation at the end of a season requires a great deal of work. They had to complete field reports and artifact inventories, carefully pack the artifacts for transportation back to Saloniki, and stow equipment as well. Amid the chaotic bustle they also had to pack their personal belongings and prepare for the journey themselves. All remembered how difficult the road between Myriophito and Saloniki was and prepared accordingly, as Ellingson describes in this June 7 letter:

We arrived last Friday night, 5 hours over roads that were terrible—there had been regular cloudbursts the day before—it was a miracle that we got here— it is 85 Kilo[meter]s, about 60 miles I think. We had been expecting mud so we had worn our old clothes, I had on that cotton dress with the short sleeves, it was dirty, too & the boys had on their high boots & breeches & were all muddy when we arrived here at 9 o'clock. . . . But—enter the tragedy—our bags were all on the truck & it hadn't arrived—so here we were looking like tramps. Gladys did have a small bag with her with soap etc. but that was all. And I was so surprised when we arrived in Salonique. It has put on its summer clothes & are the people smart looking? Well I should say. Well anyway we washed our faces, & came back to the Med[iterranean] P[alace] [see figure 1.9] for dinner & sneaked in the back way in our unseemly raiment. The orchestra at the M[editerranean] P[alace] was playing, & it sounded marvellous [sic] to us country folks. The tables at the Mediterranean Palace are all moved out on the sidewalk by the water now, & it's lovely. . . . Then oh joy of joys—I had my first hot bath for 2 1/2 months.

The work was not over at this point. According to Greek antiquities law and the terms of the permit under which he worked, Robinson did not own the artifacts he had uncovered; they belonged to the Greek government and people. The permit required Robinson to deposit all the material he had excavated at the national archaeological museum in Saloniki, housed in a building known as the New Mosque (figure 3.19). After the population exchange of 1923 that brought Greek refugees to Greece from Turkey and sent Muslims to Turkey from Greece, the city of Saloniki turned the mosque into an archaeological museum.[12] Over the next week or so, Robinson had his staff of graduate students unpack the artifacts, conduct some preliminary conservation on them, and prepare them for storage in the museum. A rare photo shows Ellingson at work with two of her colleagues in the museum's workspace (figure 3.20). Although Ellingson is clearly visible, all three figures have a ghostly appearance as the camera shutter had to remain open longer in the low light of the room making any motion blur the moving figures.

After the frenetic pace at the end of the season in Myriophito, Robinson allowed his graduate-student staff to slow their work and enjoy the urbane and sophisticated atmosphere of Saloniki. The city is one of Greece's largest; in 1931 residents had access to the latest cosmopolitan fashions, music, and movies (figure 3.21). Ellingson was dazzled by all she saw and heard and delighted in sharing in an urban night life she and the others had been denied at Myriophito, as she explains in this June 7 letter:

> It was the opening night of the Med[iterranean] Palace Roof Garden. We had dinner & danced. It was simply marvellous [sic]—had the time of our lives. The roof garden is lovely.

In an undated letter, Ellingson sounds almost breathless as she tries to describe their evening activities in Saloniki:

> Then at 4 we started off again, walked down to the tower & had something to eat at one of the café-effects, then we went to the movies—Greek movies (with French also)—Tarzan. Then we came home & changed for dinner. Then dinner put on the street in front of the Med[iterranean] P[alace], then we walked down to the tower, & took a boat for an hour, & went around by a couple of dance places—it [the Saloniki waterfront] looks lovely at night just like Venice so Gladys says. Then we finished up by going up to the roof garden for a few dances—also very enjoyable. . . . It's taking me longer to do

Figure 3.19. View of the former mosque and later National Museum in Saloniki.
Photo courtesy of the University of Evansville Archives

Figure 3.20. Mary Ross Ellingson, forefront in the bottom right-hand corner of the photo, and several of her colleagues at work in the storeroom of the National Museum in Saloniki. The shelves behind them hold a collection of ancient Greek pots in various stages of the conservation process.
Photo courtesy of the University of Evansville Archives

Figure 3.21. Ellingson's photo of the view of the Saloniki waterfront from the city's citadel.
Photo courtesy of the University of Evansville Archives

my terracottas than I thought it would but we are having such a good time I don't mind staying here longer.

Saloniki was home to a community of ex-patriot Americans, British, French, and Canadians. The ex-pats welcomed the visitors into their midst. Ellingson describes one extravagant party the excavation team was invited to in an undated letter:

The Americans in Salonique were having a party (cabaret effect) & they had invited us to come. They had the best entertainment features [and] dances, too. A couple of Americans who speak French, & they cracked the best jokes half in English & half in French. They came out dressed in slickers & umbrellas, & sang "Singing in the Rain" & a whole lot of good old American songs. They were a howl, & you'd have to go a long way before you'd get anybody as good. There were about 20 Americans. There was also an English party, about 10, & one Canadian in it with them, whom I met.

Eventually Ellingson and the others did complete their work and the time for departure arrived. The team scattered as each pursued their own travels in Europe. Helen Boyle, Ellingson's best friend from home (see figures 1.2 and 3.22) came to Saloniki to join Ellingson and begin a leisurely trip across the continent to England, from where they were scheduled to sail home. On June 14 the friends departed Saloniki for Athens. From there they visited sites across Greece (see figure 3.23) before crossing the Adriatic Sea to Italy. Stops in Naples, Pompeii, Rome, Venice, Paris, and London followed. As they visited museums, archaeological sites, and trendy shops, Boyle talked

Figure 3.22. Ellingson with her best friend, Helen Boyle, in a photograph taken in Edmonton before the Olynthus excavation. Ellingson holds a string she has attached to the camera's shutter release to take a "selfie."
Photo courtesy of the University of Evansville Archives

frequently about her upcoming wedding, which seems to have never been far from her mind despite everything they were seeing and experiencing:

> From an undated letter: "Helen is being married in Sept. to Hugh somebody in Regina."
> From a July 12 letter written in Venice: "Oh I forgot to tell you if she has a large wedding, I am to be one of the bridesmaids. Helen got 6 yellow hats at the market for the bridesmaids . . . (She won't know until she gets home if it is to be a large wedding.)
> From a July 26 letter written in Paris: "Helen has decided to get married about Sept 14 now instead of 22."
> From the same letter: "And Wednesday we are going to lunch at Helen's aunt-in-law-to be's home [in London]."

Graham accompanied them on the first leg of their trip to Rome before leaving them to pursue his own travels. Coincidentally, Ellingson ran into him again in London, according to a letter dated July 26:

Figure 3.23. Mary Ross Ellingson standing under the cyclopean architecture at the Greek site of Tiryns. Helen Boyle probably took this photo.

Photo courtesy of Barbara Petersen

I went to the British Museum yesterday (Helen went to another) & as I was going in who should I meet but Walter. So we went in & were sitting on a bench discussing things in general, & who should rush up but Gladys & Arthur Parsons. So we had a good reunion. We are all going to dinner at the Parsons' tomorrow.

The July 26 letter is the last during her trip, and at the end she sums up her entire journey:

Gee we've had a marvellous [sic] trip—everything's just been lovely.
Heaps of love 'n' kisses
Mary.

The End of the Story

I set down the last letter and looked at the mess on my desk. My head was spinning. It was time to go home, but I took a few minutes to gather up the letters, photos, and news clippings and put them back as I had found them. Over dinner I intended to tell my wife, Christine, about all I had seen and read. As a fellow archaeologist, she could appreciate Ellingson's tales as much as I had. I believed that would be the end of the story, however. What I could not have understood at that moment is that I had just made the discovery of a lifetime. The photo album and its contents would change the course of my entire career.

Notes

1. Compare Ellingson's experiences discovering Greek culture with her near contemporary and another American woman, Eva Palmer-Sikelianos, *Upward Panic. The Autobiography of Eva Palmer-Sikelianos*. Translated by John P. Anton (Philadelphia: Harwood Academic Publishers, 1993), 53–56.

2. "Edmonton Girl Finds Interest in Archaeology," *The Albertan*, September 18, 1931.

3. "Excavations in Old Greece Are Recounted," *The Evansville Courier and Press*, March 3, 1940, 4.

4. For a brief summary of this tragic period in Greek history, see Richard Clogg, *A Short History of Modern Greece* (New York: Cambridge University Press, 1979), 117–22.

5. Figure 3.6 is cropped; in the original photo the woman sits with other elderly women, all spinning wool. The scene brings to mind the words of Eva Palmer-Sikelianos: "Spinning with a distaff is a most sociable occupation, especially when old women gather round their neighbor's fire-place to sit spinning and gossiping at the

same time, which aways seemed a pleasanter way of paying a visit than our stand-up-and-do-nothing tea parties." Palmer-Sikelianos, *Upward Panic*, 76.

6. For more on the impact of the refugee settlement in Aegean Macedonia, see John Shea, *Macedonia and Greece: The Struggle to Define a New Balkan Nation* (Jefferson, NC: McFarland and Company, 1997), 105–7.

7. Stephen L. Dyson, *Ancient Marbles to American Shores: Classical Archaeology in the United States* (Philadelphia: University of Pennsylvania Press, 1998), 194.

8. This estimate comes from Tom J. Winnifrith, *The Vlachs: The History of a Balkan People* (New York: St. Martin's Press, 1987), 3. Winnifrith gives an excellent account of the development of the Vlach language and the history of the Vlach people.

9. Anna Wichmann, "The Vlachs: The Proud Greeks Who Speak a Romance Language," *The Greek Reporter* (December 21, 2021), https://greekreporter.com/2021/12/21/vlachs-greece/, accessed October 4, 2022.

10. This excerpt gives a taste for the letter, the full text with Ellingson's account of more of her misadventures as well as a meticulously detailed account of the ceremony is presented in appendix I.

11. Ellingson has made a mistake in her Latin here. The ending should be ablative: *Bello.*

12. The museum was moved out of the building in 1965 and today the former mosque is a civic building used for public displays. To see modern photos of the building, including one that was taken from nearly the same angle as Ellingson's, see http://wikimapia.org/1479811/Geni-Mosque.

PART II

〜

SEXISM AND SCHOLARSHIP

Figure P.2.   Sarah Freeman, J. Walter Graham, and an exuberant Gladys Weinberg (left to right) on a lunch break at Olynthus. Beside Graham sits a wicker basket containing their lunch.

Photo courtesy of the University of Evansville Archives

CHAPTER FOUR

~

The Men

In the days that followed, the stories I had read and the images I had seen continued to swirl around in my head. Ellingson's letters offered much information about the archaeological process and the context in which Robinson's crew worked at Olynthus, but her stories had gaps. I had grown to like Ellingson and her fellow excavators based on all I learned of them the afternoon I found the photo album and could not simply let them go; I wanted to know more. The story seemed incomplete without knowing what happened to them after they left Olynthus in 1931. It was not a conscious decision at first, I just started researching some of the people she discussed. Starting with the men, most of whom I had heard of before, I read up on their careers and was able to piece together what influence their time at Olynthus had on them. Seemingly innocuous at first, my curiosity to answer questions about Ellingson's friends and colleagues would grow more obsessive as I read. Each answer led to new questions.

J. Walter Graham and David Robinson

After the 1931 season at Olynthus, Graham, and Robinson's fates were linked for years to come. Unlike some of the other graduate student staff from that season, Graham remained under Robinson's tutelage and completed his dissertation on the domestic architecture of classical Greece, receiving a PhD from Johns Hopkins University in 1933.[1] With jobs scarce in Depression-ravaged America, Robinson looked after Graham offering

him a paid research assistantship so that Graham could help him with the
Olynthus publications.[2] During the 1931 season Graham had taken on the
responsibility of inventorying lamps and loom-weights;[3] he now worked the
inventory into a full catalog including comparisons to contemporary lamps
from other sites. Robinson published this in 1933 as a separate chapter in
Olynthus V, giving Graham full credit as the chapter author. When Robinson
became aware of a faculty position at Washington University in St. Louis,
Missouri, he pushed those he knew at the university to hire Graham but, for
reasons that are not clear, Graham did not follow through on the process and
chose to remain a research assistant at Johns Hopkins.[4]

During the following two years Graham's personal and professional life
changed rapidly. When he returned to Olynthus in 1934 Robinson promoted
him to assistant director and put him in charge of the lamps again as well
as the "smaller finds."[5] Mylonas, Robinson's previous second in command
on site, was not able to come to Olynthus that season, which helps explain
Graham's promotion.[6] Robinson seems to have been off-site a lot that season,
leaving Graham in charge of day-to-day operations. Following up on his own
interest in the houses, he had the crew focus on carefully recording specific
data about their architecture to provide information for a future *Excavations
at Olynthus* volume.[7] After the excavation season wrapped up in July, Graham
traveled to London, where he married a fellow Johns Hopkins graduate student
and alumna of Vassar College, Annie Christine Hare, who was focusing her
studies on Latin.[8] Eventually the two would have two daughters and a son.[9]
In 1935 he found a teaching position at the University of Missouri where he
remained for the next twelve years.[10]

Robinson and Graham published *Excavations at Olynthus VIII* jointly in
1938; Graham was the first person to share the authorship and the title page
of one of the *Olynthus* volumes with Robinson. In the introduction to the
volume they state that *Olynthus VIII* incorporates material from Graham's
1933 dissertation which is greatly augmented with data from the 1934 excavation season.[11] Joseph Shaw, a later student of Graham's, has claimed that the
names of the authors should have been reversed to acknowledge Graham's
majority contribution to the volume.[12] *Olynthus VIII* is the most renowned
of the Olynthus volumes. In a review that appeared just one year after the
volume's publication, Lucy T. Shoe[13] made a bold prediction about the volume's lasting value that has proven true in the decades that followed:

> [T]he study of the Hellenic house as set forth here will remain for some
> time the reference work on domestic architecture of the late fifth and early
> fourth centuries B.C. It would be hard to overestimate the importance of this

contribution to our knowledge of Greek architecture and civilization, filling as it does one of the most tantalizing gaps in our previous information. . . . The authors are to be congratulated on a carefully recorded, well assimilated, correctly evaluated, and well documented presentation of material which makes a real addition to our evidence for one of the outstanding periods of Greek civilization.[14]

Graham had developed a better system of recording where excavators found artifacts than the one Robinson had used in 1928, a system used in the 1931, 1934, and 1938 seasons. The new recording technique was so well-thought-out that even today it is possible to use the publications and excavation records in the archives at the University of Mississippi to determine in which rooms Graham, Robinson, and their team found specific artifacts, allowing modern archaeologists to reconstruct the use of individual spaces within each house. More than a half century after the completion of the Olynthus excavations, archaeologist Nicholas Cahill was able to examine the variation in artifacts found in the different buildings and interpret what this tells us about the status, economic decisions, and even the aspirations of the residents.[15] For Graham *Olynthus VIII* and the archival records used to produce it were, and continue to be, a triumph.

In 1947 Graham was able to return to his native Canada, taking a position at the University of Toronto where he remained for the rest of his career. While teaching in Toronto Graham served as the Keeper of Classical Collection in the Royal Ontario Museum of Archaeology significantly improving the displays there. Up until that point his work at Olynthus had defined Graham's career, but after his return to Canada Graham turned his attention to the Bronze Age Minoan architecture, making himself an expert on the subject after repeated trips to Crete and publishing the celebrated work *The Palaces of Crete* in 1962. He retired from the University of Toronto in 1972 and passed away in 1991 after having suffered for some time from Parkinson's disease.[16]

As Graham's career developed, Robinson went from being his mentor to his colleague, then to a friend, and finally to an enemy. Throughout most of the rest of Robinson's life, the two men's professional and private lives remained intertwined. After the 1931 season, Robinson returned to Baltimore and focused on publishing more additions to the *Excavations at Olynthus* series as well as numerous articles on Olynthus and other subjects. He had two more field seasons at Olynthus in 1934 and 1938 and hoped for more, but war forced him to postpone those plans. During World War II and the Greek civil war that followed until 1949, Robinson was the president of the

Maryland Branch of the Greek War Relief Association and a member of the Council for the Restoration of Greece, raising money to help the Greek people and nation recover from all they suffered during the 1940s.[17] Robinson returned to Greece in 1947 to investigate the possibility of reopening excavations at Olynthus, but quickly realized that it would not be feasible.[18] While in Saloniki he worked with the staff of the archaeological museum to locate and dig up boxes of artifacts that they had hidden to keep safe during the conflict. Some of the Olynthus pieces had been broken in the process of hiding and rediscovering them, so Robinson paid to have them mended.[19] In the end the 1938 season at Olynthus proved to be the last excavation he would ever direct, and Robinson spent the rest of his life preparing publications on the Olynthus material. He completed the fourteenth and final volume in 1952.[20] He considered writing a fifteenth volume to summarize and synthesize his life's work at the site,[21] but he had made little progress on it by the time of his death and seems to have abandoned the project.

The 1931 season was pivotal. Reviewers received the volumes published after that season with more enthusiasm than they had the earlier volumes as Robinson's recording techniques had improved and his exclusive focus on houses and daily life were something fairly new for classical archaeology. Illustrating how unique this focus was, one reviewer stated,

> [Olynthus] offers little in the way of public buildings, major sculpture, or civic documents. As if with conscious singleness of purpose, Olynthus is concentrated on the private life of the individual, and on the several subjects which grew from it, i.e., on his dwelling, its multifarious contents, its place in a [city] plan. In this sphere Olynthus is unrivaled, and the fourteen volumes are indispensable.[22]

Another reviewer addressed the harsh commentary on Robinson's pre-1931 Olynthus publications, offering him absolution for his post-1931 work:

> Some earlier volumes have been criticized for not giving "archaeological contexts" in full. In [Excavations at Olynthus] X the place of discovery at least is given with most items, usually a particular room of a house, or a grave; and Professor Robinson expresses concern at lack of precise information in some cases.[23]

As the final volumes of the series appeared in print the accolades mounted. One reviewer wrote of *Olynthus XII*, "Prof. Robinson and his collaborators are to be thanked and congratulated once more on a solid contribution to our knowledge of Greek life. No pains have been spared in presenting this uniquely interesting material."[24] Another reviewer summed up the feelings of many at seeing the last volume in the *Excavations at Olynthus* series appear in print:

> It is a little overwhelming to realize that the excavation of this extensive significant site has been brought to a conclusion and that all the finds have been published. There may still be room for more excavation at Olynthus or in its vicinity, but this can hardly detract from credit due an excavator who has carried out a great project with vision, determination, and tremendous energy.[25]

The lasting impact of Robinson's work on classical archaeology has to do with not only the scale at which he excavated but also at which he published. Many reviewers used the word "perseverance" when describing Robinson's energetic and unrelenting drive to excavate and publish the site completely. A few numbers may give some indication of Robinson's accomplishments. In the final season, he estimated that his crew was removing sixty tons of earth each day.[26] During his four field seasons he uncovered over six hundred graves and more than one hundred houses; no other Greek site can boast the excavation of so many domestic structures even today. The entire cost of the four field seasons at Olynthus was $50,000 of which Robinson contributed $20,000.[27] It took Robinson twenty-three years to publish the fourteen volumes of the *Excavations at Olynthus* series and these run for a total of 4,499 pages of text with 1,902 illustrations describing 11,221 artifacts.[28] Shortly before Robinson's death, King Paul of Greece awarded him the Cross of the Royal Order of the Phoenix in honor of his archaeological accomplishments and his contributions to the modern country of Greece.[29]

While all of this is impressive, valid criticisms of Robinson's excavation remain. Even with the increased number of supervisors, Robinson did not have enough people directing and controlling his workers to record all the data he uncovered and the excavation techniques they employed had become old-fashioned by 1931. Robinson's dig winds up on the wrong side of any comparison with the supervisor/worker ratio and techniques employed in the contemporary excavation in the Agora of Athens.[30]

Even though he received a great deal of recognition for it, Robinson was never fully satisfied with his shift in focus away from public architecture to private. In a letter to Graham from 1947, long after praise of his work had begun to appear, Robinson makes the rather stunning statement, "I often wish that I'd never put the time and sacrifice into Olynthus. . . . Naturally, I too was disappointed not to find better houses and I've spent endless time and money trying to locate temples."[31] Despite all he had accomplished,

Robinson could not escape the traditional idea that classical archaeology was primarily about life in public, not life in private.

The Olynthus excavations were not Robinson's only legacy; he also trained a new generation of classical archaeologists. George Hanfmann, one of Robinson's former students, claimed, "Professor Robinson's greatest pride was to be a teacher and he gloried in saying of younger scholars: 'He was my student.'"[32] During his many years at Johns Hopkins, Robinson made the Department of Art and Archaeology into a top destination for graduate students interested in classical archaeology. He supervised the writing of a staggering forty-one master's theses and seventy-four dissertations on classical and archaeological topics. Robinson conferred degrees on many of the most influential members of the next generation of classical archaeologists[33] and used his connections to help them acquire jobs. Robinson helped by publishing the work of several of his students, including Mylonas and Graham, in the *Excavations at Olynthus* series. He also started and edited the *Johns Hopkins University Studies in Archaeology* series and used it as a vehicle to publish the dissertations of some of his other students. Each year Robinson would attend the annual meeting of the Archaeological Institute of America where he would, as one scholar remembers, "hold court" surrounded by his former students, now colleagues.[34]

Not all Robinson's former students shared feelings of goodwill toward him, nor did he retain similar feelings toward some of them. Loyalty was a characteristic he valued most highly in his students and his rage was implacable when he felt betrayed. Robinson had a very public spat with Graham and another former student, Paul A. Clement, after each wrote a negative review of an *Excavations at Olynthus* volume.[35] Clement joined the Olynthus team in 1934, several years after he had completed his dissertation under Robinson at Johns Hopkins, spending the season cataloging the coins.[36] Together Robinson and Clement published the coins in *Excavations at Olynthus IX*, for which they shared the authorship, making Clement the only other person besides Graham whose name appears on the cover page of an *Excavations at Olynthus* volume next to Robinson's. Robinson responded in print to Graham and Clement's critiques by calling them "petty inaccurate rude reviewers";[37] the lack of commas in his text only highlights the breathless rage Robinson felt, as if he did not want to take the time to pause between insults. In the same response to their reviews, Robinson dismisses their comments on his work by adding that both Graham and Clement's statements were "unauthorized and breaking the rule of the [American] School [of Classical Studies at Athens] that no information can be printed by any member of the staff without the consent of the Director." He is, in fact, mistaken, as both men based their critiques on published data, which they cite.

The sense of betrayal Robinson felt is understandable as Graham was harsh in his assessment of his former mentor's excavation and analysis of the domestic structures at Olynthus after Graham had left the project, suggesting the older archaeologist added little new information to the understanding of the subject. In a review of *Excavations at Olynthus XII*, Graham compared Robinson's work with that described in the volume he coauthored with the man, *Excavations at Olynthus VIII*:

> Most of this new Olynthus volume is devoted to the houses excavated in 1938, a rather generous "supplement" (p. v) to Olynthus, VIII, The Hellenic House. Indeed, the question may well occur whether the size and cost of this "μέγα βιβλίον,"[38] especially under present conditions, is warranted by the amount of new evidence.[39]

It was not just that Graham had written a bad review that bothered Robinson but that he had written a bad review of his former mentor's work. In a letter Robinson wrote to Graham after seeing his review he states, "[I]t is generally considered bad etiquette for a student to review or criticize the work of his own chief. It almost seems like a case of spite, at least of ungratefulness."[40] Robinson was giving voice to an unspoken expectation of many in the field about respect for their intellectual fathers.

Robinson took Clement's review of *Excavations at Olynthus VIII* as a personal attack. The reason the review so galled him was that Clement states *Excavations at Olynthus VIII* was based on Graham's dissertation supplemented by data he gathered during the 1934 season when, according to Clement,

> Graham was again at Olynthus, the de facto field director for the third campaign of the Johns Hopkins University's excavations on the site. Conscious at that time of the responsibility he was to assume for the publication on domestic architecture at Olynthus he made every effort to augment and to correct the data pertinent to the solution of problems connected with that publication—and his success was notable, within limits imposed by circumstances beyond his control.[41]

Even though Robinson and Graham are both listed as authors on the title page of *Olynthus VIII* with Robinson's name first, Clement never uses Robinson's name in the text of his review, giving all the credit for what he assesses to be an excellent work to Graham alone. Clement also absolves Graham of any shortcomings with the caveat about "circumstances beyond his control," which one who knew the personalities of those involved might interpret as interference from Robinson. As if that was not slight enough, in his review

Clement repeatedly points out interpretations of evidence that differed from the earlier volumes and for which he felt the volume VIII interpretations were always superior. Therefore, according to Clement, Graham did a better job interpreting the evidence than the author of the other volumes on the architecture at Olynthus, Robinson.

While it is not difficult to understand Robinson's resentment, it is a little more surprising to see how time failed to soften his hurt feelings at all; the wounds remained fresh for years. Robinson published the acerbic rebuttal to the two reviews quoted above in 1950, three years after Graham's review appeared and a full eleven years after Clement's. Three years later, in 1953, Robinson still fumed at Graham:

> You will be the death of me. I can't understand your disloyal and bellicose (a word used by one of your friends) and unfriendly attitude after all I have done for you financially and otherwise. . . . I do not mind friendly criticism and suggestions but as I told you at Olynthus when you acted as if you were in charge and asked me to let you publish Olynthus (into which I have put more than $100,000)[42] and sulked, I was responsible and no one else according to the contract. I have always appreciated your great help and thank you, but Olynthus is mine, not yours.
>
> But what I want to say again is that the Olynthus volumes and material are copyrighted in my name and nothing can be used without my permission. . . . Better consult your lawyer before you use unauthorized . . . copyrighted material.[43]

Robinson's tendency to destroy his relationships with his graduate students is well represented by the table of contents of a pair of companion volumes. In 1951 and 1953, Mylonas published two massive studies on topics that interested Robinson. The title of the set, *Studies Presented to David Moore Robinson on His Seventieth Birthday*, demonstrates his purpose. Names in the table of contents of each volume are like a who's who of early 1950s archaeology and art history showing the depth of respect Robinson still commanded. Just a few of these contributors include V. Gordon Childe, Spyridon Marinatos, W. F. Albright, William Dinsmoor, Gisela Richter, and C. H. V. Sutherland. The names that are missing, however, say even more about Robinson and his recklessness with his friendships. Some are familiar from the previous chapters including J. Walter Graham, Paul Clement, Arthur Parsons, Alexander Schulz, Sarah Freeman, Mary Ross Ellingson, Wilhelmina van Ingen Elarth, Eunice Couch, Herbert Couch, Gladys Weinberg, and Gladys's husband and also veteran of the Olynthus excavation, Saul Weinberg. Aside from Mylonas, who organized the project, only one other person who spent time with Robinson in the field at Olynthus over the four seasons of the project contributed to volumes lauding Robinson, the archaeologist William McDonald. Robinson's students are not completely absent from the volumes; in addition to Mylonas and McDonald, four other former students of Robinson wrote something.[44] Considering the statistics quoted above, that he supervised forty-one theses and seventy-four dissertations, a total of six former-student contributions speaks to the nature of the relationships Robinson had with his former graduate students.

Robinson's temper not only led him into a conflict that destroyed his friendships with his students, it also cost him his job at Johns Hopkins in 1946. The circumstances that precipitated Robinson's departure from the university are murky, but there is no question that his anger was a major contributing factor. As Jennifer K. West, one historian of archaeology who has studied Robinson's papers at the University of Mississippi, concluded his dismissal was "[a]t least in part due to the fact that he was a 'difficult' person."[45] James Stimpert, an archivist at Johns Hopkins, shared a secondhand story that offers a few more details. However, he stressed that the full veracity of the story is difficult to confirm from the letters that remain in the university's archives as they are worded very carefully so as to avoid the charge of libel. According to the story Stimpert heard, and based on his investigation in the archives, Robinson believed that some of the artifacts he brought back to the university from a trip to Egypt belonged to him personally, while the university administration believed they belonged to the university. The disagreement turned ugly when Robinson removed artifacts from campus in perhaps an aggressive attempt to test the strength of the administration's claims. Rather than involve lawyers in the matter, as the administrators had to admit that their records on the Egyptian artifacts were incomplete, they forced him to retire citing the fact that he was past the mandatory retirement age. To mollify him, the administration named him a Professor Emeritus of Art and Archaeology,[46] a merely ceremonial position, and gave him a year's pay. It is not clear if Robinson had tenure at Johns Hopkins; he began work there in 1904 long before the tenure system became popular in American academia. The Johns Hopkins administration would have found it easy to dismiss an untenured faculty member. Perhaps not surprisingly, Robinson found someone else to blame for these events. In a letter, he suggests that Graham's public statements about the Olynthus material challenging some of Robinson's interpretations led to his forced retirement.[47]

Robinson had trouble finding another position. This is a rather unexpected development as he was a highly respected archaeologist by this time, he had many students who were in positions to help him, and colleges and universities across the country were eager to hire professors because of the glut of students arriving on campuses thanks to the GI Bill. One can only wonder if his reputation for being a "difficult person" preceded him. Desperate for another academic appointment Robinson found an opening at the University of Mississippi, an institution that was in a totally different class from Johns Hopkins. The university was equally desperate, having a position they could not fill; they had already offered the job to eight other archaeologists and classicists all, of whom declined because of the inadequate compensation the university was offering. Robinson took the job at half his Johns Hopkins salary. He spent the rest of his career at Ole Miss finishing the publication of his Olynthus excavation volumes and teaching classes on art and archaeology. His classes were popular and always well enrolled.[48] In October 1957, Robinson became ill and stepped away from his teaching duties; the following January he died.[49] At the time of his death, Robinson owned an extensive collection of antiquities, which in his will he divided between Harvard University, the American Numismatic Society, the University of Mississippi, and various individuals; the University of Mississippi received all of his papers.[50] In an unexpected move, considering the fractious way he departed the university, Robinson included a bequest in his will for Johns Hopkins University to establish two trust funds. One fund was to help underwrite the costs for Hopkins students going to study at the American School of Classical Studies at Athens and the other to be used by the university's press. The trusts have since been rolled into other university funds and no longer exist independently.[51]

George E. Mylonas, Arthur Parsons, and Alexander Schulz

Robinson remained on much better terms with Mylonas, Parsons, and Schulz. He and Mylonas in particular had a lifelong friendship, while Parsons and Schulz moved on to other projects, slipping out of Robinson's immediate social circle. Mylonas held several temporary teaching positions in the United States after the 1931 season at Olynthus. In 1933, Washington University in St. Louis, Missouri, hired him as faculty in the Department of Art and Archaeology where he became department chair in 1939 and remained until his retirement in 1969.[52] In a letter he sent to Robinson, Mylonas credits his former advisor with using his influence and connections to get Mylonas the position;[53] this was the same position Robinson had first sought for Graham but in which Graham was ultimately not interested.[54] Holding a permanent position helped Mylonas become a naturalized U.S. citizen in 1937, although he continued to spend much of his time in Greece.[55] Mylonas did not participate in the 1934 season at Olynthus as he was excavating at the Greek site of Eleusis but he returned in 1938, during which time he held the excavation permit jointly with Robinson.[56] During the latter half of his career, Mylonas worked at the Bronze Age citadel of Mycenae, famed as the home of the mythical king Agamemnon, becoming one of the noted excavators of the site. In recognition of his work at Mycenae, he was allowed to be buried there after his death from a heart attack in 1988.[57] The Archaeological Institute of America awarded Mylonas its Gold Medal for Distinguished Archaeological Achievement in 1970,[58] making him, along with Gladys Davidson Weinberg, one of two staff members at Olynthus in 1931 to win this prestigious distinction. Mylonas continued an interest in Olynthus, contributing to *Excavations at Olynthus XII*, and remained a good friend to Robinson. The two-volume work he edited, *Studies Presented to David Moore Robinson on His Seventieth Birthday*, demonstrates the deep respect and affection for Robinson that Mylonas had. The feeling was reciprocated. In item four of his will, Robinson bequeathed an ancient Greek vase from his collection to Mylonas as well as $20,000, with the request Mylonas put the sum toward his research. Robinson specifically made the bequest to Mylonas personally, not to any institution with which he was affiliated. The will mentions no other former student of Robinson's.[59]

Parsons, on the other hand, broke away from Robinson to pursue his career. Arthur and Gladys Parsons were fellows at the American School of Classical Studies at Athens in 1931–1932. The couple returned to Olynthus in 1934 to aid in that year's excavation, but Arthur Parsons had lost interest in Olynthus for his dissertation research.[60] Between his two seasons at Olynthus, Parsons had become involved in the American School excavations at Corinth and in the Athenian Agora.[61] Parsons rose to be the assistant director of the School from 1939 to 1941.[62] With the Italian invasion of Greece in 1940, the Parsons and others at the American School became determined to aid the Greeks in the war effort. At Gladys Parsons's suggestion, members of the American School raised money to build a truck, which they used to ferry supplies to the front as well as to transport wounded and exhausted soldiers.[63] Arthur Parsons drove the truck on some of these dangerous missions.[64] Once the Germans took control of the Greek invasion, the Parsons fled.[65] Despite the chaos of war, Parsons managed to complete his dissertation in 1942 based on data he gathered during excavations on the slopes of the Athenian Acropolis,[66] which he published the following year.[67] Although he was away from Greece for much of his tenure and worked simultaneously with the U.S. State Department, Parsons was appointed the nominal head of the American School from 1941 to 1946. After the war Parsons served as a liaison officer and representative for the United States to the United Nations Security Council International Investigating Committee in Athens.[68] He died of a heart attack in the fall of 1948.[69]

It is not clear if Alexander Schulz ever took the motorcycle tour of Europe that he told Ellingson he was planning after the excavation season at Olynthus ended. In 1931 he joined the Parsons at the American School at Athens. He later spent nine months working with, and learning from, the highly respected artifact conservator and restorer, Apostolos Kontogeorgis, while working on some of the Olynthus material in the museum in Saloniki.[70] Both men appear in the group photo, figure 3.3. Schulz completed his MA in 1935 with a thesis on the burial customs of prehistoric Greece, a work that makes very little mention of Olynthus.[71] He never published his thesis. Schulz clearly enjoyed conserving artifacts and reassembled one of the ceramic bathtubs that the team had excavated at Olynthus and which the Greek government had allowed Robinson to bring back to Johns Hopkins. The bathtub had been smashed into sixty-five pieces, making it a large and challenging jigsaw puzzle.[72] With the advent of World War II, Schulz joined the navy and upon his discharge in 1945, returned to the University of Illinois to pursue his doctorate in classical archaeology. He was distracted from his goal, however, when the faculty head of the university's Classical, Oriental, and Egyptian Museum died in a boating accident and Schulz was appointed temporary custodian until a faculty replacement could be found. The "temporary" appointment was renewed every year between 1945 and 1950, and Schulz tirelessly threw himself into caring for the neglected collections and augmenting the displays. Devoting himself to work in the museum forty hours a week left little time to write his dissertation, and he abandoned the project in 1950.[73] Schulz married and moved to Florida to become a farmer. He passed away in 1973.[74]

Georg von Peschke and Euripides Melanides

Both the men who remained in Greece, the artist von Peschke and the photographer Melanides, disappear for the most part in the years following World War II. Von Peschke clearly enjoyed his first experience drawing the Olynthus material and working with archaeologists and wanted to continue. The relationships he established with Gladys and Saul Weinberg as well as with George and Lela Mylonas during that season grew and deepened in subsequent years to the point that the two couples became some of his closest friends.[75] When he and Robinson returned to Athens after wrapping up the Olynthus excavations in 1931, Robinson introduced the artist to his colleagues at the American School, whom von Peschke instantly impressed and charmed. Some of people at the School bought von Peschke's paintings and a few still hang in the School's halls. In 1931, he joined the excavations at Corinth as the chief architect, a position he maintained until his sudden death in 1959 and later worked at the site of Isthmia near Corinth as well. His star dimmed after the war, however, as interest in his artistic work faded and after his death he was quickly forgotten. Von Peschke's work has been rediscovered, however, and the Phillips Museum of Art at Franklin and Marshall College held an exhibit of his paintings in 2012.[76] In what is perhaps not a surprising development, von Peschke's relationship with Robinson grew tense in later years. At one point, he sent a watercolor caricature of himself to Gladys Weinberg. In the tiny artwork he coopts the imagery and story of his namesake, St. George, who slew the dragon. Instead of a shield, von Peschke holds a comically oversized painter's palette and the saint's lance is replaced by a large paintbrush. Von Peschke labeled the drawing in German "The Struggle with the Dragon." He does not label whom the dragon represents but Kostis Kourelis, the scholar who rediscovered and published the drawing, thinks von Peschke did not have to label the fantastic creature as his audience, Weinberg, would have recognized the monster as an allusion to Robinson.[77]

After Ellingson returned to the United States in 1931, she exchanged letters with the photographer Melanides who sent her some pictures he had taken at Olynthus in which she appeared.[78] Melanides continued to work with Robinson during the 1934 and 1938 seasons, photographing architecture and artifacts from the excavation.[79] With the approach of World War II, his hometown of Saloniki suffered a great deal as first the Axis powers bombed strategic positions in preparation for their capture of the city in 1941, only to be followed by Allied bombing prior to the city's liberation in 1944.[80] The rooftop garden of the Mediterranean Palace Hotel where Ellingson and her colleagues spent evenings dancing in 1931 was blown off in one of these raids. Ellingson enquired of Robinson if he had news of Melanides as she feared for his safety with this destruction in Saloniki but, unfortunately, Robinson's response does not survive and so it is not clear how Melanides and his photography business fared during the conflict.[81] He did survive the war, however, and in the last mention Robinson makes of him he was helping Robinson photograph some of the Olynthus artifacts Robinson had salvaged from the museum's wartime hiding places in 1947.[82]

Ellingson, Weinberg, and Freeman

The men involved in the Olynthus dig had varied careers after 1931, nonetheless their work that season was pivotal. For some, the Olynthus experience launched them in a direction they never could have anticipated. For others, their desire to escape David Robinson sent their careers on unexpected trajectories. Being men, tracking their post-Olynthus movements was fairly easy as during the twentieth century male archaeologists left large footprints in the published and archival record. After seeing the impact the season had on them, I could not help but wonder if the experience had affected the three women and their careers as profoundly. Finding their fates was going to require more work—female archaeologists have much lighter records in libraries and archives—but at this point I very much wanted to know.

Notes

1. J. Walter Graham, "Domestic Architecture in Classical Greece," PhD diss., Johns Hopkins University, 1933.

2. "Miss Annie C. Hare Is Married in London to Dr. J. Walter Graham, Archaeologist," *New York Times*, July 26, 1934, 16.

3. David M. Robinson, "Mosaics from Olynthus," *American Journal of Archaeology* 36, no. 1 (1932): 16, no. 2.

4. Robinson describes this episode in a letter dated January 10 or 17 (the last digit is smudged), 1953, now in the Graham folder, Box 6, David M. Robinson Collection, Special Collections, University of Mississippi Libraries. A copy is now on file at the University of Evansville Archives.

5. David M. Robinson, "The Third Campaign at Olynthus," *American Journal of Archaeology* 39, no. 2 (1935): 210, no. 1.

6. David M. Robinson, *Excavations at Olynthus XIII: Vases Found in 1934 and 1938*, Johns Hopkins University Studies in Archaeology 38 (Baltimore: Johns Hopkins University Press, 1950), vi.

7. Paul A. Clement, "Review of *Excavations at Olynthus, Part VIII: The Hellenic House, a Study of the Houses Found at Olynthus with a Detailed Account of Those Excavated in 1931 and 1934* by David M. Robinson and J. Walter Graham," *L'Antiquité Classique* 8 (1939): 474.

8. "Miss Annie C. Hare Is Married," 16; Joseph W. Shaw, "James Walter Graham 1906–1991," *American Journal of Archaeology* 96, no. 2 (1992): 325.

9. Homer Thompson, "In Memoriam: J. Walter Graham 1906–1991," *Ákoue* (Fall 1991): 15.

10. Shaw, "James Walter Graham," 325.

11. David M. Robinson and J. Walter Graham, *Excavations at Olynthus VIII: The Hellenic House; a Study of the Houses Found at Olynthus with a Detailed Account of*

those Excavated in 1931 and 1934, Johns Hopkins University Studies in Archaeology 25 (Baltimore, MD: Johns Hopkins University Press, 1938), v.

12. Shaw, "James Walter Graham," 325.

13. Later to marry and become Lucy Shoe Meritt.

14. Lucy T. Shoe, "Review of *Excavations at Olynthus, Part VIII: The Hellenic House, a Study of the Houses Found at Olynthus with a Detailed Account of Those Excavated in 1931 and 1934* by David M. Robinson and J. Walter Graham," *American Journal of Archaeology* 43, no. 4 (1939): 707–8.

15. Nicholas Cahill, *Household and City Organization at Olynthus* (New Haven, CT: Yale University Press, 2002), ix and 61–64.

16. George E. Mylonas, "Biographical Sketch," in *Studies Presented to David Moore Robinson on His Seventieth Birthday*. Vol. 1, edited by George E. Mylonas (St. Louis, MO: Washington University, 1951), xvii; Shaw, "James Walter Graham," 325; Thompson "In Memoriam," 15.

17. Mylonas, "Biographical Sketch," ix.

18. David M. Robinson, *Excavations at Olynthus XIV: Terracottas, Lamps, and Coins Found in 1934 and 1938* (Baltimore, MD: Johns Hopkins University Press, 1952), vii.

19. Letter from Robinson to Graham, October 30, 1947, Graham folder, Box 6, David M. Robinson Collection, Special Collections, University of Mississippi Libraries.

20. Linda M. Medwid, *The Makers of Classical Archaeology* (New York: Humanity Books, 2000), 258.

21. Robinson, *Olynthus XIV*, v.

22. Sterling Dow, "Review of *Excavations at Olynthus. Part XIV* by David M. Robinson," *American Historical Review* 58, no. 3 (1953): 58.

23. Richard E. Wycherley, "Review of *Excavations at Olynthus. Part X: Metal and Minor Miscellaneous Finds: An Original Contribution to Greek Life* by David M. Robinson," "*Excavations at Olynthus. Part XI: Necrolynthia: A Study in Greek Burial Customs and Anthropology* by David M. Robinson," *Journal of Hellenic Studies* 62 (1942): 104.

24. Richard E. Wycherley. "Review of *Excavations at Olynthus XII: Domestic and Public Architecture* by D. M. Robinson," *Journal of Hellenic Studies* 66 (1946): 135.

25. Robert Scranton. "Review of *Excavations at Olynthus, Part XIV: Terracottas, Lamps, and Coins Found in 1934 and 1938* by David M. Robinson," *Classical Philology* 49, no. 2 (1954): 144.

26. Cahill, *Household*, 61.

27. Louis E. Lord, *A History of the American School of Classical Studies at Athens 1882–1942* (Cambridge, MA: Harvard University Press, 1947), 261.

28. William A. McDonald, "Review of *Excavations at Olynthus Part XIV: Terracottas, Lamps and Coins Found in 1934 and 1938* by David M. Robinson," *Classical Journal* 50, no. 2 (1954), 94.

29. University of Mississippi, "Biographical Sketch of David Moore Robinson," (2000), https://classics.olemiss.edu/wp-content/uploads/sites/159/2011/01/Robinson_biography.pdf, accessed September 19, 2022.

30. Stephen L. Dyson, *Ancient Marbles to American Shores: Classical Archaeology in the United States* (Philadelphia: University of Pennsylvania Press, 1998), 194.

31. Letter from Robinson to Graham, October 30, 1947, Graham folder, Box 6, David M. Robinson Collection, Special Collections, University of Mississippi Libraries.

32. George M. A. Hanfmann, *The David Moore Robinson Bequest of Classical Art and Antiquities* (Boston: Harvard University Press, 1961), 3.

33. Mylonas, "Biographical Sketch," xi–xxi.

34. Jennifer K. West, "Observations on Selected Papers of David Moore Robinson from the University of Mississippi Archives" (MA thesis, University of Mississippi, 1995), 125.

35. Clement, "Review of *Excavations at Olynthus, Part VIII*," 474–77; and J. Walter Graham, "Review of *Excavations at Olynthus XII: Domestic and Pubic Architecture by D. M. Robinson*," *American Historical Review* 53, no. 1 (1947): 145–46.

36. Robinson, "The Third Campaign at Olynthus," 210, no. 1.

37. Robinson, *Excavations at Olynthus XIII*, 36.

38. "big book."

39. Graham, "Review of *Excavations at Olynthus XII*," 145–46.

40. Letter from Robinson to Graham, October 30, 1947, Graham folder, Box 6, David M. Robinson Collection, Special Collections, University of Mississippi Libraries.

41. Clement, "Review of *Excavations at Olynthus, Part VIII*," 474.

42. Robinson is exaggerating here, although in truth he was very generous in underwriting the excavation; see Louis E. Lord, *A History of the American School*, 261.

43. Letter from Robinson to Graham, January 10 or 17, 1953, Graham folder, Box 6, David M. Robinson Collection, Special Collections, University of Mississippi Libraries.

44. The students of Robinson who contributed to the two volumes include George Mylonas, George M. A. Hanfmann, William A. McDonald, Donald W. Prakken, William C. McDermott, and Elmer G. Suhr.

45. West, "Observations on Selected Papers," 121.

46. "Dr. Robinson Dies; Archaeologist, 77," *New York Times*, January 3, 1958, 21.

47. Letter from Robinson to Graham, October 30, 1947, Graham folder, Box 6, David M. Robinson Collection, Special Collections, University of Mississippi Libraries.

48. West, "Observations on Selected Papers," 121, 126.

49. "Dr. Robinson Dies," 21.

50. West, "Observations on Selected Papers," 118–28, has a summary of Robinson's later career as well as an assessment of his complex personality.

51. Greg Britton, editorial director of Johns Hopkins University Press, personal communication, June 22, 2022. Britton discovered a memo discussing the bequest in the Press' files from William Patterson to a Mr. Baker. The memo is undated but was probably written in 1958 after Robinson's death.

52. "G. E. Mylonas, 89, Archeologist Who Led Greek Excavations, Dies," *New York Times*, May 2, 1988, D14.

53. This letter is now in the Mylonas folder, Box 12, David M. Robinson Collection, Special Collections, University of Mississippi Libraries.

54. Letter from Robinson to Graham, January 10 or 17, 1953, Graham folder, Box 6, David M. Robinson Collection, Special Collections, University of Mississippi Libraries.

55. Raymond Dessy, *Exile from Olynthus: Women in Archaeology.com. Mentoring and Networking in Greece, 1927–1928*, 2005, 16, http://scholar.lib.vt.edu/faculty_archives/dessy/T_HOME-PAGE.htm, accessed June 1, 2014.

56. Robinson, *Excavations at Olynthus XIII*, vi.

57. Linda M. Medwid, *The Makers of Classical Archaeology*, 211–12; Spyros Iakovidis, "George Emmanuel Mylonas, 1898–1988," *American Journal of Archaeology* 93 (1989): 237; "G. E. Mylonas, 89," D14.

58. Archaeological Institute of America, "Seventy-Second General Meeting of the Archaeological Institute of America," *American Journal of Archaeology* 75, no. 2 (1971): 194.

59. The will is a public record on file at the Chancery Clerk in the Lafayette County Courthouse, Oxford, Mississippi.

60. Robinson, "The Third Campaign at Olynthus," 210, no. 1.

61. See Arthur W. Parsons, "The Long Walls to the Gulf," in *Corinth, Results of Excavations Conducted by the American School of Classical Studies at Athens III.2: The Defenses of Acrocorinth and the Lower Town*, edited by Rhys Carpenter and Antoine Bon (Princeton, NJ: American School of Classical Studies at Athens 1936), 84–127.

62. Lucy Shoe Meritt, *History of the American School of Classical Studies at Athens 1939–1980* (Princeton, NJ: American School of Classical Studies at Athens, 1984), 33; Mylonas, "Biographical Sketch," xix.

63. Susan H. Allen, *Classical Spies: American Archaeologists with the OS in World War II Greece* (Ann Arbor: University of Michigan Press, 2011), 31.

64. Allen, *Classical Spies*, 47.

65. Ibid., 66–67.

66. Arthur W. Parsons, "Klepsydra and the Paved Court of the Pythion" PhD diss., Johns Hopkins University, 1942.

67. Arthur W. Parsons, "Klepsydra and the Paved Court of the Pythion," *Hesperia* 12, no. 3 (1943): 191–267.

68. Meritt, *History of the American School*, 33; Mylonas, "Biographical Sketch," xix.

69. "Dr. Arthur Parsons," *New York Times*, October 1, 1948, 26.

70. Wayne T. Pitard, "Alexander the Great: How Grad Student Alexander Schulz Became a Key Figure in the Museum's History," *Spurlock Museum Magazine* (Fall 2012): 6.

71. Alexander H. G. Schulz, "The Burials and Burial Customs of Prehistoric Greece" (MA thesis, Johns Hopkins University, 1935).

72. "Student Rebuilds Ancient Bathtub," *Baltimore Sun*, November 24, 1935.

73. Pitard. "Alexander the Great," 6.

74. Wayne T. Pitard, personal communication.

75. Kostis Kourelis, "Flights of Archaeology: Peschke's Acrocorinth," *Hesperia* 86 no. 4 (2017): 436.

76. Kostis Kourelis, "Byzantium and the Avant-Garde: Excavations at Corinth 1920s–1930s," *Hesperia* 76 (2007): 423–24; Kostis Kourelis, *Peschke: Colors of Greece* (Lancaster, PA: Franklin and Marshall College, 2012); and Kourelis, "Flights of Archaeology: Peschke's Acrocorinth."

77. Kourelis, "Flights of Archaeology: Peschke's Acrocorinth," 776–77.

78. October 20, 1931, letter from Euripides Melanides to Mary Ellingson, the original is in the possession of Barbara Petersen, a copy is in the archives at the University of Evansville.

79. Robinson, "The Third Campaign at Olynthus," 210, n. 1; David M. Robinson and George E. Mylonas, "The Fourth Campaign at Olynthus," *American Journal of Archaeology* 43, no. 1 (1939): 48, n. 1.

80. "Italians Raid Salonika," *New York Times*, January 27, 1941, 2; "Allies Bomb Salonika Bases," *New York Times*, October 28, 1943, 3.

81. March 13, 1941, letter from Mary Ellingson to David Robinson, Box 5, David M. Robinson Collection, Special Collections, University of Mississippi Libraries; a copy is filed in the archive at the University of Evansville.

82. Robinson, *Excavations at Olynthus XIV*, vii.

CHAPTER FIVE

~

The Women

The pictures Ellingson collected offer insights into a specific moment in the lives of those being photographed. One of her snapshots shows herself, Weinberg, and Freeman (figure 5.1), and according to the label on the back, it was taken in a park near Johns Hopkins. Although it lacks a date, it most likely comes from the winter of 1930–1931 as the three were preparing to depart for Olynthus. Each woman is in a pose that seems typical based on the descriptions in Ellingson's letters, Freeman with chin down offering a demure look, Weinberg's head is thrown back in a hearty laugh, Ellingson's chin is up and a broad smile lights up her face. Ellingson wrote in the margin of the photo "the 3 archaeologists." At the moment that photo was snapped, each woman appears confident she would be able to achieve the future career in archaeology that she envisioned. At that moment, their confidence was well founded.

I knew the female archaeologists at Olynthus must have had an experience in pursuing their careers that differed from that of the men because of their gender, but I wanted to know how. What I discovered was that the stories of Ellingson, Weinberg, and Freeman are illustrative of the opportunities and obstacles all women of their generation encountered when seeking a career in archaeology, the sciences, or academia as well as the varied strategies women developed to help them work in fields dominated by men. When they had begun their undergraduate and graduate careers, all three women had a greater chance of becoming college professors than the members of the first generation in the field, and it is clear from the letters of their mentor and advisor David Robinson that this is what he was expecting and was the

Figure 5.1. Ellingson wrote on the margin of this photo, "The 3 archaeologists." From left to right Sarah Freeman, Gladys Weinberg, and Mary Ross Ellingson in a park near Johns Hopkins in late 1930 or early 1931.

Photo courtesy of Barbara Petersen

path for which he was grooming all his graduate students, both male and female. The employment landscape in higher education shifted throughout the 1930s, however, offering fewer opportunities for women, a situation that worsened after World War II. As the door slowly began to close on women who wanted to be professors and archaeologists, they had to develop what one historian of women in archaeology, Mary Ann Levine, has called "alternative career styles," ways of remaining in their chosen field without following the traditional route leading directly to a professorship.[1] Often women wound up on the margins of the field still doing useful and sometimes significant work but never gaining the kind of focused attention that those with university positions did. To make sense of the professional and personal choices each of the three female excavators made after they left Olynthus, it is useful to understand a little of the evolution in attitudes toward women in higher education as well as the change in career opportunities available to them that took place between the 1920s and 1970s. Ideas about marriage and family also evolved during that time as expectations of women developed and redeveloped rapidly before and after the war. Ellingson, Weinberg, and Freeman had to negotiate a swiftly changing United States and Canada and in doing so each found her own unique path toward the life she wanted.

Changes in Career Opportunities and Family Expectations for Women

When Ellingson and her female friends were students, the signs were good that they would be able to get a job in academia once they completed their doctorate, if that was what they wanted. Between the late nineteenth century and the time Ellingson went to Olynthus in 1931, women had made enormous strides in their participation in higher education as undergraduate (figure 5.2)[2] and graduate students (figure 5.3)[3] in both Ellingson's home country of Canada and adopted country of the United States. Likewise, more women were joining American college and university faculties,[4] which figure 5.4 shows.[5] We have no indication that Ellingson, Weinberg, or Freeman ever consulted or were even aware of the statistics and trends illustrated by the graphs in figures 5.2–5.4, but it seems plausible that they were cognizant in an anecdotal way that an increasing number of women had the opportunity to enter the ranks of university students and faculties. What all three graphs indicate, however, is that the upward trends for women in higher education were beginning to reverse within just a few years of the time the three spent at Olynthus. The percentage of women within the total undergraduate population in the United States peaked in the early 1920s at 47 percent followed by a precipitous drop starting in 1931. In Canada the apex of female undergraduate enrollment occurred in the early 1930s at 24 percent before slowly dropping. The percentage of women receiving PhDs in both countries reached a high level in the early 1920s, then began to decline. Women as a percentage of the overall faculty in the United States topped out in the late 1930s before also decreasing. Between the time the three aspiring women professors had started their undergraduate degrees and completed their doctorates, the world of higher education had been transformed in ways that would not help them achieve their goals. The mismatch between Ellingson's expectations and the changing academic world around her is well illustrated by a pair of letters written independently on the same day by two different people. On April 11, 1931, Ellingson wrote to her family about the careful way she had to excavate a badly decayed grave; the letter brims with the excitement of someone who is learning skills she hopes to employ in her career. In a letter with the same date, Edward Capps, chair of the Managing Committee of the American School of Classical Studies at Athens, suggested the School set a ratio of men to women when awarding fellowships in order to cut down on the number of women studying archaeology at the American School. He complained that there was

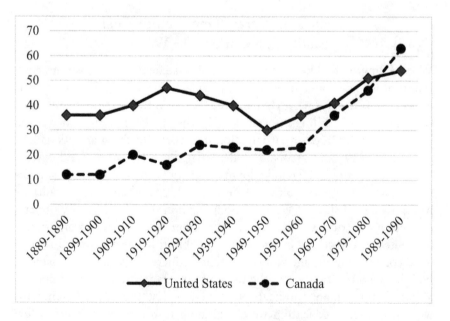

Figure 5.2. Percentage of women among undergraduates at American and Canadian institutions.

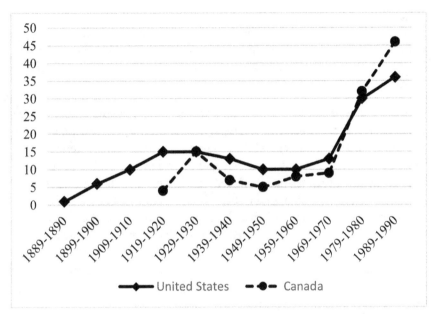

Figure 5.3. Percentage of women awarded PhD's at American and Canadian institutions.

"a dearth of men archaeologists and a superfluity of women," adding that it would be difficult for "the latter [to] get jobs."[6]

Several intertwining factors led to the decline of female participation in higher education, particularly as professors, between the 1920s and 1940s. While these factors are laid out here, at their heart was simple sexism; many people held stereotypes about the ability of women to be college professors. Writing in the mid-1970s, a time when notions about the inherent abilities of women were rapidly evolving, the chair of the chemistry department at Trinity College in Washington DC, Lilli S. Hornig, described the stereotypes she had endured over the previous few decades and which she still encountered:

> Women get good grades but have no imagination. They do well in humanities but not in science. They are good at routine work but do not have ideas. They may have jobs but they should not have careers.[7]

By the time Hornig wrote these words, this ideological belief was already many decades old. In 1941, sociologist C. Robert Pace published results of a survey focused on the careers of hundreds of recent coed graduates from the University of Minnesota. Pace concludes,

> Among the men the job characteristics most clearly related to satisfaction had to do with advancement, opportunity, and the future—suggesting a permanent

and sustained vocational drive. Among the women the job characteristics most clearly related to satisfaction had to do with prestige and pleasantness— suggesting a lack of sustained or permanent vocational ambition. Women were most satisfied when their jobs possessed prestige and provided contacts with pleasant people.[8]

Because this is hard data from a scientifically conducted survey, Pace's results justified contrasting stereotypes about men and women: men are aggressive and goal driven while women lack these characteristics and instead prefer to feel important and spend their days with "pleasant people."

These sexist attitudes and beliefs led to institutionalized, self-perpetuating discrimination within higher education. Because women wanted to feel prestigious and liked contact with people, the reasoning went, they made good instructors, while because they lacked drive and focus, they made bad research-ers. In the 1920s and 1930s, female professors were given higher teaching loads and lower salaries than their male counterparts who, it was assumed, needed more time to conduct and publish their research.[9] With minimal time for non-teaching activities, female professors conducted less research and published fewer articles and books, the yardstick by which their intellect was measured. Among archaeologists, women wrote fewer successful research grants than men because women were rarely allowed to lead field projects as fieldwork

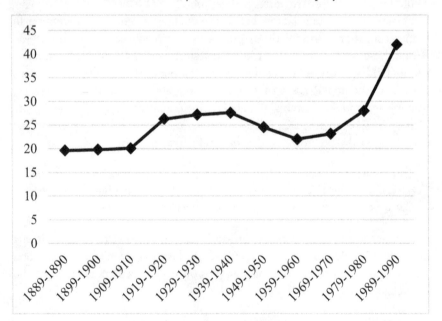

Figure 5.4. Percentage of women faculty at American colleges and universities.

was primarily a man's job; instead they were often relegated to cataloging artifacts rather than leading excavations.[10] The lower number of publications and grants simply proved the stereotype that women were intellectually incapable of original research and lacked the sustained drive and vision necessary to publish it. As a result, they deserved higher teaching loads and less research time, a conclusion that closed the loop of circular reasoning.[11]

A few extraordinary and lucky women were able to find a way to teach while still researching and publishing in archaeology and the sciences. Their success, however, led to what has been dubbed the "Madame Curie Complex," the idea that if French physicist Marie Curie could teach, publish, discover polonium and radium, and win the Nobel Prize twice, there was no reason other female scholars should not be equally capable.[12] Should a woman prove to be less a researcher than Curie, then she did not deserve time to conduct research. Naturally few male professors could match their accomplishments to Curie's, but they were not being measured against her as the women were. In 1924 Goucher College history professor Ella Lon gave a presentation to the American Association of University Women based on a survey she had conducted of the chairs in a variety of departments across the United States seeking to understand their attitudes toward women faculty. While most respected their female professors as teachers, she reported, they lamented their lack of doctorates, publications, and more up-to-date knowledge of their fields. Lon's solution to this problem was that female professors simply had to try harder to become Curie despite their heavy teaching loads; that would be the only way to prove the intellectual abilities of all women. Lon failed to understand that this was not a realistic resolution to an institutionalized problem.[13]

The lack of research and publications developed into a serious problem for women beginning in the 1920s with the introduction of the tenure system. The American Association of University Professors (AAUP) issued its first statement on tenure in 1925 followed by a revised statement in 1940.[14] As the AAUP's idea came to be applied at most colleges and universities, newly hired professors would have seven years to prove they were good researchers and competent instructors. After seven years if they lacked validation by their peers through peer-reviewed publications, they were clearly not cut out to be college professors. With their higher teaching loads and difficulties finding grant money, conducting original research, and publishing in multiple venues, the tenure system squeezed many women out of colleges and universities.[15] It is no coincidence that the percentage of female professors begins to decline after the AAUP's endorsement of the tenure system.

Figure 5.4 shows the dramatic rise in the number of women on college faculties in the United States between 1910 and 1940, with particularly large growth between 1910 and 1920. What would seem to indicate prog-ress in gender equality actually led to backlash. University officials began to worry about the feminization of their institutions; since women were inferior researchers, as proven by the smaller number of publications they produced, male faculty with longer publication lists made an institution more prestigious. During the 1920s and 1930s, universities began to seek male can-didates for jobs more frequently than female candidates. In an ironic twist, even women's colleges started to aggressively recruit male faculty.[16] The per-centage of women on faculties continued to grow, nonetheless, until around 1940 when the result of this hiring policy finally began to be manifest in the statistics. As the graph in figure 5.4 indicates, the highs in the percentage of women faculty reached around 1940 would not be equaled again for another four decades.

With the onset of the Depression in 1929, discriminatory hiring against women inside and outside of academia only increased as the number of jobs available decreased. Since women were believed to only be seeking jobs, while men were seeking careers, and because it was the role of men to support their families financially, in the early years of the Depression some politicians sought to drive women out of the workplace to decrease their competition with men for jobs. The mayor of Syracuse dismissed all women from city government whose husbands had employment. The North Dakota legislature created a ban on women working at state educational institu-tions. In Maryland a new law required that any woman working at a public school be fired once she married.[17] Across the public and private spheres, the number of job opportunities for women decreased dramatically.[18] American colleges and universities adopted another mechanism to limit the number of women faculty they employed: anti-nepotism policies. If a husband worked at a university it was deemed unfair to hire his wife. While such policies began to appear in the 1920s, their popularity increased during the Depres-sion and many institutions retained them long after the financial crisis had ended.[19] Archaeologists Madeline D. Kneberg and Tom Lewis, specialists in the American Southeast, became involved in a relationship not long after Lewis hired Kneberg to work in the University of Tennessee archaeology lab in 1938. The two chose not to formalize their relationship in order to avoid the invocation of the university's anti-nepotism rule. Upon Lewis's retire-ment in 1961, the two married after what Kneberg described as "the longest courtship on record."[20]

The low point in the percentage of American female undergraduates came in 1949–1950 according to figure 5.2. The Canadian data in that graph show a similar dip in the same years although the drop is not as dramatic as it was in the United States as the Canadian female undergraduate population showed more stability in the period between 1930 and 1960. The percentage of women receiving doctorates in the United States and Canada hit bottom during the 1950s (figure 5.3), while the percentage of women on American faculties bottomed out around 1959–1960 (figure 5.4). Although the downward trends had begun prior to World War II, they accelerated in the United States after the war primarily because of the GI Bill, a government program that offered financial support to veterans who wanted to go to college. The male undergraduate and graduate populations quickly skyrocketed as 97 percent of the people taking advantage of the American GI Bill in the 1940s were men. Institutions favored returning male veterans, quickly filling all available class seats and leaving few for women. Women had to prove their abilities were far superior to men to gain admittance to the few remaining spots.[21] The end result was a dramatic drop in female undergraduates, which led a few years later to fewer female graduate students and ultimately a dearth of female professors.

While all these factors influenced the career options available to Ellingson, Weinberg, and Freeman, probably the single biggest factor with which they and other female scholars of their generation had to contend was the question of whether to marry and have children, the point of marriage at the time. As archaeologist Jane Kelley points out, "women arrive at their penultimate childrearing years about the same time they are well into their PhD program or beginning the critical period of career development," the period requiring them to focus on publishing their dissertations and finding their first jobs.[22] Many archaeologists have long held a prejudice against children at an excavation as archaeological sites can be dangerous places for the uninitiated and children are seen as a distraction.[23] Few archaeologists bring their children on a dig and the few men who do rely on their wives to tend to the children, keeping them away from the site. In the past, this prejudice extended beyond fieldwork. American Plains archaeologist Alice Beck Kehoe relates a story of attending an archaeological conference in the 1960s with her infant son. A senior archaeologist spotted her in the back of the room with the sleeping child in her lap and demanded she leave the room to avoid a potential disruption of the proceedings. When Kehoe refused, the unnamed archaeologist had security officials carry her, still seated in the chair holding her baby, out of the room.[24]

Immediately before and after World War II, the commonly held belief was that women could either have a career or a family but not both. In 1941 the sociologist Pace illustrated the stark black and white nature of this decision when he stated flatly, "[U]ndoubtedly there are some women who have as intense vocational ambitions as men. But probably most women want to get married."[25] Women, therefore, could only be in the workforce temporarily, pursuing a job until they married rather than pursuing a long-term career. Such a scenario presented a particular problem within academia where, ideally, one would work at one position for many years if not for life. For this reason, some department chairs were hesitant to hire a single woman and at some universities the expectation was that once a woman married she would either resign or be forced to resign.[26] When Nobel Prize–winning geneticist Barbara McClintock was beginning her career in the botany department of the University of Missouri in 1936, her enraged chair called her into his office and pointed to a wedding announcement in a local newspaper mentioning a Barbara McClintock. He was prepared to fire her on the spot until she was able to convince him of the truth, that the announcement was not about her but about another woman who by coincidence happened to have the same name.[27]

During the first thirty years that Ellingson, Weinberg, and Freeman were alive, the percentage of female college graduates with a bachelor's degree or higher who married increased at a much faster pace than for the general population of women in the United States. Between 1912 and 1937, the increase in the percentage of women graduates who wed was over 20 percent while for all American women the figure was a mere 3 percent (figure 5.5).[28] The data in figure 5.5 are based on surveys of graduates from Mount Holyoke, a women's college, but evidence from other colleges and universities show similar patterns.[29] During this same period, the women who took their vows were also marrying at an increasingly earlier average age.[30] These changes in marital demographics correlate with the drop in the number of women in bachelor or advanced degree programs. Whether more women chose to tie the knot rather than go to college or increasing discrimination against women in higher education led more women to give up the goal of going to college or graduate school and marry instead is currently an unsolvable chicken-and-egg problem. Nonetheless, just one year after their adventure at Olynthus, across the United States, 78 percent of college women, and 92 percent of all women, were marrying with those numbers continuing an upward trend. This is not to say women who wed saw themselves as left with no other options and were thus reluctantly walking down the aisle. Marriage, it seems, could be a fulfilling pursuit. In his 1941 survey of nearly one thousand male and female graduates from the University of Minnesota, Pace reported that the people who had the highest satisfaction with their current jobs were housewives and that married women were more satisfied with what they were doing than single women.[31] A compromise a few female archaeologists found

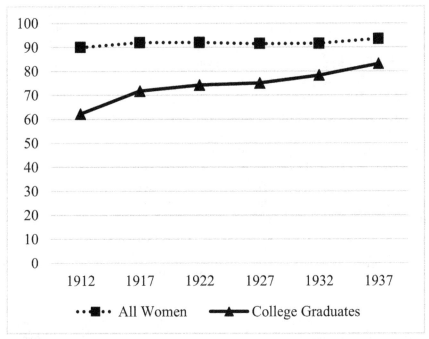

Figure 5.5. Percentage of graduates from Mount Holyoke College who married compared to all women born in the United States.

was to marry a fellow archaeologist who would pursue an academic career. While meeting the expectations of a mid-century American housewife and finding someone to look after the children, she could also participate with her husband in fieldwork and in post-excavation analysis and publication, allowing her to remain active in the field. Most men who have directed excavations in Greece were married and their wives provided valuable and usually unacknowledged logistical and technical support.[32] Robinson's wife Helen is one example, having played such a role during the Olynthus excavation.

At a time when most women had to choose between a family and career, however, some chose their careers over marriage. Virtually no data exist to enlighten us as to why some women made this highly personal decision. Some may have felt they were making a sacrifice while others may have reveled in the freedom of being single; nonetheless not marrying offered some advantages to women researchers and professors. At a time when women had to face the high bar set by the Madame Curie Complex, being able to focus on her research without being distracted by caring for a house, husband, and children certainly allowed a woman who chose this path to excel.[33] A book celebrating early women archaeologists presents the biographies of twelve pioneers in the field. The editors of the book note that of these only three married and only two had children, to make their mark the other nine women, or 75 percent, chose to forgo marriage.[34]

Naturally a woman's intellectual pursuits did not have to end with marriage. As life spans grew longer and as the average age of marriage fell, a growing number of women found themselves with years, even decades, of time to pursue their own interests as their children went to school and eventually left home. Women returning to the workforce later in life became an increasingly common phenomenon after World War II.[35] Precedents exist within the field of archaeology. In 1939, Mildred Mott Wedel, an archaeologist whose research focused on the Native American cultures of the American Plains and Southwest, married a fellow archaeologist and retired from the field. She returned twenty years later, picking up her career where she had left it, expanding her research focus, and publishing popular accounts of archaeological research.[36] Even before World War II, archaeologist Boyd Hawes had followed a similar path. She had this advice for women aspiring to work in the field:

> A woman should expect her intellectual life to be interrupted, i.e. she should be prepared to give the first 10 years after marriage . . . to her family interests. . . . Perhaps she can keep alive her intellectual interests and return to them with new zest and judgment after ten years. Throughout life a woman's work should be more or less interruptible or family and society will suffer. Her happiness in accepting this interruption will depend largely on her having anticipated it as part of the Good Life.[37]

Ellingson, Weinberg, and Freeman faced all these challenges when pursuing their careers. Each reacted differently to them and found a unique way to be satisfied with her career and home life. Their stories nicely illustrate the three most common directions women in archaeology and the sciences went after receiving their doctorates: one married a fellow archaeologist and made a career in the field, in the lab, and in museums; another chose not to marry but had the support of a patron who helped her find work in publishing and, eventually, in a museum; and a third left the field to raise children but returned to academia later in life to become a professor. Careers like these have been documented too rarely.[38]

Gladys Davidson Weinberg and Sarah Freeman

Both Weinberg and Freeman wound up on the margins of the university system. Neither fulfilled Robinson's dream for them that they be full-time, tenured professors, a position for which he and their Hopkins education had prepared them. No record survives to indicate if the two women shared his career plan for them. Weinberg had a severe stutter that would have brought challenges to teaching and may have guided her career decisions.[39] Nonetheless, Weinberg and Freeman used research assistant and curatorial positions quite successfully to further their goals. Their stories are worth recounting for the creative and sharply contrasting ways they developed their own "alternative career styles" in the face of the same expectations and discrimination Ellingson faced. The choices they made particularly about marriage had a large effect on opening or closing career opportunities to each woman.

After her season at Olynthus, Weinberg did not remain under Robinson's tutelage and decided not to pursue the vases she had cataloged for her dissertation project. She spent the 1931–1932 academic year in Baltimore and then returned to Greece, studying at the American School in Athens and participating in the excavations at the ancient port city of Corinth between 1933 and 1937.[40] Weinberg completed her dissertation in 1935 focusing on the "small finds" from Corinth as her unit of study, an assignment typical of women at the time.[41] Weinberg had trouble finding a publisher for her dissertation and feared losing a $100 deposit all doctoral graduates were required to pay to Johns Hopkins University, refundable as long as they published their dissertations within two years of graduation. In response to a despondent letter from Weinberg in which she announced her intention to publish her dissertation on the shoe-string budget provided by her $100 deposit, Robinson wrote, "I think it would be very foolish to publish a hundred dollars' worth of your excellent dissertation."[42] Presumably he was concerned about the limited number of copies that would be produced and the poor quality that the limited budget would impose. In the same letter, Robinson describes steps he took to get Weinberg an extension on the two-year deadline from the Johns Hopkins administration. Even after the expiration of the deadline and the loss of the deposit, Robinson continued to encourage his former student to publish. After much delay because of World War II, Weinberg eventually published a revised version of her dissertation in 1952.[43]

Saul Weinberg was a fellow Johns Hopkins graduate who spent the 1937 season at Corinth with Gladys Davidson. Slightly younger than his future wife, the Chicago native had participated in the 1934 season at Olynthus, gaining his first taste of fieldwork under Robinson. Saul Weinberg had gradu-

ated in 1936 and was soon an integral part of the staff at the Corinth excavation, producing several important interim articles on the excavation and
eventually two volumes in the *Corinth* series. He quickly became a respected
archaeologist and a prolific scholarly writer.[44] The Weinbergs married in 1942
amid the chaos of World War II. As all archaeology in Greece had shut down
during the war, Gladys Weinberg joined the Foreign Service Auxiliary of the
United States State Department as a librarian and translator in Athens and
Istanbul.[45] Rumors persist that she also worked for the American wartime spy
agency, the Office of Strategic Services, the precursor to the postwar Central
Intelligence Agency.[46] Her husband joined the U.S. Army Signal Corps and
was stationed in England, France, and Belgium.[47]

After the war Gladys Weinberg's career was inextricably linked to Saul's.
With all the barriers women faced in finding academic positions at the time,
in addition to Gladys Weinberg's stutter, it certainly made more sense for
Saul Weinberg to seek an academic position rather than, and without the
competition from, his wife. Prior to the war the strong strains of antisemitism
in American academia made such a dream elusive. In 1940, Jewish faculty
made up only 2 percent of all the faculty members at American colleges and
universities. Fortunately for the Weinbergs, the postwar years saw a reversal
in antisemitic employment practices as some institutions of higher learning
increased the number of Jewish men they were hiring.[48] Progress was uneven,
however, as the number of Jewish women added to faculties was much more
modest. Hopkins even implemented a quota on the enrollment of Jewish
undergraduates just as the war ended in 1945, leaving it in place for the next
six years.[49] One can only wonder how Gladys and Saul Weinberg felt about
the antisemitic policy of their alma mater.

While looking for an academic position, the Weinbergs returned to
Greece where he took on the position of the assistant to the director of
the American School.[50] In 1948, the University of Missouri at Columbia
hired Saul Weinberg to fill the post Graham had just vacated to return
to Canada and Weinberg remained on the faculty there for the rest of his
career re-founding the Department of Art History and Archaeology in 1960.
He helped build the department into a significant center for the training
of a new generation of classical archaeologists.[51] Gladys Weinberg did not
compete with her husband for an academic job; instead the couple worked
as a team in the field and she pursued her own research interests. In 1957,
they founded the Museum of Art History and Archaeology at the University
of Missouri with Saul Weinberg as the director and Gladys as the assistant
director and curator.[52] In the 1950s, Saul Weinberg led several excavations
in Greece with the help of his wife.[53] Although they worked together well,

Gladys Weinberg established her own professional identity independent of her husband. She edited the popular magazine *Archaeology* from 1952 to 1967, ensuring that articles were scholarly, well written, and interesting to the general public.[54] While working on small finds from Corinth, Weinberg was struck by how little interest excavators took in the glass fragments they had found, a type of material that few had studied in depth prior to World War II. She soon made herself a leading expert on ancient and medieval glass and became so curious about the origins of glass production that she, with Saul Weinberg's assistance, organized a joint excavation of the University of Missouri and the Corning Museum of Glass at two sites in Israel with evidence for glass manufacturing—Jalame and a site near Shavei Zion—during the 1960s.[55] Ancient glass expert Paul Perrot lauded Weinberg for focusing on the "minutiae of scholarship" and "emphasizing the study of those aspects [of archaeology] which for some may hold little glamour," pointing out how neglected the study of glass had been.[56] Between the late 1960s and the mid-1980s, the Weinbergs worked together on a significant Hellenistic site in the Upper Galilee of Israel, Tel Anafa. The Archaeological Institute of America awarded Saul and Gladys Weinberg its Gold Medal for Distinguished Archaeological Achievement in 1985.[57] The Israel Museum in Jerusalem awarded the couple the Percia Schimmel Award the following year.[58] Gladys continued to work at Corinth until she suffered a stroke, losing her ability to speak. Six years later in 2002, Weinberg died in Columbia, Missouri.

In an email she sent me after the first edition of the book came out, Weinberg's daughter, Miriam Dyak, shared a memory of talking with her mother days before her stroke, which I quote with her permission:

> One of our last long conversations, jet lagged in the middle of the night in an Athens hotel, was about how much she missed the old days and old ways of excavation that were romantic and fun. . . . [S]he felt computers were ruining the spirit of the work.

Weinberg was the last surviving member of the team that excavated at Olynthus in 1931 and the sentiments reflected in Dyak's email show that despite her feelings about Robinson, she looked back on her career, especially the early part, with great fondness and nostalgia.

For Weinberg marrying a fellow archaeologist allowed her opportunities not open to Ellingson. She was able to help Saul Weinberg on the excavations he directed and received his support in those she wanted to conduct. Since Saul Weinberg joined a faculty in a department determined to grow, Gladys Weinberg could help him increase department resources by aiding in the founding of the university museum and by curating its collections. Remaining within this academic and archaeological world also gave Weinberg access to an excellent library, a base from which to apply for grants and raise money for excavations, and the moral support of others interested in similar subjects, all of which made her career advancement possible. Marrying a male archaeologist as a way to remain active in excavation and research was a career option some women discussed openly. Alice Beck Kehoe recollected hearing the charge that some student archaeologists were seeking their MRS (Mrs.) degree as a pathway to remain active in the field.[59] Although she is writing about the generation that followed the women at Olynthus, it does not seem a stretch to assume that similar discussions took place in the 1930s and 1940s.

Freeman took a very different path from Weinberg since she chose not to marry. She continued in the field after participating in the Olynthus excavations but also chose to search for a subject other than material from Olynthus for her dissertation. During the fall of 1931, she remained in Athens as a student at the American School with the Parsons and Schulz. Like Weinberg, she was drawn to participate in the Corinth excavation. Eventually she wrote her dissertation about a Roman-era temple excavated at that site, Temple E, putting the training she had gotten at Olynthus in surveying and architectural drawing to good use. Freeman continued working with the Corinth team for years to come.[60] She graduated from Johns Hopkins with her PhD in 1934 during the height of the Depression when jobs were scarce and discrimination against women inside and outside of higher education was increasing. With what appeared to be no prospects for a job, she remained in Baltimore for a year until Robinson hired her as his research assistant at Johns Hopkins, supporting her as he had Graham. Freeman held this position from 1935 to 1944,[61] aiding Robinson in the publication of the Olynthus volumes, a position for which she was eminently suited.[62] During the 1920s and 1930s, the number of university research assistantships increased, especially in the sciences, and women often filled these positions.[63] The opportunity Freeman took advantage of was part of a growing trend. While research assistantships could help a recent graduate survive until she found a more permanent job, the disadvantage to these positions was that the pay was low or nonexistent, funding could unexpectedly disappear, and there was little chance for advancement within a university.[64] Still, Johns Hopkins University was a vibrant place for Freeman to work as it had an unusually large number of highly educated women, some recent graduates and others the spouses of male faculty members, who worked in the medical and science labs as well as in individual departments helping prepare publications. Together they formed a supportive community.[65] In 1944, Freeman finally found a permanent position and was able to leave her research assistantship to become the curator of fine arts at the Johns Hopkins museum.[66] During her nearly three decade tenure there, she cataloged two extensive collections of ancient coins and medals donated to the museum, becoming an acknowledged expert on the subject and publishing extensively.[67] She remained a loyal assistant to Robinson, helping him to publish more Olynthus volumes even when that was no longer her job. Freeman's choices differed from Weinberg's, but she also made a niche for herself as a professional in the field. Since Freeman did not have a husband to support her financially or professionally, having a powerful supporter like Robinson was vital to her success. She worked as a museum curator until her retirement in 1972. Twelve years later, Freeman suffered a horrific death when men entered her home, locked her in a closet, robbed her, and fled. Her mailman called the police nine days later when he noticed all the uncollected mail; officers discovered the body still in the closet. Two men were convicted for the crime.[68]

Mary Ross Ellingson

Ellingson's archival footprint for her time at Olynthus is vast. For the single year 1931, the year she went to Greece, I have located approximately thirty-six letters that she wrote or that mention her, 152 photographs, and eight newspaper articles. The amount of material illustrating her life in the years that follow does not compare. For the period between 1932 and her death in 1993, a total of sixty-one years, I have identified in various archives approximately twenty-eight letters, eleven photos, and twelve newspaper articles that touch on her activities. The woman whose personality bursts out of the archives in 1931 becomes more elusive and harder to see in the years that follow. Clues, however, do survive.

After returning to Baltimore from England at the end of the 1931 season at Olynthus, Ellingson spent the rest of 1931 and the beginning of 1932 writing her master's thesis, *The Terra Cottas of Olynthus*, which earned her a master's degree in classical archaeology in 1932. While Robinson must have given her access to the excavation records, most of the thesis was based on her own notes, photographs, and the plaster casts of some key pieces she had made independent of Robinson's records (see figure 2.11). The catalog in her thesis is a well-documented history of the evolution of Greek terracotta figurines from the sixth to the mid-fourth century BCE. For each of the 392 figurines, she provides a catalog number as well as the contextual information: when the piece was found in a building she gives the building number, room letter, and the piece's depth below the surface. When it comes from a grave, she gives the cemetery designation and grave number when an individual grave could be delineated. Each entry has measurements of the figurine and a description of the individual piece along with a list of similar pieces uncovered at other sites or of similar artistic representations in other media. These "*comparanda*," as they are called, were of particular importance because they had been securely dated by archaeologists working at these other sites, allowing Ellingson to date the similar pieces from Olynthus. Figure 5.6 shows one of the plaster casts Ellingson made while at Olynthus, which is now in the collections of the University of Evansville. In her catalog entry about this piece, she identified the figure as a dancer found in the East Cemetery. It stands 24.6 centimeters high, and she noted traces of red paint on the dancer's hair and red and black paint on her clothing. Ellingson dated this figurine to the early fourth century BCE based on dated *comparanda* from other sites. She points out that the artist who made this figure was trying so hard to show the spinning of the dancer that he made a figurine that is quite unbalanced. The break in the middle of the plaster visible in figure 5.6 occurred after Ellingson had made the cast, further showing how unbalanced the original design was.[69]

Ellingson's chronologically organized catalog was a useful contribution to the fields of archaeology and art history.[70] It gave further examples of terracotta figurines known from other sites, offered variations on those known examples, and publicized some previously unknown types. Her analysis of the larger issues surrounding the use of these types of artifacts was also important. Among other conclusions, she observed that terracotta figurines were found in both houses and graves. Until her time, most archaeologists believed that the purpose of these figurines was to accompany the dead in their graves or as offerings to deities in their temples. Ellingson was able to show beyond a shadow of a doubt that while many terracotta figurines did end up in graves, many living people at Olynthus also displayed some for decoration and some for worship in their homes. She also noted that nearly all types of terracotta figurines were found in both homes and graves, indicating they were not made exclusively for funerary use. Robinson's publication of the terracotta figurines found during the 1928 season in *Excavations at Olynthus IV* was only a catalog with no analysis. Ellingson's thesis catalogs the figurines from the 1931 season as thoroughly but is more valuable than *Excavations at Olynthus IV* because of the accompanying analysis.

After completing her thesis Ellingson left graduate school. Her reasons are not clear, but she had been contemplating a temporary departure for a year. In an undated letter from Olynthus that must have been written at some point in April of 1931, she explains to her mother, "I wouldn't consider

Figure 5.6. Plaster cast of a fourth century BCE terracotta figurine representing a woman dancing.

Photo by the author

going back to Hopkins for the 2nd year (I mean for Ph.D.) right away but would work maybe a year or two before going on with my Doctor's work." On May 25, 1932, a telegram arrived for her in Baltimore offering her a job as a lecturer teaching Latin and Classical studies at Mount Royal College in Calgary, a junior college affiliated with Ellingson's alma mater, the University of Alberta.[71] In a letter a month later, Robinson thanked Ellingson's old mentor from the University of Alberta, W. H. Alexander, for assisting her in getting the job even though he had no direct evidence for Alexander's involvement.[72] Still, his assumption was probably correct as Ellingson would have reached out to Doc Alik once she had decided to leave Johns Hopkins, and he would likely have known about the position at an affiliated institution. He would also have been an obvious person for her to ask for a letter of recommendation.

Ellingson thrived at Mount Royal, although her duties kept her extremely busy. A letter from the school's dean written in 1939 and placed in her University of Evansville personnel file shows she was a good teacher as he wrote, "[A]ll who were associated with her either as colleagues or as students are unanimous in considering Miss Ross one of the best and most popular teachers on staff." A photograph from this period (figure 5.7) shows her surrounded by her students, posing in humorous stances. All appear to be happily enjoying the moment with her. Despite how relaxed she looks in the photo, Ellingson worked constantly both inside and outside the classroom. In addition to teaching duties, her position required her to help supervise the women's residence hall and extra-curricular activities. The hectic schedule kept her from contemplating publishing her thesis. Masters degree recipients did not regularly publish theses in the 1930s, but Ellingson's had potential. We have no indication if she wanted to return to Olynthus for either the 1934 or 1938 seasons, but between her duties and the difficulty of not being a student and, therefore, eligible for financial aid to go to Greece, it is not hard to imagine she hardly contemplated such a move. Perhaps because she worked all the time, she had little time to think about her future and her time in Calgary wound up lasting longer than the year or two she had envisioned. It was not until 1938 that she made good on her determination to return to Johns Hopkins to complete her PhD work.

Ellingson spent the academic year 1938–1939 in Baltimore writing her dissertation, *The Terra-cotta Figurines of Macedonia and Thrace*.[73] For this document she created a second catalog and compared terracotta figurines excavated at other sites in northern Greece and Bulgaria to those she and other members of Robinson's team found at Olynthus. The first portion of her dissertation is less interesting as it relates information about figurines

Figure 5.7. Mary Ross Ellingson (bottom, center) surrounded by her seemingly-happy students at Mount Royal College in Calgary in a photo taken between 1932 and 1938.
Photo courtesy of the University of Evansville Archives

found at sites other than Olynthus, information which came from previously published sources. More useful is a pair of tables she added as appendixes that list specific graves and rooms within houses along with all the terracotta figurines found in those locations during the 1931, 1934, and 1938 seasons at Olynthus. These tables make all three volumes of the *Excavations at Olynthus* series mentioning terracotta figurines much easier to use because rather than making the figurines the unit of study, as the catalogs do, the tables make the individual houses and graves the units of study. As with her thesis, the most interesting part of her dissertation is the analysis.[74] While she discusses the movement of certain artistic motifs in terracotta figurines across the Balkans, her most valuable conclusions are again based on the Olynthus material and particularly the data in the two tables. Using those tables, she generates some descriptive statistics that allow her to move beyond a simple art-historical analysis of the figurines and into an archaeological analysis of their use within Olynthian society. For instance, she reconfirms what she had stated in her thesis: that the people of Olynthus placed terracotta figurines in temples, graves, and their homes, a view still not widely held at the time of her writing. She found identical figurines, some made from the same molds, excavated in graves and houses, proof that one design was not made for one specific use but rather that individuals had some choice as to what they did with them. Figurines in the homes are of two types: religious motifs such as seated goddesses that were probably worshiped and apotropaic or decorative images, such as dancers (see figure 5.6 as well as figures 2.11 and 2.12) and caricatures. Most frequently excavators uncovered figurines in the entrance courtyard, *andron*, or *pastas* of the houses, indicating these were the areas in which the people of Olynthus preferred to worship and display these artifacts. Patterns of human behavior also emerge from the placement of figurines in graves. Of the more than six hundred graves Robinson's crews found, about half had some kind of grave good and only a total of fifty-eight had terracotta figurines, indicating they were not common grave offerings. More children than adults had figurines in their graves leading Ellingson to conclude that, contrary to what some had argued, figurines with motifs such as roosters, pigs, tortoises, monkeys, and sphinxes did not have a symbolic significance but rather were toys. At the time she was writing, virtually no archaeologist in Greece saw evidence for children in the archaeological record. Children were not a subject archaeologists acknowledged as worthy of study making her conclusion surprising and innovative. Her discussion of the context of the figurines' find spots offers us a glimpse of human behavior that is simply impossible to discern from a catalog of figurines. According to the material in her personnel record, her dissertation earned her a PhD from Johns Hopkins in the spring of 1939.

One benefit of graduate school is the opportunity to make and keep friendships that can help with career advancement. Some female archaeologists in particular have found they can build networks with other women, each helping the others to succeed in a male-dominated profession. Circumstances curtailed Ellingson's ability to strengthen her network ties with other women. Of her friends from the excavation, only Robinson, Weinberg, and Graham returned to Baltimore as Ellingson worked on her thesis during the fall of 1931 and spring of 1932. Freeman, Schulz, and the Parsons spent the year in Athens at the American School. The von Peskes lived in the city too, beginning work on drawing material from Corinth. Mylonas taught at another American university that year. By 1939, Weinberg, Schulz, and Graham had all graduated and left Johns Hopkins. Mylonas had found a permanent position in St. Louis. That academic year only Robinson and Freeman, who was working for Robinson as a research assistant, remained in Baltimore. While Ellingson was fond of Robinson, her negative feelings toward Freeman may have left that connection cold. Ellingson lost touch with her archaeology friends while she worked at Mt. Royal College in Calgary, perhaps because her demanding schedule allowed little time for corresponding. No surviving evidence shows she connected with any of the other classics or archaeology graduate students while she worked on her dissertation in Baltimore in 1939.

During the time she was writing her dissertation, she would normally have been expected to spend a year as a fellow at the American School in Athens. All her Olynthus friends had done their time at the School. To this day, it remains difficult for an American or Canadian to break into the field of Greek archaeology without having been a fellow at the School. We do not know if she had a desire to go, but again circumstances conspired to ensure she could not. The quota on fellowships for women the leadership of the American School imposed in 1931 has already been mentioned, limiting her chances of attending. In 1935, the Managing Committee at the American School imposed another impediment, it reserved all fellowships for United States citizens. It would be nearly two decades before Canadians would be welcomed again at the School.[75] Lacking United States citizenship, Ellingson was barred from taking the next step to advance her career by attending the American School.

As the 1939 academic year closed in late spring and Ellingson completed her dissertation, two opportunities arose, between which she had to choose. It was one of the most consequential decisions she was to make in her life. One was an offer of a temporary job, the other an offer of marriage.

Marriage or Career?

First, the job offer. In April or early May 1939, the University of Alberta contacted Ellingson. Her former teacher, Geneva Misener, had been granted a sabbatical for the 1939–1940 school year. Misener intended to spend the year conducting research and writing at the University of California, Berkeley. Her old friend and Ellingson's mentor, William Alexander, had recently left the University of Alberta for a teaching position at his American alma mater and likely had invited Misener to spend her sabbatical year there.[76] Someone, no doubt either Misener or Doc Alik, mentioned Ellingson's name as good temporary replacement for Misener. It had to have felt like a gratifying offer, a chance for Ellingson to come full circle in her intellectual journey, returning to the place that had kindled her deep love of ancient Greek culture and to fill the shoes of someone who had influenced her so much. The position lasted only a year, meaning she would have to be looking for another position while she taught and the possibility she would be unemployed at the end of her sabbatical replacement year was strong, but at the moment she had no other academic job lined up.

Around the same time she was contemplating the opportunity to return to Canada to work, another option arose. According to Ellingson's eldest daughter, Barbara Petersen, the landlady of the boarding house where Ellingson lived invited her to a dinner party in February of 1939. The unsuspecting graduate student found her hostess had invited only two other guests, another landlady friend and that woman's tenant, Rudolph Conrad Ellingson.[77] "Rudy" was the youngest son of a chemistry professor and department chair at St. Olaf College in Northfield, Minnesota, and had received his PhD in chemistry from Johns Hopkins in 1938. Since that time, he had worked as an instructor at Johns Hopkins as he sought a job in industry.[78] The two landladies had set up the two single intellectuals, enticing them with a free meal. Although he was three years younger than her, the pair hit it off and began dating. The pace of their courtship accelerated in April or May of the same year when the pediatric nutrition manufacturer, Mead Johnson in Evansville, Indiana, offered Rudy Ellingson a job and his own lab to direct.[79] The only way to keep their relationship going was to propose marriage.

Ellingson's last name gives away the choice she made that spring, there is no suspense, but the terms under which she made that decision are worth exploring as they not only helped lead her to that decision but also helped her shape her marriage as she wanted it. If she chose to take the one-year job in Alberta, she would probably have been choosing to remain single. Long-distant relationships are always hard but especially so when Rudolph Ellingson would be busy settling into a new job and town and setting up a new lab and the still single Mary Ross would have been preparing new courses she had probably not taught before. Just as she lost touch with her friends under the workload at Mt. Royal, keeping a nascent relationship going from afar through letters would have been unlikely or impossible.

As a single woman, then, looking for work once the 1939–1940 school year ended, Dr. Mary Ross would have been facing a very difficult situation. While she probably never saw graphs like those shown earlier in this chapter, she must have been aware anecdotally that the number of faculty positions for women was shrinking. Without American citizenship, she would have been limited to looking for work in Canada. She would still not have a publication once she came back on the job market in 1940. Her professional network was thin. Without time at the American School on her *curriculum vitae*, her credentials claiming she was a Greek archaeologist were not hefty, hung only on her degrees from Johns Hopkins and her one season at Olynthus.

She could look to Freeman as an example of what single life might hold. Her friend-enemy depended on Robinson's patronage and her American School connections to work in the field. We cannot know how attractive Ellingson found the first, but the second was not possible.

The societal pressure on her to wed was much more intense than it is in the United States and Canada today. While she had traveled across Europe with her best friend Helen Boyle, Boyle spoke incessantly about her upcoming nuptials, even shopping for wedding accoutrement along the way. And while at first glance the story of the two landladies setting up a dinner party to introduce the two singles they knew may seem charming, again it indicates the pressure others were placing on them. Time was also applying pressure. According to 1940 United States Census data, the average age of first marriage for a woman was around twenty-two. Ellingson was twenty-two when the Greek photographer Melanides proclaimed her "a queen among women"; nearly a decade had passed since then as she became more of an outlier each year. Ellingson seems to have genuinely wanted children of her own. Her biological clock, as the rather cruel cliché goes, was ticking.

Once engaged, Robinson believed Ellingson's career in archaeology and academia was over; like many at the time, he was certain that a career and marriage were mutually exclusive life choices. He wrote of his ambivalent feelings at Ellingson's decision to marry in a letter to Alexander on May 27, 1939, not long after he had learned of her engagement. He states, "I spent a lot of time on her and it seems too bad that it is to be lost but after all I advised her to get married as she is such a nice girl and probably marriage is better than being a teacher."[80]

Although Robinson and the society around her told Ellingson that she could have either marriage or a career, but not both, she remained unconvinced. As mentioned earlier, Margriet Haagsma pointed out that Misener insisted, to the shock of others in Edmonton, that a woman could have a career and marriage. The Edmonton of Ellingson's youth was a vibrant, growing, energetic town where new ideas emerged to overcome old problems and prejudices. The idea that it was either a marriage or a career must have felt arcane to Ellingson. She had also befriended the Parsons at Olynthus in 1931. Gladys Parsons worked with her husband in the field that year and when he returned to Olynthus in 1934. She was at his side working together in the Athenian Agora and at Corinth and when he was appointed assistant director of the American School in 1939. Marriage was not the end for her. From his subsequent actions, it appears Rudy Ellingson understood and supported her career goals, making him a good partner. Taking the job in

Edmonton would close doors. Marrying, however, could give her the opportunity to craft the life she wanted, even if challenges intruded.

The wedding took place in August in the bride's family home in Edmonton after which the couple moved to Evansville and established a home there. Ellingson immediately began exploring her new surroundings to determine how she could be a wife and professional in the field, waiting on the birth of her first child to see if she could be a wife, professional, *and* a mother. She was following a trend during the first half of the twentieth century as an increasing number of American women continued to work after marriage and only stopped with the birth of their first child.[81] Similar to today, after earning a PhD the next step toward becoming a professor is to publish one's dissertation as this establishes a candidate as a promising scholar. Ellingson intended to pursue that path as a series of letters between her and Robinson in October and November 1941 make clear.[82] Robinson was supportive and expressed his confidence that her dissertation was worthy of publication if she could condense it a bit and supply illustrations.[83] Other opportunities were presenting themselves, however, which were making it difficult for her to focus on this publication project. In the 1940s there was only one college in Evansville and the surrounding area, Evansville College, later to become the University of Evansville. Contracts in her file indicate that she had found a temporary adjunct professor position teaching art history at the college in 1940 and 1941. She may have been hoping that this would turn into a permanent position but that did not occur. Once Evansville College stopped offering her temporary positions, Ellingson took on a volunteer position in 1944 that allowed her to use her skills and that demanded a great deal of her time. According to her personnel record, she became the chair of the Department of Archaeology at the Evansville Public Museum where she organized exhibits and events on local archaeology, particularly about a major pre–Columbian Native American site in Evansville known as Angel Mounds. She also set out to organize and catalog the museum's archaeological collection. At some point in the 1940s, Ellingson must have given up on the idea of publishing her dissertation as discussions of the topic disappear from her letters.

Balancing the demands of career and home proved difficult. In a letter to Robinson, Ellingson confides, "[m]y housekeeping has gone by the board in the meantime but that's all right."[84] After two or three miscarriages, she finally gave birth to a healthy daughter, Barbara, in 1945 (see figure 5.8). Barbara remembers spending time at the Evansville Public Museum with her mother, but by 1949 Ellingson felt the need to give up her work there to concentrate on her family. The Ellingsons adopted a second daughter in 1951.[85]

As their children grew and developed a sense of self-sufficiency, however, Ellingson became restless like so many educated women of her generation. A contract in her file shows she returned to teach Latin part time at Evansville College in 1960. In 1963 she joined the college faculty on a permanent basis teaching courses in Latin for the foreign languages department and English vocabulary derivatives from Latin and Greek roots for the English department.[86] Four years later a rapid increase in student population led to the renaming of the institution to the University of Evansville.[87] Since I also work for the same university, I have met several of Ellingson's former students and in casual conversations they always repeat that her vast knowledge, wit, and dignity made her a respected and well-liked teacher. Surprisingly, those former students when asked all stated that Ellingson never mentioned her participation in the Olynthus excavation to them and all expressed surprise to learn of her adventurous past. The University of Evansville was more of a teaching than a research institution, so there was little pressure on Ellingson to publish any of her archaeological work, which may be one reason she never mentioned this part of her life to her students. By the time she retired in 1974, Ellingson had been promoted to full professor and granted tenure even though she had no publications; at the University of Evansville she was being evaluated on her ability to teach, not research. She lived in Evansville another twenty years before her death in 1993.

The "alternative career style" Ellingson pursued left her on the margins of the field and academia for much of her career. While she put in a great deal of work at the Evansville Public Museum and helped to preserve and present the archaeological collection there, her position was unpaid and so lacked any prestige or permanence. She was an adjunct professor for several years depending on the fluctuating staffing needs of the local college, but her status as a recently married woman no doubt denied her the opportunity for a regular position as the expectation was that she would soon become pregnant after which point it was assumed she could no longer work. Only when her children were old enough was she able to pursue a tenure-track professorship; it cannot be a coincidence that in 1963, the year Ellingson started working on a permanent basis at Evansville College, her oldest daughter turned eighteen. Since moving from Evansville was not an option as her husband had a good job that he clearly enjoyed there, teaching at Evansville College was Ellingson's only avenue for pursuing her desire of being a professor. Since that institution was a teaching college and not a research institution like Johns Hopkins, working there left her outside of the archaeological world as she was not expected to conduct research nor to publish. No one has attempted to quantify how many women who received their PhDs before or after World

Figure 5.8.   Mary Ross Ellingson with her daughter Barbara in 1945.
Photo courtesy of Barbara Petersen

War II returned to university faculties in the 1960s when the number of undergraduates skyrocketed as the baby boomer generation came of age, but Ellingson's story may be fairly common.

Eight Words

That should have been it. I had read all Ellingson's letters. I had satisfied my curiosity about what happened to Ellingson and her colleagues in the years after their work at Olynthus. It had all been a great deal of fun, but it was time to let it go and get back to my own research. Besides, researching the history of archaeology was not the kind of work that earned an archaeologist respect in the field or tenure.[88]

Still, eight words I had seen on one form in Ellingson's file would not allow me to move on so easily. While trying to discover more about her career, I had visited the University of Evansville Archives and come across a personnel form Ellingson had filled out in September 1973. In that year the university required professors to complete a form outlining their credentials. Under the section on publications Ellingson listed two entries, *Olynthus VII: The Terra-Cottas of Olynthus Found in 1931* and the first chapter of *Olynthus XIV: Terracottas, Lamps and Coins Found in 1934 and 1938*. After giving the title of *Olynthus VII*, she added eight words: "the work is acknowledged as mine in introduction." I remember holding that form, feeling incredulous: Ellingson was claiming to be the author of one of the *Olynthus* volumes and of a chapter in another. Having read them in graduate school, I knew her name did not appear on the cover page of these two volumes, only Robinson's did. I had tried to forget about the form and those words in the days and weeks that followed, but they were not so easily dismissed. Ellingson's story was not over yet; there was a mystery to solve.

Notes

1. Mary Ann Levine, "Creating Their Own Niches: Career Styles among Women in Americanist Archaeology between the Wars," in *Women in Archaeology*, edited by Cheryl Claassen (Philadelphia: University of Pennsylvania Press, 1994), 22–23.

2. The American data in this graph are based on the fall enrollment numbers for the given academic year as reported in *120 Years of American Education: A Statistical Portrait*, edited by Thomas D. Snyder (National Center for Educational Statistics, U.S. Department of Education, Office of Educational Research and Improvement, 1993), 75. http://nces.ed.gov/pubs93/93442.pdf. Canadian data comes from M. Wisenthal, "Section W: Education," in *Historical Statistics of Canada*, edited by F.

H. Leacy. Ottawa, Statistics Canada, 1983, https://www150.statcan.gc.ca/n1/pub
/11-516-x/sectionw/4147445-eng.htm, accessed July 1, 2022; Lesley Andres and
Maria Adamuti-Trache, "You've Come a Long Way, Baby? Persistent Gender Inequality in University Enrolment and Completion in Canada, 1979–2004," *Canadian
Public Policy / Analyse de Politiques* 33 no. 1 (2007): 96; Statistics Canada, *Education
in Canada, Catalogue no. 81-229-XPB* (Ottawa: Minister of Industry, 1996), 57. The
Canadian data are incomplete. When data for the same year were absent, the graph
shows data from the following year.

3. American data from Thomas D. Snyder, editor, *120 Years of American Edu-
cation*, 75; Canadian data from Wisenthal, "Section W: Education," and Barry R.
Chiswick, Nicholas Larsen, and Paul Pieper, "The Production of PhDs in the United
States and Canada," *IZA Discussion Paper Series* No. 5367 (2010): 40.

4. Margaret W. Rossiter, *Women Scientists in America: Struggles and Strategies to
1940* (Baltimore: Johns Hopkins University Press, 1982), 215–16; Carol S. Hollenshead, Stacey A. Wenzel, Barbara B. Lazarus, and Indira Nair, "The Graduate Experience in the Sciences and Engineering: Rethinking a Gendered Institution," in *The
Equity Equation: Fostering the Advancement of Women in the Sciences, Mathematics, and
Engineering*, edited by Cinda-Sue Davis, Angela B. Ginorio, Carol S. Hollenshead,
Barbara B. Lazarus, and Paula M. Rayman (San Francisco: Jossey-Bass Publishers,
1996), 126.

5. Judith G. Touchton and Lynn Davis, *Fact Book on Women in Higher Education*
(New York: Macmillan Publishing Co., 1991), 222.

6. Quoted in Natalia Vogeikoff-Brogan, "The Modern Greek Exam, 'Professor
Blank's' Method, and Other Stories from the 1930s." *From the Archivist's Notebook*,
October 1, 2013, http://nataliavogeikoff.com/category/women-studies/, accessed June
30, 2022.

7. Lilli S. Hornig, "Affirmative Action through Affirmative Attitudes," in
Women in Academia: Evolving Policies toward Equal Opportunities, edited by Elga
Wasserman, Arie Y. Lewin, and Linda H. Bleiweis (New York: Praeger Publishers,
1975), 9.

8. C. Robert Pace, *They Went to College: A Study of 951 Former University Students* (Minneapolis: University of Minnesota Press, 1941), 56.

9. Levine, "Creating Their Own Niches," 16; Cynthia Irwin-Williams, "Women
in the Field: The Role of Women in Archaeology before 1960," in *Women of Science: Righting the Record*, edited by G. Kass-Simon and Patricia Farnes (Bloomington:
University of Indiana Press, 1990), 25.

10. Irwin-Williams, "Women in the Field," 14; Lucia Nixon, "Gender Bias in
Archaeology," in *Women in Ancient Societies: An Illusion of Night*, edited by Léonie J.
Archer, Susan Fischler, and Maria Wyke (New York: Routledge, 1994), 16.

11. Rossiter, *Women Scientists in America*, 168.

12. Julie Des Jardins, *The Madame Curie Complex: The Hidden History of Women in
Science* (New York: Feminist Press of the City University of New York, 2010), 5–8.

13. Rossiter, *Women Scientists in America*, 165–66.

14. American Association of University Professors, "Academic Freedom and Tenure," *Bulletin of the American Association of University of Professors* 26, no. 1 (1940): 49–54.

15. Rossiter, *Women Scientists in America*, 194–95.

16. Rossiter, *Women Scientists in America*, 168 and 176; Hollenshead et al., "The Graduate Experience," 126.

17. Chase Going Woodhouse, "Women," *American Journal of Sociology* 37, no. 6 (1932): 958–59.

18. Mary E. Cookingham, "Combining Marriage, Motherhood, and Jobs before World War II: Women College Graduates, Classes of 1905–1935," *Journal of Family History* 9, no. 2 (1984): 189.

19. Rossiter, *Women Scientists in America*, 195–96.

20. Lynne P. Sullivan, "Madeline D. Kneberg Lewis: Leading Lady of Tennessee Archaeology," in *Grit-Tempered: Early Women Archaeologists in the Southeastern United States*, edited by Nancy M. White, Lynne P. Sullivan, and Rochelle A. Marrinan (Gainesville: University Press of Florida, 1999), 86–87.

21. Carol S. Hollenshead et al., "The Graduate Experience," 126.

22. Jane H. Kelley, "Being and Becoming," in *Rediscovering Our Past: Essays on the History of American Archaeology*, edited by Jonathan E. Reyman (Aldershot: Avebury, 1992), 86.

23. D. Z. Chase, "Archaeology, the Academy, and Women: Finding One's Own Path." *Heritage* 4 (2021): 1730. For a deeper discussion of attitudes toward children and fieldwork, see C. D. Lynn, M. E. Howells, M. J. Stein, "Family and the Field: Expectations of a Field-Based Research Career Affect Researcher Family Planning Decisions." *PLoS ONE* 13 no. 9 (2018): https://doi.org/10.1371/journal.pone.0203500, accessed August 20, 2022.

24. Alice Beck Kehoe, *Girl Archaeologist: Sisterhood in a Sexist Profession* (Lincoln: University of Nebraska Press, 2022): 49.

25. Pace, *They Went to College*, 56.

26. Rossiter, *Women Scientists in America*, 139.

27. Sharon B. McGrayne, *Nobel Prize Women in Science. Their Lives, Struggles, and Momentous Discoveries* (New York: Brick Lane Press, 1993), 144.

28. Cookingham. "Combining Marriage, Motherhood, and Jobs," 179.

29. Levine, "Creating Their Own Niches," 36.

30. Cookingham. "Combining Marriage, Motherhood, and Jobs," 178–79 and 186; Barbara Sicherman, "College and Careers: Historical Perspectives on the Lives and Work Patterns of Women College Graduates," in *Women and Higher Education in American History*, edited by John M. Faragher and Florence Howe (New York: W. W. Norton, 1988), 142–43.

31. Pace, *They Went to College*, 41 and 56.

32. Nixon, "Gender Bias in Archaeology," 16–17.

33. Nixon, "Gender Bias in Archaeology," 17; Levine, "Creating Their Own Niches," 16–17.

34. Getzel M. Cohen and Martha S. Joukowsky, editors, *Breaking Ground: Pioneering Women Archaeologists* (Ann Arbor: University of Michigan Press, 2004), 557.

35. Cookingham. "Combining Marriage, Motherhood, and Jobs," 179.

36. Alva Myrdal and Viola Klein, *Women's Two Roles. Home and Work*, 2nd ed. (London: Routledge and Kegan Paul, 1968), 44–45; Sicherman, "College and Careers," 143.

37. Quoted in Vasso Fotou and Ann Brown, "Harriet Boyd Hawes, 1871–1945," in *Breaking Ground: Pioneering Women Archaeologists*, edited by Getzel M. Cohen and Martha S. Joukowsky (Ann Arbor: University of Michigan Press, 2004), 235.

38. For a lament of the interest in the history of women in classical archaeology and for an assessment of the employment landscape for women in the field, see Tracey Cullen, "Contributions to Feminism in Archaeology," *American Journal of Archaeology* 100, no. 2 (1996): 412.

39. Miriam Dyak, personal communication.

40. Archaeological Institute of America, "Archaeological Institute of America Award for Distinguished Service Gladys Davidson Weinberg," *American Journal of Archaeology* 90, no. 2 (1986): 173.

41. Gladys R. Davidson, "Miscellaneous Finds from Corinth, 1896–1933" (PhD diss., Johns Hopkins University, 1935).

42. David Robinson to Gladys Weinberg, October 21, 1942, Box 5, David M. Robinson Collection, Special Collections, University of Mississippi Libraries, a copy is in the archive at the University of Evansville.

43. Gladys D. Weinberg, *Corinth, Results of Excavations Conducted by the American School of Classical Studies at Athens XII: The Minor Objects* (Princeton, NJ: American School of Classical Studies at Athens, 1952).

44. Sharon C. Herbert, "Saul S. Weinberg, 1911–1992," *American Journal of Archaeology* 97, no. 3 (1993): 567.

45. Aleisa Fishman, "Gladys Davidson Weinberg 1909–2002," in *Jewish Women in America: An Historical Encyclopedia*, edited by E. Paula Hyman and Debora D. Moore (New York: Routledge, 1997), 1462; and Susan H. Allen, *Classical Spies: American Archaeologists with the OS in World War II Greece* (Ann Arbor: University of Michigan Press, 2011), 256 and 304.

46. Pierre de Miroschedji, Obituary for Gladys Davidson Weinberg, *Israel Exploration Journal* 52.2 (2002): 97. In an email she sent me on January 17, 2016, Weinberg's daughter, Miriam Dyak states, "Just to confirm, I'm pretty sure that Gladys was indeed a spy in WWII."

47. Herbert, "Saul S. Weinberg," 567.

48. Harriet Pass Freidenreich, "Joining the Faculty Club: Jewish Women Academics in the United States," *Nashim: A Journal of Jewish Women's Studies and Gender Issues* 13 (2007): 68.

49. Jason Kalman, "Dark Places around the University: The Johns Hopkins University Admissions Quota and the Jewish Community, 1945–1951." *Hebrew Union College Annual* 81 (2010): 233–79.

50. I have heard the rumor repeated by several people that had Saul Weinberg not been Jewish, he would have been considered to head the American School. Such a rumor is impossible to confirm and no one who has told me this rumor was willing to state it on the record.

51. Herbert, "Saul S. Weinberg, 1911–1992," 567; Archaeological Institute of America, "Saul S. Weinberg," *American Journal of Archaeology* 90, no. 2 (1986): 174.

52. Obituary for Saul Weinberg, *Israel Exploration Journal* 43, no. 2/3 (1993): 199; Paul N. Perrot, "Gladys Davidson Weinberg (1909–2002)," *Journal of Glass Studies* 44 (2002): 211–15.

53. Herbert, "Saul S. Weinberg," 567.

54. Perrot, "Gladys Davidson Weinberg (1909–2002)," 211.

55. Fishman, "Gladys Davidson Weinberg 1909–2002," 1462.

56. Perrot, "Gladys Davidson Weinberg—A Tribute," *Journal of Glass Studies* 24 (1982): 9. Studying this type of "minutiae" represents a technique some women in archaeology and the sciences used to carve out a niche for themselves. By focusing on some topic that had previously received little scholarly attention, they would not be competing with men. See Levine, "Creating Their Own Niches," 17.

57. Archaeological Institute of America, "Archaeological Institute of America Award," 173–74.

58. Obituary for Saul Weinberg, *Israel Exploration Journal* 43.2/3 (1993): 199; Paul N. Perrot, "Gladys Davidson Weinberg (1909–2002)," 211.

59. Kehoe, *Girl Archaeologist: Sisterhood in a Sexist Profession*, 150.

60. Sarah E. Freeman, "The Excavation of a Roman Temple at Corinth" (PhD diss., Johns Hopkins University, 1934) and "Temple E at Corinth," in *Corinth, Results of Excavations Conducted by the American School of Classical Studies at Athens* I.2: *Architecture*, edited by Richard Stillwell, Robert L. Scranton, and Sarah E. Freeman (Princeton, NJ: American School of Classical Studies at Athens 1941), 166–236.

61. Special Collections, Milton S. Eisenhower Library, Johns Hopkins University, "Freeman (Sarah Elizabeth) 1906–1986, Papers 1944–1969, MS. Gar30," n.d. http://old.library.jhu.edu/collections/specialcollections/manuscripts/msregisters/ms-gar30freeman.pdf, accessed August 1, 2013.

62. David M. Robinson and J. Walter Graham, *Excavations at Olynthus VIII: The Hellenic House; A Study of the Houses Found at Olynthus with a Detailed Account of Those Excavated in 1931 and 1934, Johns Hopkins University Studies in Archaeology* 25 (Baltimore, MD: Johns Hopkins University Press, 1938), ix; David M. Robinson, *Excavations at Olynthus X: Metal and Minor Miscellaneous Finds, an Original Contribution to Greek Life, Johns Hopkins University Studies in Archaeology* 31 (Baltimore, MD: Johns Hopkins University Press, 1941), xi.

63. Rossiter, *Women Scientists in America*, 205–6.

64. Levine, "Creating Their Own Niches," 23.

65. Rossiter, *Women Scientists in America*, 207.

66. George Mylonas, "Biographical Sketch," in *Studies Presented to David Moore Robinson on His Seventieth Birthday*, Vol. 1, edited by Geroge Mylonas (St. Louis, MO: Washington University, 1951), xvii.

67. Max B. Spiegel, "The Garrett Collection: Coins, Medals, and Archives at the American Numismatic Society," *American Numismatic Society Magazine* 5, no. 3 (2006). https://numismatics.org/pocketchange/ferry/; "In Memoriam: Sarah Elizabeth Freeman 1907–1986," *Ákoue*, Spring 1986.

68. "Man Convicted of Murdering Retired Professor," AP News Archive, July 7, 1987, http://www.apnewsarchive.com/1987/Man-Convicted-of-Murdering-Retired -Professor/id-7498088409c4759742230947017034d8.

69. Published in David M. Robinson, *Excavations at Olynthus VII: The Terra-Cottas of Olynthus found in 1931* (Baltimore, MD: Johns Hopkins University Press, 1933), #182, 51–52.

70. For an independent assessment of her thesis, see Walter R. Agard, "Review of *Excavations at Olynthus, Part VII: The Terra-Cottas Found in 1931* by David M. Robinson," *Classical Journal* 30, no. 3 (1934): 173–74; Valentin Müller, "Review of *Excavations at Olynthus* by David M. Robinson," *Classical Philology* 31, no. 1 (1936): 92–93; George W. Elderkin, "Review of *Excavations at Olynthus, Part VII: The Terra-Cottas Found in 1931* by David M. Robinson," *American Journal of Archaeology* 38, no. 3 (1934): 497.

71. The original telegram resides in the archives at the University Evansville. Additional information from "Excavations in Old Greece Are Recounted." *The Evansville Courier and Press*, March 3, 1940, 4.

72. David Robinson to W. H. Alexander, June 21, 1932. The original letter is in the possession of Barbara A. Petersen and a copy is on file in the archives at the University of Evansville.

73. For an independent assessment of her dissertation, see Reynold A Higgins, "Review of *Excavations at Olynthus: Part XIV, Terracottas, Lamps and Coins Found in 1934 and 1938* by D. M. Robinson," *Journal of Hellenic Studies* 75 (1955): 180; Reynold A. Higgins, "Review of *Excavations at Olynthus: Part XIV, Terracottas, Lamps and Coins Found in 1934 and 1938* by D. M. Robinson," *Antiquaries Journal* 35 (1955): 97; Sterling Dow, "Review of *Excavations at Olynthus. Part XIV* by David M. Robinson," *American Historical Review* 58, no. 3 (1953): 586–87; William A. Mc-Donald, "Review of *Excavations at Olynthus Part XIV: Terracottas, Lamps and Coins Found in 1934 and 1938* by David M. Robinson," *Classical Journal* 50, no. 2 (1954): 94–95; Robert Scranton, "Review of *Excavations at Olynthus, Part XIV: Terracottas, Lamps, and Coins Found in 1934 and 1938* by David M. Robinson," *Classical Philology* 49, no. 2 (1954): 143–44; R. M. Cook, "Review of *Excavations at Olynthus: Part XIV, Terracottas, Lamps and Coins Found in 1934 and 1938* by D. M. Robinson," *Classical Review* 5, no. 3/4 (1955): 326–27; R. C. Wood, "Review of *Excavations at Olynthus: Part XIV, Terracottas, Lamps and Coins Found in 1934 and 1938* by D. M. Robinson," *American Journal of Archaeology* 57, no. 3 (1953): 227–28.

74. Helen M. M. Ross, 1939. "The Terra-cotta Figurines of Macedonia and Thrace" (PhD diss., Johns Hopkins University, 1939), 132–45.

75. Natalia Vogeikoff-Brogan, "The Modern Greek Exam, 'Professor Blank's' Method, and Other Stories from the 1930s." *From the Archivist's Notebook*, October 1, 2013, http://nataliavogeikoff.com/category/women-studies/, accessed June 28, 2022.

76. Letter David Robinson to W. H. Alexander dated May 27, 1939. The letter is currently in the possession of Barbara Petersen; a copy is on file in the archives at the University of Evansville.

77. Barbara Petersen, interview with the author on December 11, 2013.

78. This information comes from a newspaper article among Ellingson's papers at the University of Evansville Archives titled "Mary Ross Is Married Quietly at Family Residence Saturday." The name of the paper is missing but someone has written "August 1939" on it.

79. Letter David Robinson to W. H. Alexander dated May 27, 1939.

80. The letter is dated May 27, 1939, and is addressed to W. H. Alexander. It is currently in the possession of Barbara Petersen; a copy is on file in the archives at the University of Evansville.

81. Cookingham, "Combining Marriage, Motherhood, and Jobs," 182; Sicherman, "College and Careers, 139.

82. October 5, 1941, letter from Mary Ellingson, to David Robinson; October 15, 1941, Robinson to Ellingson; November 4, 1941, Ellingson to Robinson; all three letters are in Box 5, David M. Robinson Collection, Special Collections, University of Mississippi Libraries. Copies are filed in the archive at the University of Evansville.

83. David Robinson to Mary Ellingson, October 15, 1941, Box 5, David M. Robinson Collection, Special Collections, University of Mississippi Libraries, a copy is in the archive at the University of Evansville.

84. Mary Ellingson to David Robinson, March 18, 1941, Box 5, David M. Robinson Collection, Special Collections, University of Mississippi Libraries, a copy is in the archive at the University of Evansville.

85. Barbara Petersen, interview with the author on December 11, 2013.

86. George Klinger, *We Face the Future Unafraid: A Narrative History of the University of Evansville* (Evansville, IN: University of Evansville Press, 2003), 105.

87. Klinger, *We Face the Future Unafraid*, 135.

88. Kehoe, *Girl Archaeologist: Sisterhood in a Sexist Profession*, 150.

PART III

~

SCANDAL: MARY ROSS ELLINGSON'S WORK PLAGIARIZED

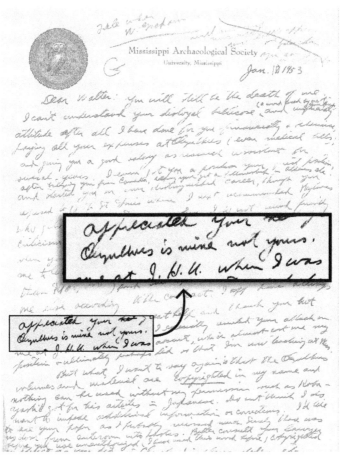

Figure P.3.   Letter from David Robinson to J. Walter Graham in which he declares "Olynthus is mine not yours."

Image courtesy of the David M. Robinson Collection, Special Collections, University of Mississippi Libraries.

CHAPTER SIX

~

A Secret Uncovered

Even though my interest was piqued, I had other research projects to work on including a book based on my own fieldwork studying Roman urban roads. The summer before I found Ellingson's materials, I had been conducting research in the streets of the Roman cities of Pompeii and Ostia and wanted to get that work written for publication. In the academic world professors have a phrase we repeat to one another, "publish or perish." For untenured faculty, as I was at the time, it is a mantra. There was no time to follow up on something that had happened so long ago and that had nothing to do with my own research and which was outside my field of study. Besides, I had already spent too much time trying to satisfy my curiosity as it was. Once again, I tried to forget about it but could not. What had started as a delightful afternoon reading Ellingson's letters was slowly turning into an obsession.

The form on which Ellingson claimed to have written *Excavations at Olynthus VII: The Terra-Cottas of Olynthus Found in 1931* as well as the first chapter of *Excavations at Olynthus XIV: Terracottas, Lamps, and Coins Found in 1934 and 1938* carried the date of September, 1973. Her file also had a photo of her from around that time (figure 6.1). I could picture her as she looked in that photo in front of a typewriter, typing the words, "[T]he work is acknowledged as mine in introduction." Why would she make such a dubious claim? Having read all the Olynthus volumes as a graduate student, I remembered seeing only the names of Robinson, Graham, Clement, and Mylonas on the cover pages of the fourteen volumes in the series, not Ellingson's. Was she lying? Was she exaggerating? Her letters had referred to her work on the terracotta figurines; was she trying to gain some of the reflected

Figure 6.1. Professor Mary Ellingson tends a potted plant in her office in the Department of Foreign Languages at the University of Evansville. This photo was taken around the time she claimed authorship of Olynthus VII and a chapter of Olynthus XIV on a university personnel form, the first time she had ever done so.

Photo courtesy of the University of Evansville Archives

glory of Robinson's accomplishment in publishing what she and the rest of the team had excavated? To find answers to these questions would require a closer look at the *Excavations at Olynthus* volumes, the relationship between Robinson and his graduate students, as well as the relationship between principal investigators and their graduate students both in archaeology and in the sciences between the 1920s and 1950s. I tried to forget about all of this because I did not have the time, I had Roman-related articles and a book to write in order to further my own career. In the end, however, the mystery of her words got the better of me.

Two Texts, One Author

I could only pretend to ignore what I had read for a few days before I found myself returning to the photos and letters I had first seen on that rainy afternoon. There was one other document I had not read that might shed some light on Ellingson's curious claim. A manila folder, discolored with age and tied with a string, had the words "Mary's Thesis" written on the tab. I untied it and began to read. It sounded vaguely familiar.

Since my university does not own any of the *Excavations at Olynthus* series, I had the librarians order volumes VII and XIV through interlibrary loan. The librarians also obtained a copy of Ellingson's dissertation from the Johns Hopkins University archives. It took weeks before I finally had all the documents in hand and was able to spread them out on my kitchen table. The title of Ellingson's thesis is *The Terra Cotta Industry at Olynthus*. The subtitle of Robinson's *Excavations at Olynthus VII* is *The Terra-Cottas of Olynthus Found in 1931*. I read the first few pages of the thesis followed by the first few pages of *Olynthus VII*. They were nearly identical. I read on, alarmed, switching from one document to the other with increasing haste. The same words kept appearing over and over:

Ellingson wrote on page seven:	Robinson wrote on page three:
The district of Olynthus is still rich in clay, and must indeed have been so in antiquity. An especially common clay used in the terra cottas is reddish in color, and heavy in weight; it was used also in local pottery and loom-weights. Twelve figurines from the same mould[13] are of this clay and surely must [be] of native fabric; there are many examples of such products.[14]	The district of Olynthus is still rich in clay, and must indeed have been so in antiquity. An especially common clay used in the terra-cottas is reddish in color, and heavy in weight; it was used also in local pottery and loom-weights. Ten figurines from the same mould (nos. 265–271 and 372, 373, 373a of *The Terra-Cottas of Olynthus Found in 1928*) are of this clay and surely must be of native fabric.

Only two differences appear between these sections. Ellingson listed the figurines from the same molds in a footnote while Robinson listed them in the text. Robinson omits two figurines that Ellingson included for reasons that are not clear. I read on.

On page 32 of Ellingson's thesis is this:

[S]tatues of gods were too big to place in the ordinary home, so they were represented merely by masks, herms, and figurines.

On page 10 of *Olynthus VII* is the following:

Statues of gods were too big to place in the ordinary home, so they were represented merely by masks, herms, and figurines.

Ellingson describes figurines showing satyrs, the half-man, half-goat companions of Bacchus, on page 28 of her work, stating, against the then-current interpretation, that the type first appeared at Olynthus. Robinson makes the same claim on page 8 of his work using the exact same words with only slightly different punctuation and spelling. Below Ellingson's version comes first:

[T]he worship of Bacchus and his attendant cortege is of Thrako-Phrygian origin; its influence spread into Macedonia at an early period. It is not improbable then that Olynthus was the first to seize upon this new idea and create a new type as a result.

The worship of Bacchus and his attendant cortège is of Thracian-Phrygian origin. Its influence spread into Macedonia at an early period. It is not improbable then that Olynthus was the first to seize upon this new idea and create a new type as a result.

I picked a page at random from *Excavations at Olynthus VII*, found the corresponding section in Ellingson's thesis, and counted the amount of text that was the same: 95 percent. Trying the experiment on other pages yielded similar results. The only changes were editorial, not substantive. Robinson repeated Ellingson's descriptions of the terracottas, her analysis of their styles and production techniques, her chronology, her synthesis placing them in the art historical and archaeological context of ancient Greece, and her conclusions. Ellingson submitted her thesis to Johns Hopkins in 1932. Robinson published *Excavations at Olynthus VII* in 1933 after Ellingson had returned to Canada to take up her position at Mount Royal College. Only Robinson's name appears on the cover page of the volume. I turned to her dissertation and *Excavations at Olynthus XIV*. Although he had edited out some of her work and had added bibliographic references not yet available when Ellingson completed her dissertation in 1939, in the first chapter of Robinson's 1952 volume as well as about half of the second chapter he published most of Ellingson's dissertation.

Ellingson had stated of *Excavations at Olynthus VII* on the 1973 personnel form she filed with the University of Evansville, "the work is acknowledged as mine in introduction." The only mention Robinson made of Ellingson, referring to her by her maiden name, Ross, was on page viii of the introduction:

> Here I should like especially to express my gratitude to Miss H. M. Mary Ross, now instructor in Classics at Mt. Royal College, Calgary, Canada. She was a loyal, tactful, and industrious member of the staff at Olynthus and successfully helped supervise the excavation of the East Cemetery. She kept a careful typewritten inventory of the terra-cottas, separate from my note-books and the daily journal, and I have made abundant use of this and her own valuable suggestions.[1]

The "carefully typewritten inventory of terra-cottas" to which Robinson refers is the same inventory to which Ellingson refers repeatedly in her letters. Robinson clearly saw the inventory as belonging to Ellingson since she made it of her own initiative and not as part of her duties as a staff member of the excavation. Despite Ellingson's claim on her personnel form, this quote does not acknowledge her as the author of *Excavations at Olynthus VII*. Robinson does mention Ellingson in the introduction to *Excavations at Olynthus XIV*, where he published her dissertation but not as an author or contributor:

> I thank especially my former students and members of my staff, Mary Ross (now Mrs. R. C. Ellingson of Evansville, Ind.), Eleanor Lay (now Mrs. Arthur Ross of Syracuse, New York), and I owe much to my deceased daughter (Mrs. Wilson).[2]

His words indicate he did not consider Ellingson's "typewritten inventory" to belong to himself or the excavation but rather to Ellingson alone. To then publish her inventory, as well as her thesis based on that inventory, without listing Ellingson as an author, coauthor, or contributor is inexplicable. Robinson had even less claim to the information Ellingson presented in her dissertation as much of it was based on terracotta figurines found at sites other than Olynthus.

I sat back in my chair not knowing what to think. Something had to be wrong. Robinson, one of the great classical archaeologists, could not have plagiarized the work of one of his graduate students. I tried to find ways to explain what I saw before me. Did an excavation permit holder have *sole* control over all excavated material in 1930s Greece? Did archaeologists routinely exploit their research and graduate assistants back then, taking credit for their work? What about the sciences where research projects also involve a team; did principal investigators use their assistants' work without giving them credit? Had the definition of plagiarism changed in the last fifty to seventy years? Did Johns Hopkins University have a policy on graduate students' and principal investigators' intellectual property rights? There had to be a simple, and ethical, explanation for Robinson's behavior, an explanation about which I understood nothing.

A Simple Explanation

I thought I had been able to put aside the discovery, but a few weeks later I was in the university library looking for a specific article relating to Roman streets and was easily distracted. Instead of locating the appropriate Roman archaeology journal, I found myself investigating the question of whether Johns Hopkins University had some type of policy about intellectual property rights and graduate student work when Ellingson was a student there. I discovered that in the late 1920s the faculty and administration at Johns Hopkins adopted the rather radical policy of requiring graduates to publish their dissertations within two years of graduation. At that time too few successful PhD candidates published their dissertations, leaving the author's work unavailable to a wider audience, some of whom may have found it interesting and useful to their own studies. This problem persists today. Johns Hopkins University introduced the policy of requiring graduates to pay the $100 deposit at this time as well,[3] and the policy remained in place at least through the 1940s. Behind the policy is a clear presumption that at Johns Hopkins University the authors of dissertations retained full intellectual property rights to the material in their dissertations. Presumably the same was true for master's theses, although publication appears not to have been required. Even after the expiration of the two-year deadline and the loss of the deposit, the author still retained the intellectual property rights to the dissertation as is clear from the fact that some, like Gladys Weinberg, Saul Weinberg, and Ellingson, continued to work toward publishing their dissertations long after their deposits were forfeited.

This was not the simple explanation I was seeking. If anything, this library research raised more questions in my mind. Did Robinson know about the Johns Hopkins policy? Was archaeology unique in some way because the excavation permit is issued to just one or two people? How did people define the word plagiarism in the first half of the twentieth century and had the definition evolved? Did Robinson ever express an opinion on intellectual property rights? There was only one place where I had any chance of finding answers to these questions. Spring break was approaching. I really needed to spend the break working on a draft of an article about Roman streets: "publish or perish." Instead I found myself asking my wife Christine if she might enjoy a brief vacation in the South, suggesting a day or two in Oxford, Mississippi, home of the University of Mississippi as well as the archive with all of Robinson's papers, might be nice. Luckily, she was game to take a road trip south.

The archivists at the University of Mississippi were very friendly and helpful. They brought us box after box of the fifty-three they have containing Robinson's letters and documents. Some of the answers I was seeking began to emerge. There can be no question that Robinson was aware of the Johns Hopkins University policies with regard to the publication of dissertations and, therefore, intellectual property rights. A number of letters passed between Robinson and his recently graduated students asking for help getting extensions on the two-year time limit and expressing fear about losing their deposit. In 1941, Robinson and Ellingson exchanged a series of four letters in which Ellingson sought help with an extension and expressed her continued intention to publish her dissertation, although in the end she was never able to accomplish this goal.[4] Letters between Robinson and several of his graduate students were on a similar theme.[5] The policy and the issue of intellectual property rights were clearly topics of constant discussion in which Robinson engaged with his graduate students.

The issue of intellectual property rights is complicated in the case of a corporate undertaking like an archaeological excavation, however. Usually a governing authority issues a permit to one principal investigator that grants not only the right to excavate but also sole possession of the intellectual property produced by that excavation. Robinson's name alone appears on the permits issued for the excavations at Olynthus in 1928, 1931, and 1934, and with Mylonas's name in 1938.[6] In addition, the rules of the American School of Classical Studies at Athens allowed the permit holder to control all information produced by the excavation.[7]

The rules at Johns Hopkins about rapid publication of dissertations and Robinson's right to control the intellectual property rights of the Olynthus material were not necessarily at odds with one another, however. Robinson seems to have been eager to grant his students permission to publish the material from Olynthus. He helped his students publish their dissertations, particularly as editor of the thirty-eight volume series *Johns Hopkins University Studies in Archaeology*, among which the work of several of his students, both those who worked on Olynthus material and those who did not, appeared. He also incorporated material from dissertations by Mylonas, Graham, Clement, and Frank Albright into various volumes and allowed them to share the credit of authorship with himself either as coauthors or as the named authors of particular chapters. In this way his students were able to retain the intellectual property rights to their dissertations while Robinson retained the rights to the Olynthus material. In *Excavations at Olynthus I*, the publication of Mylonas's dissertation and the only volume in which Robinson's name does not appear on the title page, Mylonas thanks Robinson for giving him access to the finds as well as unpublished notes, excavation diaries, and photos. Robinson had read the manuscript, thus making certain that Mylonas was using his material in a way in which Robinson approved.[8] This collaborative process allowed the intellectual property rights of both the student and the mentor to be respected, a process Robinson clearly endorsed in the case of the publication of Mylonas's dissertation. While having many publications can build the reputation of a scholar, having many successful graduate students does as well and this was certainly a yardstick by which Robinson measured his own success;[9] Robinson was eager to help his students publish.

Perhaps definitions of plagiarism had changed and what seems unacceptable now was acceptable in the 1930s, 1940s, and 1950s. While it is difficult to make a statement about all American academics in the period between the late 1920s and early 1950s, Christine and I found evidence among Robinson's papers showing he defined plagiarism as most in academia would define it today. In a letter addressed to the chancellor of the University of Mississippi in 1956, Robinson commented on a draft code of ethical behavior for students that the chancellor had circulated. Ironically, one of the issues Robinson felt was not sufficiently addressed was that of plagiarism. To illustrate how important this issue was, he reported questions students had asked him informally and in so doing he defined the meaning of plagiarism to himself: "Is it honest to erase on a drawing or term paper or examination another name and substitute his or her own—*à la* Shakespeare for Marlowe?"[10] In the same letter Robinson claimed that it was a moral imperative that universities fight ethical transgressions such as plagiarism. He states,

> I quite agree with the President of Columbia University, [Grayson] Kirk, who at Johns Hopkins University the other day said what the Greeks long ago said, "moral integrity is still our [a university's] most important product, and if we or our students are ever allowed to forget it, our society will have been dealt a moral blow."[11]

Plagiarism was not just a technical issue for undergraduates, according to Robinson, but instead was a moral issue for professors, the university, and everyone in society. It is quite remarkable that just four years before he wrote these words, he had published large portions of Ellingson's dissertation under his own name. Equally astonishing is the simple fact that he could be savage when he felt his intellectual property rights had been violated, as illustrated by his running battle with James Ramsey over the publication of the *Res Gestae* inscription[12] and his accusations against Graham and Clement about publishing information from Olynthus without his permission.[13]

In light of Robinson's understanding of plagiarism, his statement thanking Ellingson at the beginning of *Excavations at Olynthus VII*, his publication of her thesis, takes on special interest. He wrote that Ellingson had "kept a careful typewritten inventory of the terra-cottas, separate from my notebooks and the daily journal, and I have made abundant use of this and her own valuable suggestions."[14] In other words, Ellingson wrote her inventory, Robinson wrote *Excavations at Olynthus VII*, and the two are separate documents, a statement that turns out to be false. It is an exceptionally strange thing to write since he makes no similar claim that anyone else was keeping records independent of the excavation records in any of the other thirteen volumes in the series; in this statement Robinson is drawing attention to the very document he plagiarized. The purpose of this statement, I suspect, is to throw any of the participants in the 1931 excavation season off the trail should they grow suspicious of his treachery. Ellingson mentions her independent inventory of the figurines several times in her letters; it was clearly something she put a great deal of time into constructing and something of which she was proud. Her fellow graduate students must have seen her working on this project and heard her talk about it as they were living and working in such close proximity. Robinson must have anticipated that if he then published a volume on the terracotta figurines with only his name on it just months after Ellingson had submitted her master's thesis on the same topic, it would have caused suspicion among the other graduate students who had been working at Olynthus. By putting in this disclaimer at the front of the volume, he could dampen suspicion by making it appear as if he had written his own catalog and analysis of the terracotta figurines at the same time Ellingson was writing hers. The addition of what he knew was a false statement to the introduction of *Excavations at Olynthus VII* in order to divert suspicion appears to be the actions of a man with a guilty conscience.

Still, I felt like I was misunderstanding something. Today there is an unspoken etiquette shared between the hard sciences and social sciences about what kind of addition to a collective work presided over by one or two principal investigators warranted acknowledgment through a listing as an author, coauthor, or contributor. Perhaps the etiquette in archaeology and the sciences had changed in the last three-quarters of a century. Determining what the rules of publishing etiquette in the social or hard sciences are today, or were in the past, is difficult as no one writes down such rules. Nonetheless people are happy to point out perceived transgressions, which help to define where the lines are drawn. Even today academics like to share stories in the halls of their universities or over drinks at private parties about the rare modern principal investigator in archaeology or the sciences, always a man in these stories, who violates those etiquette rules. According to these stories, he treats his graduate students like slaves, driving them to write up portions of his research so that he may publish it under his own name, offering the real authors a thank-you in a footnote only if they are lucky. This practice is supposed to be nearly extinct today, but it is supposed to have been common in the past. Female graduate students and research assistants of the previous generations in particular are supposed to have been vulnerable to this type of misbehavior. Perhaps that explained Robinson's treatment of Ellingson—he was simply embodying the contemporary culture of archaeology and the sciences.

Two strands of anecdotal evidence allow us to draw a broad picture of what the publishing etiquette was, especially in relation to women's contributions to research projects, in the years before and after World War II. The first strand is actual practice; we can see who received credit in scientific, archaeological, and specifically Greek archaeological publications. One excellent source for comparison material for the *Excavations at Olynthus* series is the publication of the excavations at Corinth, the first volume of which appeared in 1929, the same year Robinson published the first *Excavations at Olynthus* volume. Additional *Corinth* volumes came out throughout the entire period he published the remaining thirteen *Olynthus* volumes. The second strand of anecdotal evidence comes from tales of those who went too far, forcing a rebuke for crossing a line about who deserved acknowledgment. The picture that emerges from these lines of evidence is similar in Greek archaeology, American anthropological archaeology, and the sciences indicating a shared etiquette of publishing women's contributions to large research projects. That culture was tiered with female authors of theses and dissertations at the top, always receiving credit for their work, research assistants in the middle, sometimes receiving credit, sometimes not, and married spouses at the bottom, receiving credit only when their husbands chose to give it, which was not very frequently.

Women who completed theses and dissertations had the most control over their own material. In her 1982 history of women in science, still one of the broadest surveys of the subject, Margaret Rossiter records no cases of a principal investigator in the sciences publishing his students' thesis or dissertation as his own work despite the fact that one section of her book is devoted to the subject of women scientists whose work was not properly acknowledged. It seems to have been the clear understanding that because a thesis or dissertation was independently written, the author controlled it. Weinberg and Freeman represent two examples of this etiquette. Weinberg's reworked dissertation was published as a stand-alone volume in the *Corinth* series with her listed as the sole author[15] and Freeman's appeared as a chapter in *Corinth I.2*, for which her name appears on the cover page and in the table of contents as the sole author of the chapter.[16] I have found only one documented example in archaeology of someone who clearly crossed a line when it came to another's master's thesis. In the late 1920s, archaeologist Florence Hawley Ellis wrote a significant thesis on Native American ceramics in the Southwest giving a chronology and demonstrating influences from the cultures of what is now Mexico.[17] When she took a job at the University of Arizona and turned her attention to publishing the thesis, a male colleague, T. T. Waterman, tried to convince her to add his name to the publication even though he had contributed nothing to it. She refused and he sought unsuccessfully to block publication.[18] The fact that this dispute was resolved in Hawley's favor shows Waterman had gone beyond the bounds of proper publishing etiquette.

Women working as research assistants on material that was not part of thesis or dissertation research were in a more precarious position than the women who were working toward their degrees. Research assistants in the sciences and archaeology both before and after World War II were usually highly educated, holding advanced degrees. Most were women who had completed their degrees but were unable to find a job teaching at a university. A mentor or friend would provide the woman a research appointment for his own benefit but also allow her to have an institutional affiliation, an advantage when seeking academic employment. Such positions might or might not be compensated. Research associates were similar to assistants, but they had a university appointment and were thus collaborating with their colleagues.[19] The anecdotal evidence indicates the normal etiquette was to offer research assistants and associates some credit, although authorship or coauthorship was not necessarily required. Ignoring a research assistant or associate completely in publication could lead to an embarrassing admonition. Rossiter records the reaction of Agnes Fay Morgan, chair of the Department of Household Science at the University of California, Berkeley, when Herbert Evans of the university's Institute of Experimental Biology suggested that one of Morgan's female faculty work with him on a research project. Morgan vetoed the collaboration for the simple reason that she feared, based on Evans's past behavior, that the research associate's contribution to the project would be "overlooked" when it came time for publication.[20] Another anecdote that demonstrates there were expectations research assistants would receive some credit is that of George Hoyt Whipple, a researcher studying iron-deficiency diseases, and his research associate for thirty-six years, Frieda Robscheit-Robbins. For years Whipple published their joint research under his name alone. When he won the Nobel Prize for his work along with two colleagues, he was chagrined that the committee did not name Robscheit-Robbins as well. From that point forward Whipple made it a point to mention Robscheit-Robbins's collaboration in the research at public appearances and in interviews and even shared the prize money with her and two other female research assistants despite the fact that he was a notorious penny-pincher. Had the Nobel committee been aware of Robscheit-Robbins's work and awarded the prize to her along with Whipple, Robscheit-Robbins would have been only the second woman, after Marie Curie, and the first American woman to receive the prize.[21]

I have encountered no similarly documented stories about any archaeologist specializing in Greek archaeology, which means either these principal investigators were generous in their acknowledgment of their research assistants and associates or transgressions occurred but no one publicized them. Perusing the *Corinth* volumes suggests that research associates received a great deal of respect as their names appear repeatedly as authors, coauthors, coeditors, and contributors. Research associates wrote the very first volume of the *Corinth* series to appear in print. Ida Thallon Hill and Lida Shaw King authored the catalog and analysis of the decorative architectural terracotta pieces excavated at Corinth.[22] Hill and King had first been offered the opportunity to work as research assistants and publish the material nearly three decades earlier before either had completed her degree. Other opportunities arose and the two moved onto other projects that earned them their degrees. Hill came back to the material later and completed the final work on it after her marriage to Bert Hodge Hill, then-director of the American School, allowed her to quit her university post and move to Athens to focus exclusively on research.[23] This pattern was typical for the excavations at Corinth; the principal investigator would put either a graduate student or a research associate in charge of a particular category of material with the understanding that that person would have the right to publish the completed work as a chapter or volume in the *Corinth* series with the proper acknowledgment.

In classical archaeology the situation for research assistants is a bit more difficult to discern, although assistants may have been at a disadvantage when compared to the research associates since they were definitely subordinate to the principal investigator, unlike the research associates who were their peers. The names of some research assistants appear on the Corinth volumes such as Freeman, who was a research assistant at Johns Hopkins and is listed as a coeditor and contributor to *Corinth I.2*, and Arthur Parsons, who was a graduate student without a dissertation project but who is listed nonetheless as a contributor to *Corinth III.2*.[24] The names of research assistants are not common in the *Corinth* volumes published in the 1930s and 1940s. Were there other research assistants who should also have been acknowledged but who never were? Naturally we cannot answer that question with the available evidence, but the fact that some were acknowledged indicates research assistants could hold some expectation of recognition.

In the bottom tier when it came to acknowledging contributions to publications were women professionals married to other professionals in the same field with whom they collaborated. The etiquette appears to have been that the amount of credit was completely up to the discretion of the husband; he controlled the intellectual property produced for any project on which they worked together. For instance, during the 1920s, the couple Frederic and Edith (née Schwartz) Clements, both of whom had PhDs in botany, traveled to remote parts of the American West gathering samples for their work on plant ecology, which Frederic Clements published under his own name. Upon his death, Edith Clements felt the need to clarify her contributions to his published work and so wrote her own autobiography laying out their shared intellectual adventures and physical misadventures.[25] In the field of American archaeology, Ann Axtell and her husband Earl Morris excavated together in the 1920s through 1940s in the American Southwest, and she wrote large portions of their technical reports although only his name appeared as author.[26] On the other hand Harold and Winifred Gladwin, also a married couple who excavated in the Southwest, published their work jointly. Alice Beck Kehoe, an archaeologist working with her husband on the Great Plains, describes a moment of crisis in their marriage when her husband handed her a handful of notes and told her to turn it into an article on which he could place his name as sole author. She refused, fearing the precedent that would set for their relationship and the future direction of her career.[27] In Greek archaeology, wives also did not always receive acknowledgment for their work. Ida Thallon Hill ghost-wrote major portions of her husband's reports on his Corinth excavations.[28] Although it has been said of archaeologist couples working in the American Southeast that their joint work is more likely to be published under the man's name rather than both the man and the woman's,[29] that truism can be extended to archaeologists working in the Mediterranean basin before and after World War II.

The etiquette of publishing in Robinson's day, therefore, was that the authors of theses and dissertations should have their names on publications of their work, research assistants and associates should receive some type of acknowledgment, although the extent was to be determined by the principal investigator, and wives would contribute to their husbands' work without necessarily expecting to be named as a coauthor or contributor. Since Ellingson was neither Robinson's wife nor research assistant or associate, the etiquette of the day was that he should have allowed her, or better yet helped her, publish her thesis and dissertation under her own name as part of the *Excavations at Olynthus* series. He had rendered such aid for his other graduate students, and it only served to enhance his reputation as a professor. While I have heard rumors of disputes between principal investigators and their research assistants about whether or not the assistants were properly recognized for their contributions to a publication, I have never heard any accusation against any scientist or archaeologist other than Robinson that they had successfully misappropriated a graduate student's thesis or dissertation. Changing etiquette did not explain Robinson's behavior.

I had been seeking a simple explanation as to why the text in Ellingson's thesis and dissertation was identical to the text in two of Robinson's *Excavations at Olynthus* volumes, any explanation other than the obvious one. According to the rules at Johns Hopkins of which Robinson was clearly aware, according to Robinson's own stated definition of the term, according to the etiquette accorded the publication of theses and dissertations in the sciences and archaeology, what Robinson had done in publishing Ellingson's material without proper acknowledgment or her permission was plagiarism. That was the simple explanation.

Thanks to a search in 2022 of the contract files at Johns Hopkins University Press, the legal holder of the copyright to all the *Olynthus* volumes, we can identify the exact moment Robinson committed plagiarism. Most of the paperwork related to the series had disappeared, but the contract for *Olynthus XIII*, a volume in which no plagiarized material has been identified yet, survives. The wording in the contract is formulaic and differs little from the wording in contracts the Press issues today. By signing the contract, Robinson affirmed that all the statements in the contract were accurate, including "[t]hat he is the sole author of the manuscript, except those portions which are shown to be quotations." When he signed the surviving contract for *Olynthus XIII*, what he was claiming was true was that he was the sole author. Johns Hopkins University Press no longer has the contracts for *Olynthus VII* or *XIV*, but it is safe to assume they were similar, if not identical, to the contract for *Olynthus XIII*.[30] When he signed the contract for *Olynthus*

VII, likely in 1932, and *Olynthus XIV*, likely in 1951, he was affirming that he was the sole author, an affirmation he knew to be false. Everything that happened from that point forward, the Press listing him as the sole author on the title page, reviewers assessing the work as his, subsequent archaeologists citing and building on his work, all unknowingly repeated the falsehood he made when he signed those two forms.

The discussion above approaches the issue of plagiarism as one of etiquette and ethics. Plagiarism as a legal matter is a very different question. So, did Robinson break the law when he signed that contract with Johns Hopkins University Press claiming to be the only author of the two volumes? No.[31] Ellingson never sought to copyright her thesis or dissertation, something virtually no graduate student did in the 1930s. If she had sought that legal protection, she would have included the symbol of the letter "c" within a circle. At the time, exactly reproducing material that lacked a copyright symbol without acknowledging the source of that material was perfectly legitimate if ethically questionable. Even if she had sought copyright protection, where and when she conducted her research and writing would have mattered. Ellingson makes clear in her letters that she was working on her interpretations as well as the catalog while she was still in the field at Olynthus. Since Robinson raised the funds for the project, contributing much of his own money, any intellectual property she produced while enjoying the project's financial support would legally have belonged to the project's principal investigator, Robinson, under United States copyright law. This would not be true once she returned to Baltimore and Johns Hopkins to finish writing her thesis, however; any original ideas she developed and wrote then belonged to her. Since she did not write her dissertation in the field on Robinson's dime, but instead as a graduate student in Baltimore, that material was also hers and she would have had a right to seek a copyright if she had chosen. Another lens through which to consider the legality of his actions is that of permission. If she allowed Robinson to use her work of her own free will and without coercion, that would also obviate any claims of lawbreaking plagiarism. No document remains, however, showing she granted such permission and considering his long history of acting without making such a request or considering the consequences of his rash decisions, I find it easy to believe he did not contact her in Calgary to ask for her acquiescence once he had decided to send her work to Johns Hopkins University Press in late 1932. Regardless, even if he did not seek her agreement, Robinson did not commit legal plagiarism because her work lacked copyright protection and she produced at least part of it while he was supporting her financially.

While Robinson did not break the law, if a professor were to represent his graduate student's thesis and dissertation as his own work in print today, even with the graduate student's uncoerced permission, that professor would have committed an ethical violation so severe that I have no doubt such action would result in the termination of that person's employment should the action be brought to the attention of a university administration. I suspect the same would have been true in American academia at any point during the twentieth century, a suspicion that is impossible to confirm as I can find no other case of an advisor publishing a student's entire thesis, and most of a dissertation, under his or her own name. Even if what Robinson did was legal, it does not mean that his actions would not warrant negative consequences. He was taking an enormous risk.

Why had Robinson treated Ellingson differently from Mylonas, Graham, Clement, and others with whom he shared the credit for authorship on the front pages of the Olynthus volumes? Ellingson returned to Johns Hopkins to complete her PhD in 1938, six years after Robinson had published her thesis under his own name; she had to have known what he had done with her thesis. Was she bitter or angry? Did she ever complain to anyone? Did she ever find out he had published her dissertation under his own name? We found answers to some of these questions among Robinson's papers at Ole Miss.

Ellingson's Reaction

Christine and I continued to pour over the papers in the Robinson Collection for hours, searching for a document or letter from the 1930s that might offer clues to how Ellingson found out and reacted to Robinson's theft of her thesis and to explain why she returned to him and Johns Hopkins in 1938. Our hopes went unfulfilled; we encountered nothing. If we are to go by the surviving record, therefore, it would appear Ellingson remained silent about Robinson and even forgave him by enrolling as one of his students again to complete her PhD. She maintained her silence for decades, never speaking with bitterness or expressing a feeling of having been used to her colleagues or students at the University of Evansville.[32] Ellingson was even given a chance to set the record straight not long before her death when she was interviewed by Marcus Diamond who was writing an article about women scholars at Johns Hopkins University. Diamond has stated explicitly that during his interview he "was looking for something outrageous, some benchmark, I suppose, against which to mark progress."[33] I suspect that Diamond was looking for exactly the type of story that Ellingson could tell about the behavior of her former advisor. By the time of his interview, most of the people involved in the Olynthus excavations had passed away so one would think Ellingson would feel free to discuss these matters openly. Diamond reports she spoke at length about her great fondness for the project and for Robinson and even shared her photo album with him.[34] He left the interview never learning her secret.

Part of the explanation for her silence is cultural. Underlying Ellingson's reaction to Robinson's decision to leave her name off the publications of the Olynthus terracotta figurines was an attitude that female scholars should not seek public acknowledgment for their work nor complain about their treatment. Ellingson told her daughter that these attitudes were common among classical archaeologists in the 1930s.[35] Although it may strike many of us who have grown up in a society that celebrates female empowerment as difficult to believe, many women internalized these beliefs and were content to work quietly in the background, leaving their male colleagues to reap the rewards of public acknowledgment. Classical archaeologist Shelby Brown has pointed out that even today female archaeologists rarely complain about any mistreatment because they love being in the field and believe the occasional sexist colleague is simply something that must be endured. Brown notes that to excavate one must be prepared to experience extreme heat, mud, and dust, inadequate funding, and sometimes poor living arrangements, conditions with which archaeologists deal by means of a macho, stoic attitude. Sexism is just one more challenge to be silently endured by female archaeologists.[36] In 1989 when trying to organize a symposium on women's contributions to, and challenges in, American archaeology, organizers had a difficult time getting women to participate as many stated they faced no challenges different from men.[37] Female archaeologists who worked in the American Southeast during the 1930s reported absolutely no discrimination occurring even though few reports and publications have female authors or contributors while many women appear in the photos taken of these projects.[38]

Those around her portray Ellingson as the embodiment of this cultural ideal, doing what she loved without seeking recognition. In the preface to *Olynthus VII* Robinson called her "loyal and tactful." In the painting von Peschke created of the crucifixion, Mary Ellingson / Mary Magdalene is serene, stoic, and steadfast as those around her are literally twisted in anguish. After Ellingson retired from the post of director of the Department of Archaeology at the Evansville Public Museum in 1949, museum director Charles Boggs sent her a letter thanking her for her service. Even though it dates to a decade after she decided to forgive Robinson and return to Johns Hopkins, the letter offers proof of how much she internalized the idea of service over self. Boggs wrote,

I have been especially impressed by the fact that you have performed quietly, efficiently and gracefully without demanding attentions or popular praise. . . . The assumption of deep common purpose in working with you has been vastly steadying.[39]

The cultural/personality explanation for Ellingson's lack of reaction to Robinson's theft of her thesis has struck many readers and reviewers of the first edition of this book as inadequate. Some have sought their own explanations and offered theories that had not occurred to me. Margriet Haagsma studied the archival record of Ellingson's time as an undergraduate at the University of Alberta and developed an intriguing interpretation on which I build here, as I believe she provides some excellent insight.[40] Haagsma sees a clash between Ellingson's expectations for having a career in archaeology despite being a woman and not being an American citizen that she developed under her professors at the University of Alberta and the reality of academic culture both in United States higher education and at the American School in Athens. Robinson was the main person who believed she could overcome these obstacles and achieve her goal as he was more interested in what she could do rather than her gender or nationality.

According to Haagsma, Ellingson needed Robinson's help to find entry into the American archaeological and academic worlds, help Robinson was willing to give. The evidence supports her hypothesis. In Robinson's 1939 letter to Alexander quoted previously, he says that he "spent a lot of time on her,"[41] seemingly because he never doubted that she could become a college professor, an unwavering trust she surely appreciated. The deep friendship the two developed during their season at Olynthus had not faded at all from his perspective, and he remained eager to support her whenever she asked. Ellingson's forgiveness is much easier to understand when the person who wronged her was so devoted to her. While Haagsma has a point about Ellingson's dependence on the more powerful Robinson, I think the genuine affection each had for the other made that dependence palatable. Haagsma also speculates that Ellingson and Robinson bonded over their treatment by the management of the American School. Robinson fought their attempts to control his excavation, and Ellingson saw them exclude her first by limiting the number of women and later by banning Canadians and all other non–United States citizens from American School fellowships. Tremendous forces blocked her entry into the academic life she had once believed she could achieve. Robinson was the most powerful patron who supported her. As she contemplated returning to graduate school to write her dissertation, she had few options and only one American ally. Forgiving him was the expedient choice but also made easier by the fact that he admired her abilities as an archaeologist and she saw him as a friend.

On the other hand, if she had wanted to report him for publishing her work under his name, to whom would she and to what end? Once the volume was in print, what was just recompense for what he had done? She could not sue him since she had never officially copyrighted the document. She might have sought his dismissal from Johns Hopkins, but that would only make her notorious. She wanted to return to graduate school to pursue her PhD in Greek archaeology; any action against Robinson could have turned her into a pariah. No action she might take would result in her name appearing on the cover page of the volume. He had all the power and she had none. Telling someone was not an option.

Grace, however necessary, may not have come easily. Ellingson had planned to spend a year or two working but instead did not return to Johns Hopkins for six years. One must wonder if for Ellingson, forgiveness required such a long time far from Robinson. Silent forgiveness, however, was only the first of three reactions Ellingson registered to Robinson's actions. She grew more confident with time.

As we sorted through the letters and documents in the archives in Oxford, Mississippi, we expanded our search beyond the 1930s. At one point, Christine nudged me and slid a letter across the table. It was from Ellingson to Robinson dated October 6, 1952, thanking him for sending her a copy of *Excavations at Olynthus XIV.* She wrote,

> Volume XIV of the Olynthus publications gave me a very pleasant surprise, – I was delighted to see my dissertation in print, and to realize that you thought it worth including in the Olynthus publications, a most logical place for it. I do thank you for publishing it and for your very gracious acknowledgement of my work, and for the volume itself.[42]

We shuffled through the box, looking for a response. We found one. "I was very glad to use your good material," Robinson replied, adding defensively, "and probably should have given you more credit but I had to change many things and to do a lot more work on it, as you noticed."[43] Considering that approximately 95 percent of the first chapter Robinson printed in *Olynthus XIV* repeats Ellingson's dissertation verbatim, his claim to have rewritten it is not convincing. Robinson's admission that he should have given Ellingson more credit shows that he knew what he had done was wrong. We could find no follow-up letter from Ellingson.

This second response to his plagiarism coming fourteen years after she decided to return to Johns Hopkins differs from the first. Robinson clearly caught her off guard, indicating they had not discussed the publication of her dissertation nor do her words suggest she had granted consent. More than surprise, however, this text is not silent grace; it is a passive-aggressive reprimand, similar to the way people from the American South can deploy the phrase "bless your heart" with such devastating effect. She does not hesitate to use the words "my dissertation" and the phrase "your very gracious acknowledgement," the latter of which feels like a honey-coated barb considering the acknowledgment Robinson wrote was one sentence that was a generalized thanks to two people in addition to Ellingson, one of whom was his daughter who he mentions had just died. At a point in her life where Ellingson described herself as "just a housewife now,"[44] she was no longer dependent on Robinson's patronage as she had been in 1934. Again, since she was out of academia at the moment, there was no one to tell of his actions since he had broken no law and with the volume in print, her name could not be added as a contributor. Redress was not possible. Still, she was not going to be as forgiving as she had been a decade and a half earlier. The power imbalance between them no longer mattered but their friendship did; her letter reads like a friend chastising a friend. One can only imagine the satisfaction Ellingson felt at receiving his sheepish response.

A forgiving and a passive-aggressive response were just two points in the evolution of her reaction to Robinson's plagiarism. Something had changed again by the time she filled out that personnel form in 1973 on which she claimed to have written the volume and chapter. That form is the only place she ever said something publicly, revealing a secret she had kept hidden for four decades. It is hard to say how she had grown in that time, but the world around her had been changing rapidly and radically in ways that must have brought back memories of her years at the University of Alberta and the momentum that had won women the right to vote. The "second wave" of feminist activism was at its height in 1973 as proponents demanded women's access to all professions, the equalization of gender roles, and recognition for previously overlooked female contributions in all aspects of society.[45] This activism culminated just a year earlier in 1972 when the United States Congress voted to send the Equal Rights Amendment to the states for approval. The constitutional amendment guaranteed gender equity in the workplace, a goal Alexander and Misener had advocated for in Canada while Ellingson was in college in the 1920s. Ellingson had decided to reveal the truth on her own terms. She filled out the form, not knowing who would see it. Much like throwing a bottle with a note into the ocean, she had no idea if it would bob forever among the waves or if someone did find it, that person would understand it. Nonetheless, on that form the Mary Ellingson of 1973 reclaimed her work for herself.

Reviews of *Excavations at Olynthus* VII and XIV

Knowing that Robinson was not the only person to write about the terracotta figurines published in the *Excavations at Olynthus* series forces us to read reviews of volume VII and the first chapter and a half of volume XIV in a unique light. The reviewers believed they were assessing Robinson's work, the work of a famed researcher with decades of excavation experience. His extensive reputation provided a yardstick by which to judge the volumes. Ellingson was a novice archaeologist and still a graduate student when she wrote what Robinson published. Critics submitted her analysis and writing to a different level of scrutiny than they would have had they understood these were the author's first two publications. Since the reviewers were unaware of the deception, their assessments make much more intriguing reading than they ever intended.

The reviews of *Excavations at Olynthus* VII were positive. Valentin Müller, a German expert on ancient Greek sculpture,[46] wrote,

> The catalogue is very carefully done. We find not only a detailed description of every specimen accompanied by the necessary statements about provenience, measurements, technique, and date but also ample references to parallels and discussions of problems concerning the particular type. . . . The catalogue is preceded by an Introduction in which Mr. Robinson draws several important conclusions from the finds. As in the other fields of archaeology, e.g., in regard to architecture, so also for our knowledge of Greek terracottas the excavation of Olynthus is proving extremely fruitful.[47]

George W. Elderkin, one of the leaders of the Princeton excavations at the Syrian site of Antioch,[48] agreed:

> The terracottas are classified and arranged within groups in chronological sequence so that there results a ceramic history of Olynthus from the sixth century to the year 348 B.C. when the city was destroyed. The story is very interesting. All types of terracottas are represented. . . . Dr. Robinson has rendered the double service of finding and publishing a highly suggestive ceramic anthology of the Olynthians.[49]

Reviewers praised both the thoroughness of the catalog and the analysis of the finds. Müller added of Ellingson's analysis, "Robinson's assertions are all very convincing generally so that little is left for criticism."[50]

Reviewers were harsher in their assessment of the first two chapters of *Excavations at Olynthus XIV*, wondering what the point was of publishing information about terracotta figurines excavated at sites other than Olynthus, most of which had already been published elsewhere, in a site report about Olynthus. Reynold Higgins, a British archaeologist and curator of Greek terracotta figurines at the British Museum,[51] wished the first chapter had been omitted.[52] Ellingson had included information about material from Olynthus in her dissertation and compared it to the material from those other sites in order to synthesize the study of figurines from across northern Greece and the Balkans. Robinson included her analysis of the Olynthus material in the second chapter of the volume, destroying the unity of her dissertation. By dividing the material in this way, he created the awkwardness that Higgins noted of a first chapter, which had nothing to do with the Olynthus figurines.

The second chapter of *Excavations at Olynthus XIV* received better reviews. Ellingson's synthesis and analysis of all the terracotta figurines found at Olynthus over the four seasons of excavation received the most interest and praise. Higgins claimed "Chapter II, 'Summary and Statistics,' perhaps the most important part of the book, supplies much material on which future students can work."[53] He was impressed with what he believed was Robinson's archaeological analysis of the figurines' find spots, leading to an understanding of what the ancient people at Olynthus were doing with the figurines, a subject he called too often "neglected" by scholars analyzing terracotta figurines as *objets d'art*.[54] "Robinson's" conclusions, based on tables and statistical evidence, particularly caught the attention of other reviewers as well. Sterling Dow, an epigrapher and excavator in the Athenian Agora,[55] was intrigued that "Robinson" could use these numeric data to prove that the "terracottas are not used chiefly as grave furniture, nor is their cult significance primary; instead, they were for decoration and amusement," challenging contemporary interpretations of their use.[56] Although the book was about lamps and coins, as well as terracotta figurines, Robert Scranton, excavator at Corinth and Athens, concluded "the section on terracottas has genuine independent significance,"[57] a statement with which most other reviewers agreed.[58] Even if the portions of the *Excavations at Olynthus* series that she wrote did not bear her name, Ellingson had a great deal about which to be proud. We will never know if she read any of these reviews or, if she did, how she felt about seeing the reviewers comment on her work, thinking it had been written by Robinson.

A Portrait

After hours in the archives finding and copying documents, our heads were spinning. I suggested we go over to the University of Mississippi Museum to take a break. That is what archaeologists do for fun. I also knew the museum housed a room filled with artifacts Robinson had bequeathed to the institution in his will and so thought it was worth a visit. A grand painted portrait hanging at the entrance to the Robinson gallery in the museum. It caught me by surprise, I recognized it but had not known it was there. Robinson had placed a reproduced image on the front of a holiday card he had sent to Ellingson in 1952. I remembered seeing the card among Ellingson's papers in Evansville, but I never really looked at the image on the card until that moment (figure 6.2). The University of Mississippi had commissioned a famed mid-twentieth-century portrait artist, Stanislav Rembski, to create the painting.[59] The portrait shows Robinson surrounded by symbols of his accomplishments, symbols he no doubt selected. He wears regalia to show his pride in being an academic; behind him is a part of a pebble mosaic he discovered at Olynthus depicting Achilles and Thetis; beside him is the head of a satyr, part of his personal collection of antiquities, resting on a base inscribed in Greek with the cryptic phrase, "criticism tests mortals"; behind him is a fragmented line of Greek text with Aeolic spellings, indicating his publications on Greek poetry and literature, particularly Sappho.[60] In his hands is a book open to the cover page with the title "Olynthus" clearly visible on the right side; the central location within the portrait's frame of the book and the bright colors in which it is painted clearly make it one of the first things the viewer notices and marks the book series as one of the achievements of which Robinson was most proud.

As we walked toward the painting, our pace slowed and we both suddenly stopped as we simultaneously realized the significance of what we saw. On the left-hand page of the open book, Rembski had painted the frontispiece of the volume with such great care and in such detail that it is easy to identify. It is the painted terracotta figurine of a dancer holding a tambourine that Ellingson had found in the East Cemetery at Olynthus. It is the figurine Ellingson described as one of "the most marvelous things I have ever seen" in a letter to her family. It is the figurine both Melanides and Ellingson photographed (see figure 2.11, far left). It is the figurine of which von Peschke made a watercolor (see figure 2.12). Robinson chose that watercolor as the frontispiece to *Olynthus VII*, his publication of Ellingson's plagiarized thesis. It is a figurine so recognizable with all the detail Rembski lavished on it in the portrait that it is still easy to identify when the portrait was reproduced

Figure 6.2. Front of a card David Robinson sent to Mary Ross Ellingson for the 1952 holiday season featuring a recently completed portrait of himself. The painting of the terracotta figurine Ellingson excavated is between Robinson's hands.

at a small enough scale to fit on a holiday card. It is proof that the cliché is true: the criminal always returns to the scene of the crime. Christine and I eventually stopped looking at the portrait and turned to one another. We understood we were the only living people who knew the portrait carried a secret message.

Robinson's choice to be portrayed with that specific volume of the *Olynthus* series was deliberate. Everything else in his portrait, from the academic robes to the cryptic Greek phrase to the head of the Satyr bears the hallmark of something deeply significant to Robinson. And with fourteen volumes in the series, each with its own frontispiece, he had a wide variety of options from which to choose for this painting. The University of Mississippi unveiled the portrait on December 20, 1952, at the end of the year that saw the publication of what Robinson told people was his final volume on Olynthus. The frontispiece of the fourteenth volume, a painting of a figurine depicting the god Hermes, would have made a logical choice for the portrait. Since this image comes from the final volume, a fact anyone familiar with the series would have recognized, it would have represented the sum of his accomplishments at the site and in its publication. By 1952, archaeologists also understood that the main legacy of Olynthus was its foundational contribution to the architectural study of the ancient Greek house, the focus of *Olynthus VIII*. The frontispiece from that volume, a reconstruction of one of the houses, would have been another likely candidate to appear in an image meant to symbolize his most significant achievement. By choosing *Olynthus VII* for the portrait, Robinson defied expectations.

But why, what was his intention? When I published the first edition of this book, I offered a suggestion that was not well received by readers or reviewers. My initial argument was that Robinson was trying to apologize to Ellingson for having used her material without acknowledgment or permission. Robinson would have known Ellingson would recognize the figurine in Rembski's portrait immediately. The figurine in the frontispiece is catalog number 185 in the *Olynthus VII* catalog, which Ellingson found in the East Cemetery.[61] On the day she excavated it, Ellingson became the first person in over two millennia to hold the dancer figurine and to notice the traces of paint that remained. She wrote the catalog entry on it and worked with Melanides to photograph it and von Peschke to paint the watercolor that became the frontispiece. Her dissertation also contains numerous references to *Excavations at Olynthus VII*, proving she had consulted the volume often and no doubt saw the frontispiece repeatedly. Even though twenty-one years passed since Ellingson found the figurine, she would certainly have recognized the dancer's sinuous pose, the tambourine, and the unusual double base on which the woman stands, all of which are clearly visible in Rembski's original portrait of Robinson, and in the much smaller version of the image on the holiday card.

The timing of Robinson's gesture in including Ellingson's thesis in his portrait is also significant. The university presented the painting to the public in December 1952. When Robinson sat for the portrait or when he told Rembski which volume of *Excavations at Olynthus* to include is not recorded but presumably it was within weeks or at most a few months of the unveiling. The letter exchange quoted earlier between Ellingson and Robinson in which he offers his meek apology for publishing her dissertation took place in mid-October 1952, about two months prior to the public presentation of the portrait. I believe this is more than a coincidence of timing. Robinson's tiff with Ellingson must have been on his mind as well as the worry that he had jeopardized their friendship at the time he was telling Rembski which symbols to include. It was the perfect opportunity for a symbolic apology. Both Robinson and Ellingson had studied art history and had taught survey courses on the entire history of art; he knew she was used to reading the symbolism in a painting. He could not be certain she would ever come to Oxford, Mississippi, to see the portrait, however, so he came up with an ingenious solution. For the 1952 holiday season, Robinson had a greeting card printed that featured Rembski's portrait in color on the front surrounded by bells and sprigs of holly, without any printed words. I surmise the intended message of this elaborate scheme was an apology for publishing her work without proper attribution and an acknowledgment that she contributed to his success. Robinson may have delighted in the knowledge that he had publicly, yet secretly, given Ellingson credit and also snickered at future art historians studying Rembski's work who would never fully understand the symbolism of the portrait, although they would think they did.

Ellingson may have received Robinson's message. They corresponded a great deal as the many letters now in the archives at the University of Mississippi prove. Robinson saved copies of those he had sent to Ellingson and her responses; she kept only a couple of his letters. In her later years she moved twice, each time to a smaller place, shedding unnecessary possessions.[62] Interestingly the copy of *Excavations at Olynthus XIV* Robinson sent her in 1952 was one item that did not survive these purges, but the holiday card did. This card must have meant something very special to her for she kept it until her death.

Few reviewers of the first edition of this book found the apology hypothesis completely convincing, offering interpretations of their own. Classicist Kathy Gaca wrote,

Even if Robinson meant the card as an apology to Ellingson, as Kaiser maintains, in other ways the card reasserts Robinson's wrongful claiming of her work. There the volume sits on his lap and in his hands, her master's thesis published as his own work. Further, given the social custom of sending holiday greeting cards, Robinson likely sent this card to other recipients too. Any colleagues and graduate students in classical archaeology who received a copy of this card would also have recognized the book, but they would have seen it as one of Robinson's volumes in the *Olynthus* series. Seen from this perspective, Robinson's 1952 holiday greeting card further represents the book as his own, thereby re-enacting his deception of 1933.[63]

Archaeologist Marianna Nikolaidou concurred and elaborated:

> We may instead be witnessing an alpha-male's disproportionate sense of entitlement, also evident in his repeated plagiarism while vociferously advocating policies to the opposite or when his strong support for protégés, men *and* women, turned to intense hostility against perceived disloyalty or antagonism.[64]

During the question-and-answer period after a lecture I had given on Ellingson's story at the University of Mississippi, a lecture I delivered just a few dozen feet from Robinson's portrait, an audience member, whose name I did not think to ask, succinctly, if crudely, summarized a common opinion expressed by reviewers and readers alike: "The painting is a f**k you to anyone who'd challenge him."

What I missed initially, and what these and other reviewers and readers noted, was that Robinson's intended audience for the portrait was not primarily Ellingson but rather a much broader group of those familiar with his life's work. On the back of the card he sent Ellingson are the words "Pavelle Color Print," an indication this was one of a set of cards mass-produced, probably by a local printer in Oxford, Mississippi, who owned one of the Pavelle company's color printing machines. Robinson likely mailed a number of these cards to family, friends, former students, and colleagues around the time Rembski presented the portrait to the public. The following year, the portrait appeared as the frontispiece in the second volume of papers Mylonas had put together to honor Robinson on his seventieth birthday. We cannot know Robinson's role in this decision, but at the very least he consented if he did not suggest it to Mylonas. Robinson wanted as many people as possible to see this image.

While I see merit in the observation that Robinson used the Christmas card to assert his claim to *Olynthus VII* and that he did not intend the holiday greeting as a personal apology to Ellingson, I am not convinced his plagiarism never bothered him. The creation of this painting, I argue, was a turning point in his feelings about what he had done to Ellingson, moving from unapologetic entitlement to guilt. Prior to 1952, Robinson had no compunction about doing whatever he wanted because, as he wrote Graham in 1953, he controlled the Olynthus material (figure P.3). With this mindset, he published Ellingson's entire thesis and most of her dissertation without seeking permission, making him the only known person in the history of archaeology to have done so. I detect a change after the final volume of the *Olynthus* series came out, a growing sense of regret. Much like the protagonist in Poe's *Tell-Tale Heart*, for whom the heartbeat of the man he murdered grows louder in his ears matching the level of his remorse, Robinson's plagiarism of Ellingson seemed to increasingly bother him. Admittedly, this is speculation that can never be proven, but the evidence is tantalizing. I suggest it was because it was Ellingson whom he had mistreated that his feelings changed. He had described her as "loyal and tactful." Boggs found her presence "vastly steadying," a feeling Robinson likely shared while they were in the field together. Von Peschke painted her as he saw her, as stoic and serene in cruel and chaotic surroundings, again personality traits Robinson must have witnessed at Olynthus. Robinson kept the letters she sent him, letters filled with her support and praise of him, showing they meant something to him as he did not keep all his correspondence. Of all the people he could wrong, she was the easiest because of her lack of power and the hardest because of her loyalty and steadfastness.

In 1952, Robinson did the first action that suggests his sense of entitlement no longer sufficed to mask his feelings of having betrayed such a kind and supportive friend. He did not have to send her a copy of *Olynthus XIV*, but he did knowing that she would recognize her text. An entitled man would simply go on with his life, not concerned with whether she found out about what he had done. His action is an admission of guilt that contradicts all his previous behavior and unshakable belief that he alone possessed all information his team discovered at Olynthus. When she called him out with words like "my dissertation" and "your very gracious acknowledgement of my work," he begrudgingly admitted he should have given her more credit, an unexpected statement from a man whose reaction to criticism was routinely an angry attack. The angry attack did come, however, as while he admitted privately to Ellingson he should have acknowledged her, he had Rembski place her thesis in his hands for the portrait to proclaim to the world, similar to his statement to Graham: "*Olynthus VII* is mine." By 1956, he was lecturing the chancellor of the University of Mississippi on teaching about plagiarism to undergraduates, citing the imperative that society was threatened by a lack of commitment to moral behavior. A privileged man might not see the contradiction, true, but a guilty man might be worrying subconsciously about how his past choices were affecting him in the present and his legacy in the future. One of his final acts suggests that the increasingly loud pulsing of guilt haunted him at the end of his life.

In 2022, a member of the editorial staff at Johns Hopkins University Press shared a document with me that he had found in the Press's records.[65] The memo dates to February 12, 1958, and was written by William Patterson. Patterson outlines a bequest left to the Press in Robinson's will after the man's death in the previous month. Robinson bequeathed $20,000 so the Press could publish "the best of the past unpublished dissertations which have been presented to the Department of Archaeology of The Johns Hopkins University." Such a bequest is unique; I am aware of no other gift in a will for the same purpose. And for a plagiarizer, it is extremely peculiar; Robinson was encouraging someone from Johns Hopkins University Press to look through unpublished Hopkins archaeology and classics dissertations, making it more likely that that person might discover his crimes. The memo states the value of Robinson's entire estate, exclusive of his antiquities collection was about $200,000, making the amount he left 10 percent of the total. I suspect the amount was also symbolic. With a Baptist minister as a father, Robinson would have been aware that giving 10 percent is a biblical "tithe." The bequest seems more like actions of a penitent rather than an entitled man. The editor at Johns Hopkins reports the fund no longer exists, having been absorbed into other budget lines at the press long ago. I tracked down Robinson's original will dated November 26, 1957, just thirty-seven days before his death.[66] Presumably, after inserting the required language about which attorney would be the executor, Robinson dictated the rest. The first item that appears to come from Robinson rather than his attorneys is this request to provide funds for publishing unpublished dissertations. It is an issue that seems to have been haunting him in the last days of his life if he insisted on mentioning it first when making his will. Just as Ellingson grew bolder about reclaiming her plagiarized work, Robinson grew more repentant for having taken it.

Time to Publish

During our visit to the University of Mississippi archives, Christine and I had gathered reams of primary source material. We were now able to definitively document the most egregious case of plagiarism in the history of classical archaeology, archaeology in general, and all the sciences. Some of the documents also allowed us to look at how and why it had happened. And we had discovered a painting with a hidden message. Normally, archaeologists have little interest in reading about the history of our discipline, but this was such an explosive story for which we had an unprecedented amount of evidence, it began to dawn on me that this might be different. Surely archaeologists would want to read an article that would so alter our understanding of a marquee excavation and a legendary archaeologist. Even if they did not want to read it, surely they should read it. Perhaps I had not been wasting my time on an obsession; perhaps I was doing research that needed to be shared. "Publish or perish." Ellingson's story had to be published.

Notes

1. David M. Robinson, *Excavations at Olynthus VII: The Terra-Cottas of Olynthus Found in 1931* (Baltimore: Johns Hopkins University Press, 1933), viii.

2. David M. Robinson, *Excavations at Olynthus XIV: Terracottas, Lamps, and Coins Found in 1934 and 1938* (Baltimore: Johns Hopkins University Press, 1952), vii.

3. E. C. Hills, "The Degree of Doctor of Philosophy," *Bulletin of the American Association of University Professors* 12, no. 3 (1927), 172–73.

4. Ellingson to Robinson October 5, 1941; Robinson to Ellingson October 15, 1941; Ellingson to Robinson November 4, 1941; Robinson to Ellingson November 7, 1941, now in the Ellingson folder, Box 5, David M. Robinson Collection, Special Collections, University of Mississippi Libraries. Copies of all these letters are on file in the archives at the University of Evansville.

5. Saul Weinberg to Robinson, October 2, 1940; Robinson to Weinberg October 5, 1940, Weinberg folder, Box 18, David M. Robinson Collection, Special Collections, University of Mississippi Libraries; Robinson to Gladys Davidson Weinberg October 21, 1942; Robinson to Davidson Weinberg November 4, 1942, Davidson folder, Box 4, David M. Robinson Collection, Special Collections, University of Mississippi Libraries. Copies of all these letters are on file in the archives at the University of Evansville.

6. David M. Robinson, *Excavations at Olynthus X: Metal and Minor Miscellaneous Finds, an Original Contribution to Greek Life,* Johns Hopkins University Studies in Archaeology 31 (Baltimore, MD: Johns Hopkins University Press, 1941), v.

7. David M. Robinson, *Excavations at Olynthus XIII: Vases Found in 1934 and 1938,* Johns Hopkins University Studies in Archaeology 38 (Baltimore, MD: Johns Hopkins University Press, 1950), 36.

8. George E. Mylonas, *Excavations at Olynthus I: The Neolithic Settlement.* Johns Hopkins University Studies in Archaeology 6 (Baltimore, MD: Johns Hopkins University Press, 1929), xi–xii.

9. George M. A. Hanfmann, *The David Moore Robinson Bequest of Classical Art and Antiquities* (Boston: Harvard University Press, 1961), 3.

10. Quoted in Jennifer K. West, "Observations on Selected Papers of David Moore Robinson from the University of Mississippi Archives" (MA thesis, University of Mississippi, 1995), 62.

11. Quoted in Jennifer K. West, "Observations on Selected Papers," 60–61.

12. See chapter 1.

13. See chapter 4.

14. David M. Robinson, *Excavations at Olynthus VII*, viii.

15. Gladys D. Weinberg, *Corinth, Results of Excavations Conducted by the American School of Classical Studies at Athens XII: The Minor Objects* (Princeton, NJ: American School of Classical Studies at Athens, 1952).

16. Sarah E. Freeman, "Temple E at Corinth," in *Corinth, Results of Excavations Conducted by the American School of Classical Studies at Athens I.2: Architecture*, edited by Richard Stillwell, Robert L. Scranton, and Sarah E. Freeman (Princeton, NJ: American School of Classical Studies at Athens, 1941), 166–236.

17. Cynthia Irwin-Williams, "Women in the Field: The Role of Women in Archaeology before 1960," in *Women of Science: Righting the Record*, edited by G. Kass-Simon and Patricia Farnes (Bloomington: University of Indiana Press, 1990), 20 and 25.

18. Mary Ann Levine, "Creating Their Own Niches: Career Styles among Women in Americanist Archaeology between the Wars," in *Women in Archaeology*, edited by Cheryl Claassen (Philadelphia: University of Pennsylvania Press, 1994), 13; Irwin-Williams, "Women in the Field," 25.

19. Margaret W. Rossiter, *Women Scientists in America: Struggles and Strategies to 1940* (Baltimore, MD: Johns Hopkins University Press, 1982), 204.

20. Rossiter, *Women Scientists in America*," 213.

21. Ibid., 213–14.

22. Ida Thallon Hill and Lida Shaw King, *Corinth, Results of Excavations Conducted by the American School of Classical Studies at Athens IV, Part I: Decorated Architectural Terracottas* (Princeton, NJ: American School of Classical Studies at Athens, 1929).

23. Natalia Vogeikoff-Brogan, "Ida Thallon Hill (1875–1954)," *Breaking Ground: Women in Old World Archaeology* (n.d.), http://www.brown.edu/Research/Breaking_Ground/bios/Hill_Ida%20Thallon.pdf.

24. Richard Stillwell, Robert L. Scranton, and Sarah E. Freeman, *Corinth: Results of Excavations Conducted by the American School of Classical Studies at Athens I.2: Architecture* (Princeton, NJ: American School of Classical Studies at Athens, 1941); Arthur W. Parsons, "The Long Walls to the Gulf," in *Corinth: Results of Excavations Conducted by the American School of Classical Studies at Athens III.2: The Defenses of Acrocorinth and the Lower Town*, edited by Rhys Carpenter and Antoine Bon (Princeton, NJ: American School of Classical Studies at Athens, 1936), 84–127.

25. Rossiter, *Women Scientists in America*," 208–9.

26. Levine, "Creating Their Own Niches," 28–29.

27. Alice Beck Kehoe, *Girl Archaeologist: Sisterhood in a Sexist Profession* (Lincoln: University of Nebraska Press, 2022), 129.

28. Vogeikoff-Brogan, "Ida Thallon Hill (1875–1954)."

29. Nancy M. White, "Women in Southeastern U.S. Archaeology," in *Grit-Tempered: Early Women Archaeologists in the Southeastern United States*, edited by Nancy M. White, Lynne P. Sullivan, and Rochelle A. Marrinan (Gainesville: University Press of Florida, 1999), 21.

30. Greg Britton, editorial director of Johns Hopkins University Press, personal communication, June 22, 2022.

31. For the discussion that follows, I am indebted to a thorough and fascinating analysis of the legal issue sent to me by Steven Holzer, a retired contract law attorney, who agreed to let me share some of his salient points.

32. George Klinger, chair of the Department of English during Ellingson's tenure, personal communication; Mike Carson, a student and later colleague of Ellingson's at the University of Evansville Department of English, personal communication.

33. Marcus Diamond to Barbara A. Petersen, February 15, 1994. This letter is now on file with Ellingson's papers in the University of Evansville Library Archives.

34. Marcus Diamond, interview with the author on March 6, 2004.

35. Barbara A. Petersen, interview with author on April 5, 2004.

36. Shelby Brown, "Feminist Research in Archaeology: What Does it Mean? Why Is it Taking So Long?" in *Feminist Theory and the Classics*, edited by Nancy Sorkin Rabinowitz and Amy Richlin (New York: Routledge 1993), 241–43.

37. Nancy M. White, 1999. "Women in Southeastern U. S. Archaeology," 21.

38. Jonathan E. Reyman, "Women in American Archaeology: Some Historical Notes and Comments," in *Rediscovering Our Past: Essays on the History of American Archaeology*, edited by Jonathan E. Reyman (Aldershot: Avebury, 1992), 71–72.

39. Boggs to Ellingson, June 22, 1949, University of Evansville Library Archives.

40. Margriet Haagsma, "Historiography and Theory." *Journal of Greek Archaeology* 5 (2020): 630–40.

41. Letter David Robinson to W. H. Alexander dated May 27, 1939. The letter is currently in the possession of Barbara Petersen; a copy is on file in the archives at the University of Evansville.

42. Mary Ellingson to David M. Robinson, October 6, 1952, Box 5, David M. Robinson Collection, Special Collections, University of Mississippi Libraries. A copy of this letter is now on file with Ellingson's papers in the University of Evansville Library Archives.

43. David M. Robinson to Mary Ellingson October 14, 1952, Box 5, David M. Robinson Collection, Special Collections, University of Mississippi Libraries. A copy of this letter is now on file with Ellingson's papers in the University of Evansville Library Archives.

44. Letter from Ellingson to Robinson dated July 16, 1949, Box 5, David M. Robinson Collection, Special Collections, University of Mississippi Libraries. A copy of this letter is now on file with Ellingson's papers in the University of Evansville Library Archives.

45. See Appendix II for more detail and Sara Evans, *Tidal Wave: How Women Changed America at Century's End* (New York: The Free Press, 2003): 2.

46. See Valentin Müller, *Frühe plastik in Griechenland und Vorderasien; ihre typenbildung von der neolithischen bis in die griechisch-archaische zeit (rund 3000 bis 600 v. Chr.)* (Augsburg: B. Filser, 1929).

47. Valentin Müller, "Review of *Excavations at Olynthus* by David M. Robinson," *Classical Philology* 31, no. 1 (1936): 92.

48. George Wicker Elderkin, *Antioch-on-the-Orontes* I (Princeton, NJ: Princeton University Press, 1934).

49. George Wicker Elderkin, "Review of *Excavations at Olynthus, Part VII: The Terra-Cottas Found in 1931* by David M. Robinson," *American Journal of Archaeology* 38, no. 3 (1934): 497.

50. Müller, "Review of *Excavations at Olynthus*," 92.

51. Linda M. Medwid, *The Makers of Classical Archaeology* (New York: Humanity Books, 2000), 152–53.

52. Reynold A. Higgins, "Review of *Excavations at Olynthus: Part XIV, Terracottas, Lamps and Coins Found in 1934 and 1938* by D. M. Robinson," *Journal of Hellenic Studies* 75 (1955): 180.

53. Reynold A. Higgins, "Review of *Excavations at Olynthus: Part XIV, Terracottas, Lamps and Coins Found in 1934 and 1938* by D. M. Robinson," *Antiquaries Journal* 35 (1955): 97.

54. Higgins, "Review of *Excavations at Olynthus: Part XIV*," 180.

55. Medwid, *The Makers of Classical Archaeology*, 96–98.

56. Sterling Dow, "Review of *Excavations at Olynthus: Part XIV*, by David M. Robinson," *American Historical Review* 58, no. 3 (1953): 587.

57. Robert Scranton, "Review of *Excavations at Olynthus: Part XIV, Terracottas, Lamps, and Coins Found in 1934 and 1938* by David M. Robinson," *Classical Philology* 49, no. 2 (1954): 143.

58. For example, William A. McDonald. "Review of *Excavations at Olynthus: Part XIV, Terracottas, Lamps and Coins Found in 1934 and 1938* by David M. Robinson," *Classical Journal* 50, no. 2 (1954): 94–95; R. M. Cook, "Review of *Excavations at Olynthus: Part XIV, Terracottas, Lamps and Coins Found in 1934 and 1938* by D. M. Robinson," *Classical Review* 5, no. 3/4 (1955): 326–27; R. C. Wood, "Review of *Excavations at Olynthus: Part XIV, Terracottas, Lamps and Coins Found in 1934 and 1938* by D. M. Robinson," *American Journal of Archaeology* 57, no. 3 (1953): 227–28.

59. David M. Robinson to Mary Ellingson, undated card celebrating the 1952 holiday season, now on file with Ellingson's papers in the University of Evansville Library Archives. To see a photo of the painting, see http://thaumazein-albert.blogspot.com/2011/12/works-from-david-m-robinson-collection.html.

60. I am indebted to Jim Ware of the University of Evansville for his analysis of the ancient Greek in this painting.

61. David M. Robinson, *Excavations at Olynthus VII: The Terra-Cottas of Olynthus Found in 1931* (Baltimore, MD: Johns Hopkins University Press, 1933), #185, 53.

62. Barbara Petersen, personal communication.

63. Kathy L. Gaca, *Byrn Mawr Classical Review*, "Alan Kaiser, *Archaeology, Sexism, and Scandal: The Long-Suppressed Story of One Woman's Discoveries and the Man Who Stole Credit for Them*," February 2, 2015. Accessed July 23, 2022. http:// http:// www.bmcreview.org/2015/02/20150203.html.

64. Marianna Nickolaidou, "Reviews of Books: Kaiser (A.) *Archaeology, Sexism and Scandal: The Long-Suppressed Story of One Woman's Discoveries and the Man Who Stole Credit for Them*." *Journal of Hellenic Studies* 137 (2017): 282–83.

65. Greg Britton, editorial director of Johns Hopkins University Press, personal communication, June 22, 2022.

66. Robinson's will is available for public viewing at the Chancery Court of Lafayette County in Oxford, Mississippi. I am deeply indebted to Tina Johnson, deputy chancery clerk, for locating and scanning this document.

CHAPTER SEVEN

~

"Unwritten History"

Now that I had a strong case against Robinson, I felt it was time to tell the world Ellingson's story by getting an article published in a scholarly journal. From my own experience getting articles and even books into print, I expected the process to follow a predictable pattern. To my surprise and consternation, it did not.

One way to begin writing an article is to simply talk about the rough idea, presenting it at a scholarly conference. This provides the author with the opportunity to get some feedback from colleagues before writing the article. I presented a paper exposing Mary Ross Ellingson's authorship of portions of the *Excavations at Olynthus* volumes at the most prestigious conference for classical archaeologists in North America, the annual conference of the Archaeological Institute of America, in January 2005 in San Diego. The paper's title was intended to be provocative, "How Women Archaeologists Were Erased from the Early 20th Century History of Archaeology: A Case Study." The paper was a great success. People crowded around when it was done to ask questions, make comments, and encourage me to publish.

The next step in getting a scholarly article published is to write a draft and send it to a journal. The editor reads the draft and decides whether to send the article to reviewers, who are other scholars in the author's field. The peer reviewers assess whether the article is worthy of publication as is, worthy after making some revisions, or does not meet professional standards in the field. The author of the article never learns the identities of the reviewers so that the reviewers may feel free to be as honest as possible in their assessment; hence the entire process is sometimes called a "blind review" or "anonymous review." If the article is approved for publication, the author works with the editor to address the issues raised by the reviewers and once the editor is satisfied the article is scheduled for publication. This process requires many months, sometimes even years.

My first rejection was swift. The anonymous reviewers said that I was not telling the whole story, and they made the accusation that Robinson had plagiarized others. More surprises awaited as I followed their suggestions and dug deeper, trying to separate myth from reality. I would write and rewrite the article a number of times, always augmenting it with new information. I had published peer-reviewed articles before, but this was to become the most controversial piece I had ever written.

Other Plagiarism Accusations against Robinson

The anonymous reviewers claimed Robinson had plagiarized several of his other graduate students in addition to Ellingson. One of the individuals they named was Graham. This is a rather extraordinary charge since Robinson listed Graham as a coauthor of *Excavations at Olynthus VIII* and published Graham's catalog of lamps found during the 1931 season in *Excavations at Olynthus V* in a chapter with Graham's name on it.[1] Since Graham did not participate in the 1938 season, and he is only recorded as working on the lamps and the domestic architecture, it is hard to imagine what he could have written what remained unpublished. Graham earned his PhD in 1933 and found a teaching position in 1935, allowing him to leave Baltimore and Robinson, which again leaves little time for Graham to have written anything else that Robinson could have pilfered. In addition, Robinson worked very actively to promote Graham's early career, so plagiarizing his work would have been counterproductive to his goal of seeing Graham succeed.[2] The only truth I can find behind this charge is Shaw's comment that Graham's name should have come first on the title page of *Excavations at Olynthus VIII* rather than Robinson's since Graham wrote most of the volume.[3] Paul Clement's 1939 review of *Olynthus VIII*, in which he only mentions Graham and not Robinson, would seem to suggest Clement also saw the work as primarily Graham's regardless of the order of the names on the cover page.[4] While Shaw and Clement's suggestions about the relative contribution of each man to the volume are perhaps true, that is certainly not a serious enough ethical breach to sustain the charge of plagiarism.

Another name the reviewers gave as a victim of Robinson's plagiarism was Gladys Weinberg who, according to one reviewer, wrote the majority of *Ex-*

cavations at Olynthus V: Mosaics, Vases, and Lamps of Olynthus Found in 1928 and 1931. On the cover page of the volume and in the table of contents, Robinson credits Graham with having written the section on lamps, Mylonas the section on pre-Persian pottery, and A. Xyngopoulos the section on Byzantine pottery. Since Donald Wilber and Freeman were in charge of architecture and, presumably, the mosaics during the 1931 season[5] and Weinberg the vases,[6] the reviewer must be claiming that Weinberg wrote the four remaining chapters on Corinthian wares, wares of uncertain origin, and the red- and black-figured pottery, totaling 201 printed pages. In the preface to the volume, Robinson writes of Weinberg, referring to her by her maiden name, "For help on the inventory of the vases (now in the Archaeological Museum of Saloniki) I am indebted to Miss Gladys R. Davidson, now fellow of the American School of Classical Studies at Athens, who also lent efficient aid in supervising a section of the excavations."[7] Robinson's statement contradicts that of the anonymous reviewer in that Robinson claims he wrote the remaining sections on the vases with only the *assistance* of Weinberg.

In the absence of documentation, we will never know which claim represents objective truth. Whatever Weinberg wrote after she returned to Baltimore in 1931 simply does not survive as she did not submit it as a master's thesis and no drafts of the volume remain among Robinson's papers or Weinberg's own, now archived at the American School of Classical Studies at Athens. As demonstrated with Ellingson's thesis, Robinson had pilfered the work of one of his graduate students prior to the writing of *Excavations at Olynthus V,* a fact that lends credence to what the anonymous reviewer reported. On the other hand, Robinson considered himself an expert on, and lover of, Greek pottery, so it seems unlikely he would have left the writing of what he must have relished as one of the best parts of the volume to a graduate student. Since the volume was assembled and published quickly, appearing in print in 1933, and these four chapters were so long, it is easy to imagine Robinson and Weinberg working on the chapters together. It may be that Robinson believed he had given Weinberg sufficient credit for her contribution in the preface, particularly as she had not written her pottery catalog entries as part of a thesis that would have accorded her more publishing rights.[8] Weinberg may have had an equally strong belief that her work on one or more of these four chapters earned her credit equal to that of her fellow graduate student and research assistant, Graham, whom Robinson credited as the author of the chapter on lamps even though Graham never submitted his work as a thesis or dissertation either. While it seems likely some of Weinberg's work appears in these four chapters, even if the amount is impossible to determine with the surviving evidence, the reviewer's claim she wrote the majority of the volume seems impossible when so much of the volume is devoted to material Weinberg clearly did not study and it seems unlikely she could have written the other four chapters completely on her own in the time available.

The anonymous reviewer who reported hearing Weinberg's stories about her time working with Robinson also stated Weinberg had said that Robinson had scoffed at the notion she could publish her dissertation under her own name. This extraordinary claim appears highly dubious, perhaps something went awry in the repeated transmission of the story. Weinberg wrote about material from Corinth, not Olynthus, thus Robinson had no control whatsoever over that material and whether or not he thought she could publish it under her own name or someone else's was irrelevant. In addition, the encouraging sentiments Robinson wrote to Weinberg about the excellence of her dissertation and his desire to see it in print are at complete odds with this secondhand story.[9]

The anonymous reviewers had more familiar names of Robinson's alleged plagiarism victims including Clement, a curious claim as Clement was one of Robinson's students who chose not to write a dissertation on an Olynthus-related topic. Instead he wrote on the ancient cults of Thessaly[10] and although he did not publish his dissertation, Robinson did not publish on this subject either. Clement joined the Olynthus team in 1934, several years after he had completed his dissertation, spending the season cataloging the coins.[11] Robinson and Clement published the coins jointly in 1938 in *Excavations at Olynthus IX*.[12] The next year, Clement published his review of *Excavations at Olynthus VIII*, which led to the feud between him and Robinson[13] and certainly an end to any collaborative projects that would have given Robinson access to his work. In addition there is no record of Clement working on any material other than the coins published in *Excavations at Olynthus IX*. Again the veracity of this charge is suspect based on the surviving evidence.

The reviewers did not stop with these three names; they had two more. One of these was William McDonald. McDonald's name is well known among archaeologists for his innovative work on the Minnesota-Messina regional survey[14] and as a professor at the University of Minnesota where he created the experimental interdisciplinary Graduate Center for Ancient Studies. Long before that as a graduate student at Johns Hopkins, he received his field training at Olynthus under Robinson.[15] During the final season at Olynthus in 1938, he was in charge of inventorying the bronzes and lamps.[16] McDonald chose not to write his dissertation on a subject related to Olynthus but instead completed *The Political Meeting Places of the Greeks* in 1940.[17] This was published three years later in the *Johns Hopkins University Studies* in Archaeology series.[18] As editor of the series, Robinson not only helped to get McDonald's dissertation into print but also found money to finance the book's publication.[19] One anonymous reviewer of my article claimed Robinson had plagiarized McDonald, publishing an edited version of his dissertation as an entry in the *Realencyclopädia der Classischen Altertumswissenschaft*, commonly called the "*RE*" or the "Pauly-Wissowa" after its earliest editors. The *RE* is the most widely respected general encyclopedia on all issues in the classical world routinely consulted by experts in the field. Robinson made his last contribution to the encyclopedia in 1938, two years before McDonald finished his dissertation. In that entry, Robinson wrote about houses, not about public space, which was McDonald's chosen subject.[20] Robinson also did not publish any general article on Greek public space in 1940 or later. Plagiarism is a strange accusation in this case as not only was McDonald's dissertation published, making detection of such an action likely, but again Robinson helped McDonald publish it in the series Robinson had created. In addition, Robinson gave McDonald permission to publish a reconstruction of a building he was working on from Olynthus that Robinson himself had not yet published.[21] If there is some truth behind this charge, I have been unable to find it.

That leaves the curious case of George Hanfmann, the final person several anonymous reviewers claimed Robinson had plagiarized. Hanfmann is best known for his excavations at the site of Sardis in Turkey while he was a professor at Harvard University and the curator of ancient art at Harvard's Fogg Art Museum. First joining the faculty at Harvard in 1935, he spent his entire professional career there. Prior to his arrival in the United States, Hanfmann completed a dissertation on Etruscan art at the Friedrich-Wilhelms-Universität in Berlin in 1934. That same year, he fled Nazi antisemitic policies taking up an invitation from Robinson to come to Johns Hopkins and serve as the Charles A. W. Vogeler Fellow in Greek Archaeology for the academic year 1934 to 1935. During his brief tenure at Johns Hopkins, he completed a second PhD.[22] Although he appears to have been unable to visit Saloniki, where the artifacts from the Olynthus excavations were stored, Hanfmann used the excavation records and Robinson's own notes in order to write about the metal objects found at the site, the basis for his Johns Hopkins dissertation.[23]

An anonymous reviewer suggested that Robinson had compiled most of *Excavations at Olynthus X: Metal and Miscellaneous Finds* from Hanfmann's dissertation. I compared the text of *Excavations at Olynthus X* to a copy of Hanfmann's dissertation I obtained from the Johns Hopkins University archives to test the validity of this claim. While the subject matter is similar, the scope of each text is significantly different. Hanfmann's catalog of metal finds from Olynthus includes 565 entries describing artifacts found in the 1928, 1931, and 1934 seasons. Robinson's catalog includes 2,683 entries describing artifacts found in all four seasons of excavation. As Robinson's text contains almost five times the number of entries as Hanfmann's, Hanfmann clearly could not have written the majority of *Excavations at Olynthus X*. Nonetheless the catalog entries repeated in both documents are nearly identical, although more than half of the entries are quite short describing the numerous beads and arrowheads found at the site, sometimes listing only an inventory number and a length or diameter. Since Hanfmann had not actually seen the material or taken his own measurements, he had to have been copying this information straight out of the excavation notebooks, the same source Robinson used. This does not explain why the remaining two hundred or so longer catalog entries are nearly identical; Robinson must have copied them from Hanfmann's dissertation.[24] Robinson had little interest in Hanfmann's forty-nine–page synthesis and analysis of the metal objects, the only sections of the dissertation outside of the catalog that he used were the discussions Hanfmann wrote preceding and following groups of artifacts, explaining the categories into which he divided them.[25] After comparing every word in *Olynthus X* with Hanfmann's dissertation, I estimate that approximately 15 percent of Robinson's text was in fact written by Hanfmann with little or no modification. Robinson did not use Hanfmann's work without acknowledgment, however. The thank-you in the preface of the volume is worth quoting in full:

> In studying the metal objects I have been much helped by my former student, Dr. George Hanfmann, now instructor in Fine Arts at Harvard, and by Dr. Sarah Elizabeth Freeman, who has rendered invaluable service in preparing for the printer the manuscript and plates and who drew the new plan on Plate XLXXII, based on our excavation plan and that of Dr. Saul Weinberg.[26]

Note that Robinson failed to mention the existence of Hanfmann's dissertation, to which there is no reference in the entire work, and that Hanfmann must share his acknowledgment in the sentence with two others.

Does this example constitute plagiarism? Since this material comes from a dissertation, the simple answer is yes according to the standards of the time. Did Robinson see it as plagiarism? That question is, of course, unanswerable, but it is easy to see how he could have justified what he was doing. Hanfmann and Robinson were working from the same notebooks to write their texts, and Robinson did not use Hanfmann's analysis, which constituted his original thoughts but instead borrowed only his catalog entries and introductory paragraphs. Also, even though Robinson repeated enormous portions of Hanfmann's dissertation, so little of the finished text of volume X was Hanfmann's that Robinson may have felt his thank-you sufficient.

Hanfmann told people. After the first edition of this book came out, I heard from some of Hanfmann's students, one of whom, John Oleson, currently at the University of Victoria, gave me permission to quote his observations. He was a student of Hanfmann's at Harvard in 1969 and found Hanfmann to be always "a very nurturing and kind professor, to both men and women." Oleson was taken off guard, therefore, when the subject of Robinson came up and "Hanfmann spoke with a bitterness that was very much out of character for him." According to Oleson, "He stated that Robinson had published his dissertation (about metal finds at Olynthus) under his own name, with no credit to Hanfmann." Hanfmann felt he could do nothing, being a German-Jewish refugee dependent on often antisemitic academics in a country hostile to immigrants on the eve of war. Oleson says he felt "horrified and surprised" at Hanfmann's revelation and reaction.[27] Other students of Hanfmann have confided the same story to me.

I cannot help but wonder if this story percolated through the community of American archaeologists working in Greece for decades, remaining close to the original in some versions and mutating in others to change the extent of Robinson's ethical violations or main character of the story to Weinberg, Graham, or some of the other supposed victims the blind reviewers mentioned. Anyone who heard the story from Hanfmann would certainly have been struck by the subtitle Robinson chose for *Olynthus X: Metal and Miscellaneous Finds, An Original Contribution to Greek Life* since Hanfmann mentioned he had worked on the metal finds. Indeed, the astute student of the man needed only to look at the first volume of Mylonas's laudatory work celebrating Robinson on his seventieth birthday. The volume lists Robinson's publications in one section and just a few pages away all his graduate students with the titles of their theses and dissertations. The title listed for Hanfmann's dissertation is *Metal Objects from Olynthus*, a title so similar to that for *Olynthus X* that it seems to confirm the plagiarism charge. This may be the main source of the accusations that dogged Robinson's memory.

As I looked again at the anonymous reviewers' comments, I was taken aback by how the rumors of plagiarism still clung to Robinson's reputation a half century after his death. I was certain no one had ever heard of Ellingson and of the people the reviewers had cited, only one had a documentable claim to the charge of plagiarism, which did not seem to me to be a strong enough reason for this vague accusation to have continued to haunt his legacy. Might the rumors be right but pertain to other people the anonymous reviewers of my draft article had not mentioned? To find out, I tracked down the names of all graduate students who worked with Robinson at Olynthus and wrote theses or dissertations under him. Between my own research and the suggestions of the reviewers I had already explored the cases of ten of his former students,[28] and I found an additional eleven names of people who had worked with him at Olynthus. Of these, seven either wrote on subjects not related to Olynthus, about which Robinson did not publish either, or if they did, he helped them publish their work under their own names.[29] One had written a dissertation with a title similar to something Robinson had published but after comparing the two texts it seemed clear they were independent.[30] Of the remaining three, the titles of Frank Albright's thesis and dissertation indicate that they covered a topic about which Robinson also wrote; unfortunately a copy of neither the thesis nor the dissertation exists in the Johns Hopkins University archives, so it is impossible to compare the texts.[31] As for the two remaining graduate students, I discovered Robinson borrowed catalog entries from both just as he had from Hanfmann.

Eleanor B. Lay, who later married and became Eleanor Ross, wrote a dissertation from which Robinson plagiarized some catalog entries. Ross participated in the 1934 season at Olynthus when she was in charge of inventorying the terracotta figurines.[32] She used this inventory as the basis for writing her dissertation, which she completed in 1936. That same year Ross joined the faculty at Syracuse University as an instructor in Latin, a post she held for several more decades.[33] Some sixteen years after Ross completed her dissertation, Robinson published the terracotta figurines found in 1934 and 1938 in *Excavations at Olynthus XIV*, incorporating edited versions of some of her catalog entries; about 75 percent of the text remains unchanged. The chapter in which it appears is a combination of Ross's catalog entries and the synthesis and analysis from Ellingson's dissertation.[34] Robinson did not use any of Ross's analysis. In the introduction to *Excavations at Olynthus XIV*, Robinson offers Ross a general thank-you but never mentions using text from her dissertation.[35] This cutting and pasting explains an observation one reviewer made of *Excavations at Olynthus XIV* the year after it was published. Unbeknownst to the reviewer, or anyone else, Ellingson wrote the first chapter of the volume and half of the second covering the terracotta figurines, Ross wrote half of the second chapter on the figurines, and Robinson wrote the remaining chapters on the lamps and coins. The reviewer stated, "The three chief divisions of *Olynthus XIV* are totally different in character and treatment."[36] Naturally this seemed odd since only Robinson's name appeared on the cover; one would have expected more consistency from a single author.

The other woman whose catalog entries Robinson copied was named Christina B. Meredith, who took the name Vestling after she married. Vestling entered the graduate program in mathematics at Johns Hopkins in the fall of 1934. After her first year she came to the Department of Art and Archaeology and in 1937 completed her master's thesis on the finger rings found at Olynthus during the 1931 and 1934 excavation seasons.[37] She did not complete a dissertation at Johns Hopkins. Because she arrived at Johns Hopkins after the 1934 excavation season and left before the 1938 season, she did not excavate at Olynthus and her thesis was based on the excavation diaries, photographs, and inventories rather than observation of the material in the museum in Saloniki or in the field at Olynthus.[38] She appears to have left academia after marrying.

Robinson published the finger rings in *Excavations at Olynthus X*. To the forty-six rings discussed by Meredith Vestling, Robinson added twelve more found in the 1928 and 1938 seasons. As in the cases of Hanfmann's and Ross's dissertations, Robinson seems only to have been interested in Vestling's catalog entries, very little of her analysis and synthesis found its way into Robinson's introduction to the rings. Also like the other two dissertations, Robinson did some editing of the entries, leaving about 75 percent of the original text.[39] Curiously, Robinson failed to mention Vestling in the preface of *Excavations at Olynthus X* at all, and no reference to her or her thesis appears anywhere in the volume. Her name never appears in anything written about Olynthus.

After I had put in many months of research, the final tally for graduate students Robinson had plagiarized was four: Ellingson, Hanfmann, Ross, and Vestling. Still, Ellingson's case was different from the rest. Robinson had copied catalog entries from Hanfmann, Ross, and Vestling, as well as some transitional material from Hanfmann, and had integrated it into the text he was writing while according to the rules at Johns Hopkins and the wider practice among archaeologists at the time, he should not have been using material from other people's dissertations without permission and proper acknowledgment. Some subsequent anonymous reviewers of my draft article did not see this as plagiarism as they were only catalog entries. Those reviewers had a strictly legal point as copyright law in the United States does not allow someone to copyright a fact. Since catalog entries record facts about artifacts, laid out in a way that is standard in the field, no one can lay claim to a catalog of archaeological artifacts as their private intellectual property. Robinson's use of those words did not constitute legal plagiarism.[40] In the case of Ellingson, however, Robinson claimed more than just the catalogs of terracotta figurines as his own. He edited her entire master's thesis very lightly and then published it as a single, unified volume including all her analysis as well as her catalog entries. He also took large sections of her dissertation, both the catalog and analysis, and published them as one complete chapter and the half of another. In no other case did he lift so much text from one source, and in no other case did he use the original author's analysis. Even by the yardstick of Robinson's own behavior, his plagiarism of Ellingson was shocking.

Why Robinson failed to give these four people proper credit will remain a mystery. It might be that he wanted the prestige of being a prolific author and simply took a shortcut to get there. Ellingson, Ross, and Vestling all married, which at the time was understood to mean their academic careers were over.[41] Precious few women were able to manage an academic archaeological career and marriage; the majority of successful professional female scholars either never married or faced a high rate of divorce.[42] Marrying and leaving the field left their academic work unpublished and forgotten and thus ripe, it appears in Robinson's mind at least, for appropriation. Why Robinson did not give Hanfmann more credit is a particularly curious question since Hanfmann was already well on his way into a promising career when Robinson published his work. It would have enhanced Robinson's status if he had put Hanfmann's name on the cover of an *Excavations at Olynthus* volume as a contributor as he had done with other of his former students; he could have appeared to be the generous patron helping his younger protégé.

The anonymous reviewers of the draft article had given me some useful ideas. Excited by these new discoveries, I wrote a completely new article. The next editor to whom I submitted it did not bother to send it to anonymous reviewers; she rejected it on sight, without offering a specific reason.

Lack of Context

I worked up a lecture on Ellingson's adventures at Olynthus and Robinson's plagiarism for a popular audience and tried it out around Evansville at any venue I could find. People who knew Ellingson would approach me, astonished by what they had learned. She had rarely spoken of her life before she arrived in Evansville. Their interest gave me the idea of writing an article for a popular magazine about Ellingson's time at Olynthus including quotes from her letters and photos from her album. Maybe it was too hard to publish a scholarly article about plagiarism, surely a popular article would do better. I wrote her story and sent it to the editor of a popular archaeology magazine. He never wrote back.

My frequently reworked scholarly article, titled "Who Wrote the *Excavations at Olynthus* Volumes?" fared little better. I felt that I was making progress when I received a rejection letter *after* the editor had sent it to the reviewers. That editor was kind enough to send me the anonymous reviewers' comments, which complained about a lack of social context for the story. It was a highly useful critique. Much of the material in the earlier chapters of this book was missing from that scholarly article. I found it difficult to explain Ellingson's full story and Robinson's plagiarism with enough background material in the limited number of words available for an article. I reworked the draft again from top to bottom and sent it off hopefully to another journal. Another rejection followed; I was not getting the balance right. "Publish or perish." My tenure review was not far off, so I had to focus on other work I knew I could publish. I returned to rework the Ellingson article in stolen moments I could find between teaching classes, grading assignments, writing up my Roman streets research for publication as articles, and, eventually, a book. Time began to slip by; the Ellingson story remained on my mind even if I was finding less and less time to work on the article.

No Story Here

My work on Roman streets was starting to gain some attention. The Archaeological Institute of America (AIA) contacted me about participating in their lecture program. The AIA has more than one hundred chapters in cities across North America as well as a few abroad. Every year they choose archaeologists doing interesting work who are good public speakers to join the ranks of their lecturers. Being an AIA lecturer is by invitation only and being asked to participate is a great honor. Speakers write abstracts for a couple of lectures. The AIA informs chapter presidents whom they will be sending and when, and makes the abstracts available to them. I wrote three abstracts. One was for a lecture about work I had done at a Roman site in Spain. Another was about my work on Roman streets focusing on the site of Pompeii, which is always a crowd-pleaser. The last was based on Ellingson's story. Presidents of the chapters I was being sent to all chose the Ellingson lecture. Audiences at all of the lectures, and at the AIA chapters where I gave this lecture the next year when I was invited back to the program, were supportive and enthusiastic. At one stop some in the audience members remained for an hour after the completion of the lecture to ask questions and discuss the implications of all they had heard. Clearly the lack of interest from journal editors was not shared by a broader audience.

So far, reasons for rejecting the article had been that I had not found everyone Robinson plagiarized and that the article lacked context. I was able to address the first critique successfully but continued to struggle with the second. A third criticism that emerged from subsequent rejections was that there was no story here; it just did not matter. According to the reasoning of some editors and anonymous reviewers, what Robinson did represented the standard behavior at that time; he did nothing wrong. Other reviewers and editors argued the opposite; Robinson was an outlier whom everyone knows was a rogue. Regardless of the reason, the conclusion was the same that there was nothing in the article that was new. Of course there is an obvious counterargument to each of these reasons for rejecting the article. If archaeologists of previous generations commonly plagiarized their graduate students, and now that behavior is considered unacceptable, we are obligated to document the shift in our own intellectual culture so that future generations will have a better understanding of how the interpretations of archaeological data produced in the past, many of which are still considered valid today, developed. As for the opposite reason for rejecting the article, that only Robinson plagiarized his students, again that is worth documenting for the exact same reason.

While editors provided these explanations as to why they did not want to publish the article, I suspect there was another implicit reason for their decisions of which they were not aware. The ripple effect of tunnel vision combined with systemic sexism from the 1930s still influences how we understand and write about excavations from that time period, focusing on the one man who directed the excavation and forgetting about the other contributors, especially the women. Even though the publication of every archaeological project is a group effort, involving the dedicated energy of many people, in Robinson's day it was common to include only the name of one man, or occasionally two men, on the cover page. If one were to ask who excavated Olynthus to any classical archaeologist today, the reply would be "Robinson." Given a moment to reflect, that person might follow up with "Graham." It is unlikely the queried individual would mention Weinberg, Freeman, or Ellingson as their names do not appear on the cover of any of the Olynthus volumes. In nineteenth and twentieth century archaeology, women often played a vital role but their contributions, if they are mentioned, are dismissed as supportive since they did not write grand syntheses nor add their names as authors to books. To find the feminine footprint in our history, we have to look harder since, like Ellingson, women often did not have the same career trajectories as men. Writing about women in North

American archaeology, archaeologist and historian Dena Dincauze makes a statement equally true of the women in classical archaeology:

> The routes to powerful positions within the profession are the same as they have always been; those routes have not traditionally been the paths women trod. Whether on account of training, personal predilection, or the obstacles of discrimination, women conventionally took other ways, ways that led to some personal fulfillment but less often to professional recognition. Such choices are part of the diversity of women's experiences in archaeology, today as well as in the past.[43]

Margaret Root, another archaeologist who has written on the history of women in the field, points out the consequences of ignoring people like Ellingson who participated in the field but did not follow the career path of her male counterparts:

> It is an unintended, but no less unfortunate, disservice to denigrate this type of archaeological achievement because it has been tainted by association with the limitations imposed by society upon the female sex—in effect a form of double prejudice. Far better to acknowledge and deplore the factors that have led to the channeling of many women's efforts into certain areas of research and scholarly production and then to dignify their work with energetic critical assessment.[44]

The next editor did not find Root's argument persuasive, even though I mentioned it in my proposal. She sent me a very polite note rejecting the article because she did not believe her readers would find the story very interesting, a statement I have no doubt she truly believed.

Unwritten History

There was one final common thread that ran through many of the letters and anonymous reviews I received that was much more disturbing than any of the previously mentioned reasons for the rejection of the draft article. American classical archaeology has an extremely strong strain of conservatism, especially in Greek archaeology. Part of this conservatism is the understanding that one does not criticize those who came before. Robinson stated this clearly to Graham nearly seventy years ago[45] and it still remains true today. Stephen Dyson blames the system whereby any American who wants credibility as, and the opportunity to become, a Greek archaeologist must attend the American School and participate in its excavations at Corinth or in the

Athenian Agora, a system that creates and feeds this conservatism. Dyson compares Greek archaeology to the work of a famed American anthropological archaeologist, stating, "Time spent at the American excavations at Corinth is more likely to encourage the development of an archaeological Confucius devoted to the word of the ancestors rather than a classical Lewis Binford, willing to challenge received tradition."[46]

Resistance to sharing Ellingson's story did not come from editors and anonymous reviewers alone. While on the road doing lectures for the AIA, I spoke at a university where one of Robinson's students had taught. Although that person had passed away long before I spoke there, several people who had trained under this person were now teaching and conducting research there and they remembered hearing stories about Robinson and Olynthus. Intense discussion followed my lecture. Many in the audience believed this was an important story that needed to be told since it offered a new view of how the Olynthus project was completed and shone a light on the role of women in classical archaeology in the 1930s. Those who had heard stories of Olynthus from their mentor disagreed and argued I should not be delivering this lecture. They saw me as embarrassing classical archaeology in general, and Robinson in particular, when none of it mattered any more as all the participants were gone and Ellingson had never gone on to make a name for herself in the field.

Journal editors and anonymous reviewers continued to reject the article while I met with intense interest in Ellingson's tale on the lecture circuit. By this time I had written several completely different versions of the article, incorporating suggestions from a number of anonymous reviewers, to no avail. Not a single editor even encouraged me to rework it and resubmit the article. In frustration I turned to a mentor of mine from graduate school, a senior scholar who understood these matters better than I. He warned me to stop trying to publish this story until I had tenure at my university. He explained that while the conservative bent of American classical archaeology was powerful, there was another issue. Robinson had helped such a large number of students through graduate school and many were now senior scholars holding positions of editors and peer reviewers at journals and publishing houses in North America. If I was able to publish Ellingson's story and angered them by embarrassing their former teacher, they might try to block publication of anything else I wrote in the future. "Publish or perish." Being unable to publish could kill the career of an untenured faculty member and even cost him or her a job. I thought long and hard about what he had said. I had a great deal of respect for him but found it hard to believe there could be such a far-reaching conspiracy of silence organized by the people who wrote the forty-one theses and seventy-four dissertations Robinson had supervised.

I started again to write another version of the Ellingson-Robinson story with a blank computer screen. Again I reread the comments from all the anonymous reviewers and editors who had rejected my past efforts and tried to address their concerns. When it was done, I sent it to a journal published outside of North America. It was rejected. One of the anonymous reviewers was adamant the editor not publish the article. The reviewer's comments did not fault the article's research, arguments, or writing. Instead he or she wrote,

[W]hat you are dealing with here is part of the unwritten history of classical archaeology. Best to leave it unwritten.

That was the final verdict, no one would publish the article. Eleven editors and more than two dozen peer reviewers had decided the story should not be told. What Robinson did to Ellingson would remain a secret. I was angry, disappointed, and bewildered. It was not the loss of my investment of time and money that hurt the most, it was the fact that even though she was long dead at this point, we were making her a victim once again. We were no better than Robinson—the journal editorial staff for covering up for him and me for reaching a breaking point and giving up on getting the word out. I gathered all Ellingson's photos, letters, and news clippings; placed them back on the storage shelf where I had found them; and covered them with office supplies. Maybe at some point in the future when classical archaeologists were ready to hear the story someone else would want to escape grading student papers and stumble across the collection. In the meantime, I would try to forget it was there.

Notes

1. J. Walter Graham, "Lamps from Olynthus, 1931," in *Excavations at Olynthus V: Mosaics, Vases, and Lamps of Olynthus Found in 1928 and 1931*, edited by David M. Robinson (Baltimore, MD: Johns Hopkins University Press, 1933), 265–84.

2. For a summary of Graham's career and of the relationship between Robinson and Graham, see chapter 4.

3. Joseph W. Shaw, "James Walter Graham 1906–1991," *American Journal of Archaeology* 96, no. 2 (1992): 325.

4. Paul A. Clement, "Review of *Excavations at Olynthus, Part VIII: The Hellenic House, a Study of the Houses Found at Olynthus with a Detailed Account of Those Excavated in 1931 and 1934*, by David M. Robinson and J. Walter Graham," *L'Antiquité Classique* 8 (1939): 474.

5. David M. Robinson, "Mosaics from Olynthus," *American Journal of Archaeology* 36, no. 1 (1932): 16 no. 2.

6. David M. Robinson, *Excavations at Olynthus V: Mosaics, Vases, and Lamps of Olynthus Found in 1928 and 1931* (Baltimore: Johns Hopkins University Press, 1933), xi.

7. Robinson, *Excavations at Olynthus V*, xi.

8. See chapter 6.

9. See chapter 4 for quotes from their letters on the matter of her dissertation.

10. Paul A. Clement Jr., *Thessalian Cults* (PhD diss., Johns Hopkins University, 1930).

11. David M. Robinson, "The Third Campaign at Olynthus," *American Journal of Archaeology* 39, no. 2 (1935): 210, no. 1.

12. David M. Robinson and Paul A. Clement, *Excavations at Olynthus IX: The Chalcidic Mint and the Excavation Coins Found in 1928–1934*. Johns Hopkins University Studies in Archaeology 26 (Baltimore, MD: Johns Hopkins University Press, 1938).

13. See chapter 4.

14. William A. McDonald and George R. Rapp Jr. (eds.), *The Minnesota Messenia Expedition: Reconstructing a Bronze Age Regional Environment* (Minneapolis: University of Minnesota Press, 1972).

15. Stephen L. Dyson, *Ancient Marbles to American Shores: Classical Archaeology in the United States* (Philadelphia: University of Pennsylvania Press, 1998), 248.

16. David M. Robinson and George E. Mylonas, "The Fourth Campaign at Olynthus," *American Journal of Archaeology* 43, no. 1 (1939): 48.

17. William A. McDonald, *The Political Meeting Places of the Greeks* (PhD diss., Johns Hopkins University, 1940).

18. William A. McDonald, *The Political Meeting Places of the Greeks*. Johns Hopkins University Studies in Archaeology 34 (Baltimore, MD: Johns Hopkins University Press, 1943).

19. McDonald, *The Political Meeting Places of the Greeks*, viii.

20. David M. Robinson, "Prähistorische und Griechische Häuser," in *Realencyclopädia der Classischen Altertumswissenschaft*, Supplementband 7, edited by August Pauly and Georg Wissowa, 224–78 (Stuttgart: E. B. Metzler, 1938).

21. McDonald, *The Political Meeting Places of the Greeks*, vi.

22. George M. A. Hanfmann, *Metal Objects from Olynthus* (PhD diss., Johns Hopkins University, 1935), 218; David G. Mitten, "George Maxim Anossov Hanfmann, 1911–1986," *American Journal of Archaeology* 91, no. 2 (1987): 259; Stephen L. Dyson, *Ancient Marbles*, 225–26 and 234.

23. Hanfmann, *Metal Objects from Olynthus*, 219; Mitten, "George Maxim Anossov Hanfmann, 1911–1986," 260; George Mylonas (ed.), *Studies Presented to David Moore Robinson on His Seventieth Birthday*. Vol. 1 (St. Louis, MO: Washington University, 1951), xviii.

24. As a fairly typical example, the entries below are for the same bronze piece and share about 85 percent of the text. The first is a direct quote from Hanfmann, *Metal Objects from Olynthus*, 100–101:

Incised Bronze Work Piece:
A. 375, pl. 109.
H. 0.055 m., W. 0.035 m.

This is an extremely intricate and brilliant piece of incising. It has to be examined from all sides in order to bring out everything that the artist has represented. There were certainly four palmettes, one at each side of the object. Fragments of two of them are preserved. Two vertically standing spirals support one palmette on each side. If viewed on the longer axis we see two calices reversed, resting on spirals, with palmettes which point in opposite directions. Later sixth century B.C.

Such intricate designs are generally archaic although they could survive for a considerable period.[1] Similar are especially compositions prevalent in Ionic schools, and the single parts of this ornament also argue for an Ionic origin,[2] although it must be admitted that Attic artists of the sixth century were equally fond of such designs.[3] It may be of interest to observe similar designs also on Chalcidic vases, since there are few possible other connections between Chalcis and Olynthus in art.[4]

1. Cf. Jacobsthal, *Ornamente griechischer Vasen*, 1929, pls. 10, c; 24, c; 137, a. Survival: pl. 132.
2. Cf. Jacobsthal, *op. cit.*, pls. 22, b; 24; 35; 39.; Ducati *Pontische Vasen*, pl. 3.
3. Jacobsthal, *op. cit.*, pls. 28, 30, 39.
4. Pfuhl, fig. 161; Rumpf, *op. cit.* pl. XII, XLV XLVIII, LVII f, LXVI f

Compare the text of Hanfmann's entry to the following quote from David M. Robinson, *Excavations at Olynthus X: Metal and Minor Miscellaneous Finds, an Original Contribution to Greek Life. Johns Hopkins University Studies in Archaeology* 31 (Baltimore, MD: Johns Hopkins University Press, 1941), 41:

Pl. V. 22. Inv. 28.375. Bronze piece with incised decoration. H. 0.055 m., W. 0.035 m. Broken.

This is an extremely intricate and brilliant piece of incising. It has to be examined from all sides in order to bring out everything that the artist has represented. There were certainly four palmettes, one at each side of the object. Fragments of two of them are preserved. Two vertically standing spirals support one palmette on each side. If viewed on the longer axis we see two calices, reversed, resting on spirals with palmettes which point in opposite directions. From the South Hill, Apotheke G 7.[192]

Such intricate designs are generally archaic, although they could survive for a considerable period.[193] Especially similar are compositions prevalent in Ionic schools, and the single parts of this ornament also argue for an Ionic origin,[194] although it must be admitted that Attic artists of the sixth century were equally fond of such designs.[195] It may be of interest to observe similar designs which also occur on Chalcidic vases, since there are only a few other possible connections between Chalcis and Olynthus in art. 196 This piece is to be dated in the late sixth century B.C.

192. Cf. *Olynthus*, II, p. 27.

193. Cf. Jacobsthal, *Ornamente griechischer Vasen*, 1927, Pls. 10 c; 24 c; 137 a. Survival: Pl. 132.

194. Cf. Jacobsthal, *op. cit.*, Pls. 22 b; 24; 35; 39. Also Ducati *Pontische Vasen*, Pl. 3.

195. Cf. Jacobsthal, *op. cit.*, Pls. 28, 29, 30.

196. Pfuhl, *Malerie und Zeichnung der Griechen*, Fig. 161; Rumpf, *Chalkidische Vasen* Pls. XII, XLV, XLVIII, LVII f., LXVI ff.

25. Compare the following two quotes. The first quote is from George M. A. Hanfmann, *Metal Objects from Olynthus*, 140:

> The Olynthian earrings show a variety which is especially surprising in view of the comparative monotony existing among the other ornaments. Eighteen varieties are represented, which may however be divided into seven main groups according to their shape. The material is usually bronze but silver earrings occurred in three graves.

The second quote is from Robinson, *Excavations at Olynthus X*, 79:

> The Olynthian earrings show a variety which is especially surprising in view of the comparative monotony existing among the other ornaments. Eighteen varieties are represented, which may, however, be divided into seven main groups according to their shape. The material is usually bronze but silver earrings occurred in three graves.

26. Robinson, *Excavations at Olynthus* X, x–xi.

27. John Oleson, personal communication, June 29, 2022.

28. Mary Ross Ellingson, Gladys Davidson Weinberg, Sarah Freeman, George Mylonas, Alexander Schulz, Arthur Parsons, J. Walter Graham, Paul Clement, William McDonald, and George Hanfmann.

29. John A. Alexander, "Potidaea" (PhD diss., Johns Hopkins University, 1939), later published as *Potidaea* (Athens: University of Georgia Press, 1963). Herbert N. Couch, "Sources for the Study of Sardis" (MA thesis, Johns Hopkins University, 1926) and "Treasuries of the Greeks and Romans" (PhD diss., Johns Hopkins University, 1927) later published as *Treasuries of the Greeks and Romans* (Menasha, WI: George Banta Co., 1929). John R. Craft, "The City Drainage at Olynthus" (MA thesis, Johns Hopkins University, 1939) and "The Civic Water Supply of Ancient Greece" (PhD diss., Johns Hopkins University, 1940). Mabel Gude, "A History of Olynthus" (PhD diss., Johns Hopkins University, 1930), later published as *A History of Olynthus, with a Prosopographia and Testimonia. Johns Hopkins University Studies in Archaeology* 17 (Baltimore, MD: Johns Hopkins University Press, 1933). Mary W. McGehee, "Replicas of Scenes on Attic Red-figured Vases" (MA thesis, Johns Hopkins University, 1926) and "Replica Scenes of Attic Red-figured Vases" (PhD diss., Johns Hopkins University, 1932). Eunice B. Stebbins, "The Letters of Augustus Preserved in Greek Inscriptions and in the Greek Writers" (MA thesis, Johns Hopkins University, 1926); "The Dolphin in the Literature and Art of Greece and Rome, Including Pre-Hellenic Civilizations" (PhD diss., Johns Hopkins University,

1927), published as *The Dolphin in the Literature and Art of Greece and Rome, Including Pre-Hellenic Civilizations* (Menasha, WI: George Banta, 1929). Lillian M. Wilson, "A Study of the Roman Toga" (PhD diss., Johns Hopkins University, 1924); *The Roman Toga, Johns Hopkins University Studies in Archaeology* 1 (Baltimore, MD: Johns Hopkins University Press, 1924); "The Loom Weights," in *Excavations at Olynthus II Architecture and Sculpture: House and Other Buildings* edited by D. M. Robinson, 118–28. *Johns Hopkins University Studies in Archaeology* 9 (Baltimore, MD: Johns Hopkins University Press, 1930).

30. Saul S. Weinberg, *The Prehistoric House of the Mainland of Greece* (PhD diss., Johns Hopkins University, 1936) and David M. Robinson, "Prähistorische und Griechische Häuser" published in 1938.

31. The thesis is Frank P. Albright, *Red Figured Vases of Olynthus Found in 1934* (MA thesis, Johns Hopkins University, 1936); Robinson published on this subject in *Excavations at Olynthus XIII: Vases Found in 1934 and 1938. Johns Hopkins University Studies in Archaeology* 38 (Baltimore, MD: Johns Hopkins University Press, 1950). Robinson acknowledges Albright in the preface but fails to mention his thesis. Albright's dissertation was "Funeral Customs of the Greeks" (PhD diss., Johns Hopkins University, 1940), parts of which seem to have wound up in Robinson's *Excavations at Olynthus XI: Necrolynthia, a Study of Greek Burial Customs and Anthropology, Johns Hopkins University Studies in Archaeology* 32 (Baltimore, MD: Johns Hopkins University Press, 1942) on which Albright is listed as a contributor.

32. Robinson, "The Third Campaign at Olynthus," 210, no. 1.

33. George Mylonas, "Biographical Sketch," in *Studies Presented to David Moore Robinson on His Seventieth Birthday.* Vol. 1, edited by Geroge Mylonas (St. Louis, MO: Washington University, 1951), xviii.

34. For example, compare the description each wrote of the same figurine. The following quote is from Eleanor B. Lay, "Terra-cottas Found at Olynthus in 1934" (PhD diss., Johns Hopkins University, 1936), 34–35:

No. 28. Inv. 121. Female mask. House A V 9, *b*, at a depth of 1.25 m. Ht. 0.187. W. 0.139. Th. 0.055. Complete except for large fragment at right base of mask and small fragment at right base of neck of figure. Coarse bluish grey clay shading to yellowish buff with numerous fine particles of mica. White slip. Blue paint on stephane and veil. Red paint on hair and eyes. Blue paint on under garment. Buff incrustation. Two holes in top for suspension.

The hair, parted in the center, is drawn to either side in fine small but distinct waves and falls to the shoulders in heavy rope-like curls. On the head is worn a stephane adorned with a palmette design and a veil descends to the shoulders and along the outer edge, widening out in a graceful curve at the shoulders and again becoming narrower as it follows the line of the upper arm to the base of the mask. The features are typically archaic, the eyes wide set, the nose long, the mouth small and placed close beneath the nose, the lips thick and protruding, the chin firm. The garment, probably a chiton, is especially indicated by the V at the neck. The upper arms are held close to the body.

At the elbow the arms are bent sharply and the hand are held over the breast, the left somewhat higher than the right. Type of the fifth century.[1]

1. Cf. OL. IV, no. 278; OL. VII, nos. 35, 383. For palmette design compare OL. IV, nos. 297–8, 410; Pottier, *Diphilos et Les Modeleurs de T. C. Grecques*, no. 203, pl. X.

Compare with this quote from David M. Robinson, *Excavations at Olynthus XIV: Terracottas, Lamps, and Coins Found in 1934 and 1938* (Baltimore, MD: Johns Hopkins University Press, 1952), 89:

30. Female mask. Inv. 34.121. From House A v 9, room *b* (*Olynthus*, VIII, pp. 96–97). H. 0.187 m. W. 0.139 m. Th. 0.055 m. Coarse bluish gray clay, shading to yellowish buff, with numerous fine particles of mica. White slip; blue paint on stephane, veil and under-garment; red paint on hair and eyes. Buff incrustation. Complete except for a large fragment at the right of the base of the mask and a small fragment at the right base of the neck of the figure. Two holes in top for suspension.

The hair, parted in the middle, is drawn to either side in fine, distinct, but small waves and falls to the shoulders in heavy rope-like curls. On the head the stephane is adorned with a palmette and rosette design as in the Cybele mould (cf. *Olynthus*, IV, 410). A veil descends to the shoulders and along the outer edge, widening in a graceful curve at the shoulders and again becoming narrower as it follows the line of the upper arm to the base of the mask. The features are typically archaic; the eyes wide set, the nose long, the mouth small and placed close beneath the nose, the lips thick and protruding, the chin firm. The garment, probably a chiton, is indicated by the V at the neck. The upper arms are held close to the body; at the elbow the arms are bent sharply and and [sic] the hand are held over the breasts, which are far apart as in early Greek art (e.g. the "Ludovisi Throne"), the left somewhat higher than the right. From the same mould as nos. 28 and 46. Cf. Olynthus, IV, 278, 284, and VII, 383; Pottier, *Diphilos et les Modeleurs de terres cuites grecques*, pl. X, 197, 203. Now in the D. M. Robinson Collection, Special Collections, University of Mississippi Libraries.

Fifth Century B.C.

35. From David M. Robinson, *Excavations at Olynthus XIV*, vii: "I thank especially my former students and members of my staff, Mary Ross (now Mrs. R. C. Ellingson of Evansville, Ind.), Eleanor Lay (now Mrs. Arthur Ross of Syracuse, New York), and I owe much to my deceased daughter (Mrs. Wilson)."

36. R. C. Wood, "Review of *Excavations at Olynthus: Part XIV, Terracottas, Lamps and Coins Found in 1934 and 1938* by D. M. Robinson," *American Journal of Archaeology* 57, no. 3 (1953): 227.

37. Christina B. Meredith, "The Finger Rings Found at Olynthus in 1931 and 1934" (MA thesis, Johns Hopkins University, 1937), 50.

38. Meredith, "The Finger Rings Found at Olynthus," 3–4.

39. The following quote from Meredith, "The Finger Rings Found at Olynthus," 29:

No. 12. Inv. 686. Location unknown. Diary reference unknown. For photograph see Plate 64.1931. Bronze ring with pointed oval bezel. Complete. L. of bezel 0.01 m. W. of bezel 0.008 m. D. of band 0.02 m.

Design at right angles to the band. Bezel very worn. Cock to the left. The feathers are done in long fine lines. The legs do not show. Compare the treatment of the dog on no. 29. The cock on no. 32 is quite different. Our cock, unlike the usual representations, has feathers all over his body and not merely on the wings and tail. This cock belongs to the less elongated Corinthian breed.[1] For a similar treatment of birds see the Mycenaean sardonyx from Vaphio[2] and the silver coin of the early fifth century from Himera.[3]

First half of fourth century B.C.
1. Cf. *Morin-Jean*, pp. 112–114, Figs. 124–127 for various breeds of cocks.
2. *Furtwängler* I–II, Plate III, No. 54; Εφ. Αρχ. 1889, Taf. 10, No. 19.
3. MacDonald, *Greek Coins in the Hunterian Collection* I, Plate XIII, No. 17.

The following quote is from David M. Robinson, *Excavations at Olynthus X*, 151:

Pl. XXVII. 477. Inv. 31.686. Bronze finger-ring. Same type as preceding. Pointed oval bezel. L. of bezel 0.01 m., W. of bezel 0.008 m., Dm. of band 0.02 m. The design would have been right side up when worn. It represents a cock to the left. The feathers are done in long fine lines. The legs do not show. Compare the treatment of the dog on no. 464. The cock on no. 467 is quite different. This cock, unlike the usual representations, has feathers all over his body and not merely on the wings and tail. He belongs to the less elongated Corinthian breed.[305]
Exact provenience unknown. First half of fourth century B.C.
305. Cf. Morin-Jean, *Le Dessin des Animaux en Grèce d'après les Vases Peints*, pp. 112–114, Figs. 124–127 for various breeds of cocks.

40. I am indebted to Steven Holzer, a retired contract law attorney, for alerting me to this quirk of United States copyright law.
41. See chapter 5.
42. Susan H. Allen, "The Archaeology of the AIA: An Introduction," in *Excavating Our Past: Perspectives on the History of the Archaeological Institute of America*, Colloquia and Conference Papers 5, edited by Susan H. Allen (Boston: Archaeological Institute of America, 2002), 18.
43. Dena F. Dincauze, "Exploring Career Styles in Archaeology," in *Rediscovering Our Past: Essays on the History of American Archaeology*, edited by Jonathan E. Reyman (Aldershot: Avebury, 1992): 136.
44. Margaret C. Root, "Introduction: Women of the Field, Defining the Gendered Experience," in *Breaking Ground: Pioneering Women Archaeologists*, edited by Getzel M. Cohen and Martha S. Joukowsky (Ann Arbor: University of Michigan Press, 2004), 13.
45. "It is generally considered bad etiquette for a student to review or criticize the work of his own chief." Letter from Robinson to Graham, October 30, 1947, Graham folder, Box 6, David M. Robinson Collection, Special Collections, University of Mississippi Libraries. A copy is on file at the University of Evansville archives.
46. Dyson, *Ancient Marbles to American Shores*, 86.

~

Epilogue

I never did publish an article about Mary Ellingson and David Robinson. I published a book. And then things got crazy. How the secret of Ellingson and her archaeological accomplishments went from literally being buried under pens and notepads to a petition to the Library of Congress is as unlikely as just about anything described in this book so far. That journey came about thanks to the heroic efforts of people inspired by Ellingson and who felt driven to see justice done and that journey is not the one I could have expected after experiencing so much rejection. Once I had returned the photo album, letters, and casts to the shelf where I had found them, I hoped I would forget they were there. Fortunately, each day as I passed the shelf on my way to my office, I could not help but be reminded of the secret so few people knew. While it would take years, the eventual first step in restarting this publication project and the restoration of Ellingson's words to her began with a tree. A dead tree.

Resurrection

Years ago, when a faculty member at the University of Evansville retired, the tradition was to plant a tree on campus to honor that person's service to the institution and its students. Back when I had first discovered Ellingson's photo album, I had also read the program for Ellingson's tree-planting ceremony, which remained among her papers. I was quite startled when I read the location of her tree. In fact, I was so surprised, I immediately went in search of it and its tiny plaque commemorating the retired professor (see figure E.1). Her tree was not fifty feet from my Tin City excavation trench. Tin City is the name of a former student-family housing complex used on the University of Evansville campus between 1946 and 1961. The thirteen surplus military barracks that made up Tin City were reserved for World War II and Korean War student-veterans who had families. As part of a class in which I teach aspiring archaeologists the techniques of the trade, I had begun an excavation at the Tin City site. Without knowing it, I had chosen a location for our trench that Ellingson's tree overlooked. The coincidence was immensely satisfying at the time I discovered it. I could almost see Ellingson's spirit embodied in that tree, watching over and guiding a new generation of eager, young archaeologists. Nearly 80 percent of the archaeology majors at the University of Evansville are female. As they graduate and enter the field, they are remaking the discipline. I cannot imagine what Ellingson would have thought of this change. Sometimes during the Tin City class period when all my students were contentedly scraping the dirt away layer by layer from their units, I would wander over to the tree and reread the plaque attached to it, seeking the strength to rework and resubmit the article about

Figure E.1.   New plaque beside Mary Ross Ellingson's replacement tree on the University of Evansville campus.
Photo by the author

Ellingson one more time. The summer after I gave up the idea of publishing the tale and put away the photo album, the tree died. The tree's death felt too real to be a mere metaphor.

The years passed and I moved onto projects other than Ellingson's until I received an email from her oldest daughter. Barbara Petersen had heard about one of the lectures I had given telling her mother's story and wanted to express her pleasure at seeing her mother's work and memory being kept alive. Guilt is a powerful motivator. I picked up the phone and called the groundskeepers to see if it was possible to replace Ellingson's dead tree and now-missing plaque; I even offered to pay whatever it would cost. After hanging up the phone, I got the photo album back down from the shelf for the first time in years and flipped through its pages. An idea began to form in my mind; perhaps my mistake had been trying to contain such a large and complicated story within the confines of a brief article; maybe Ellingson's story was big enough to be a book.

Clearly, my fellow classical archaeologists found this narrative to be so edgy or so insignificant that it did not deserve to appear in print, which meant finding a publisher was going to be tricky. I spent months searching for an editor who embraced rather than rejected edgy and controversial archaeological research finally finding one at Rowman and Littlefield. After putting together a proposal with some sample chapters, I sent it off with fingers crossed. What I could not have known was that the editor to whom I addressed the proposal had just left the company for a new job. The envelope landed on the desk of a newly appointed assistant editor. Andrea O. Kendrick had just been promoted from the manufacturing to the editorial side of the company. Until the editor she was supposed to be working for could be hired, she was told to answer the phone, open the mail, and pass along any promising proposals to another editor. No one defined "promising" for her. When she saw the envelope, she recognized the logo of the University of Evansville. Kendrick graduated from the University of Evansville just four years earlier with a degree in archaeology and gender and women's studies, and had taken several of my courses. A book on both archaeology and women's studies, which uncovered a scandal, and which was authored by her former professor looked promising to her. She passed this proposal along to another editor, who was not impressed. Publishers want books that easily fit into one category or genre, the editor helping Kendrick could not determine how they could market a book that cut across categories. As the proposal was originally written, it was hard to determine if it was archaeology, women's studies, biography, history, or something else. Still, he could see how strongly Kendrick felt about this, so he worked with her to create a pitch for the Rowman and Littlefield editorial board. The editorial board members appeared both bemused to have a newly-promoted junior editor pitching a book to them and skeptical about how they might market the book. Nonetheless, Kendrick's determination won them over, and they authorized her to move forward, offering guidance about how to work with an author to create a product they could sell. Eventually, Rowman and Littlefield hired an editor who would be Kendrick's supervisor. By that time, the project was so far along that her new boss allowed Kendrick to continue to lead all facets of the publication and marketing process through to completion. It was the first book Kendrick took from proposal to store shelves. Today on one wall of her house Kendrick has her framed college diploma next to a poster advertising the first edition of this book, her two most proud accomplishments so far.[1]

Once the book came out, so did the reviews. One of the early reviewers, Vanderbilt University classicist Kathy Gaca, did something unexpected when she wrote for the *Bryn Mawr Classical Review* in 2015, she demanded action. In the review she stated, "Given the strength of Kaiser's case, Johns Hopkins University Press and Johns Hopkins University should acknowledge Mary Ross Ellingson as the author of the volume and chapter in question." The reason Gaca was insistent on Johns Hopkins University Press in particular acknowledging Ellingson is because they hold the copyright for all fourteen volumes of the *Excavations of Olynthus* series. For reasons never made explicit, but which I suspect had to do with who was paying to publish the volumes, David Robinson allowed the Press to hold the legal copyright. Although Robinson is most associated with those fourteen volumes, he did not actually own the intellectual property contained inside them. Johns Hopkins University Press renewed the copyright on the volumes in the 1980s and so remains the legal owner of the material.[2] Gaca was the first reviewer, but not the last, to call on Johns Hopkins University Press to take responsibility for undoing Robinson's deception. Fans of the book also wrote to me stating they had written Johns Hopkins to act. No response was forthcoming from the Press.

The years went by, and eventually Rowman and Littlefield contacted me about writing this revised edition of the book. The idea prompted me to enquire with Johns Hopkins University Press about any response they might have to the calls of Gaca and others. My query wound up on the desk of a perplexed editorial director, Greg Britton. Britton had never heard of Ellingson or Gaca, knew nothing about the scandal, and was aware of no mail from the general public demanding the Press deal with this matter. Once he had verified the plagiarism accusations, he agreed that it was the responsibility of Johns Hopkins University Press to do something. The question became what accountability and restitution might look like. Robinson and Ellingson were long dead. The publication of site reports does not make money, normally the cost of publication is underwritten by grants and donations, so there was no monetary claim possible. The works are long out of print and the Press has no plans to reissue them, so changing the name of the author of *Olynthus VII* on the cover page is not possible, nor adding Ellingson's name as a contributor to *Olynthus XIV*. The only option that seemed to remain lay with the Library of Congress, the official arbitrator of copyright issues. After carefully checking with constituents around the Press and the university who might have a stake in the issue, Britton submitted a petition to the Library of Congress to make the two authorship changes to the two *Olynthus* volumes.[3] A response from the Library of Congress had not been issued by press time, but it is difficult to see how such a request could be refused given the clear evidence of plagiarism, the fact that the current copyright holder is making the request, and no has yet objected. When the change of author is made, it will be the first time in history that a plagiarized author will have her name restored to the title of her work.

Still No Story Here

I felt the need to conclude the first edition of this book with a defense of why it was necessary to publish an account of Ellingson's deeds and Robinson's misdeeds. Unfortunately, I still feel that need. One would think the public support of reviewers would be enough to convince everyone that Robinson should be exposed and Ellingson should be acknowledged. Still, I continue to receive pushback. To date, none of the journals to which I initially sent the article proposal about Ellingson and Robinson has published a review of the first edition of this book. They all received copies, Kendrick at Rowman and Littlefield made certain of that, and one of these journals even listed it in its published "Books Received" list. Nothing followed.

In private, colleagues have expressed discomfort with the publication of this work, but few can clearly articulate why. I cannot explain their discomfort if they cannot, still I have a feeling it comes from the ingrained tradition of not publicly criticizing senior archaeologists, living or dead, embedded in American archaeology in Greece discussed in the previous chapter. It may also spring from an instinctive desire to protect the American School of Classical Studies at Athens, a deeply beloved institution, and hold it above reproach. While no one at the School participated with Robinson in the deception, and it is likely officials there were unaware of his actions, meaning the School has no culpability in this matter, some felt its portrayal in these pages to be harsh. While I understand this instinctive reaction, I would hope that a desire to critically evaluate the history of classical archaeology would eventually allow us to set aside our discomfort and have frank and honest conversations about from where the discipline is coming.

Several editors and peer-reviewers of the doomed article, as well as people who contacted me after the book initially came out, supported discussing Robinson's transgressions, they just felt that looking at his relationship with Ellingson was superfluous. It would be better, they insisted, to focus on the stories of how Robinson wronged well-known and much-beloved archaeologists rather than on how he treated a young female graduate student who left the field. George Hanfmann's name has come up repeatedly. He led important excavation projects, published extensively, and shepherded many students through graduate school to finally hold careers in the field, unlike Ellingson. While Robinson pilfered some of Hanfmann's work just as he took Ellingson's, Hanfmann also had to endure an age of fashionable antisemitism. Writing about Ellingson, however, does not obviate the opportunity to write about anyone else. The discipline of archaeology will be stronger if we fill in the gaps and correct the mistakes in our history by featuring the other people who faced barriers based on identity and record how they dealt with them. A book about Ellingson should be seen as an example and even an invitation to highlight others who have been written out of history. Indeed, I would go further to say it is the responsibility of those of us who hold positions of authority, particularly tenured professors, and those with knowledge of such injustices to use our privilege to shine a light on the memory those restrained by prejudice.

The desire to ignore Robinson's appropriation of Ellingson's work has its roots in another source, one not unique to archaeology. We have a deep ambivalence toward the act of plagiarism and the people who plagiarize. Thomas Mallon opens his book *Stolen Words*, in which he relates many famed examples of the theft of people's writings, by stating, "No, it isn't murder. And as larceny goes it's usually more distasteful than grand. But it *is* a bad thing. Isn't it?"[4] Entrepreneurs have capitalized on these mixed feelings by turning them into a joke they can sell. By typing the phrase "plagiarism saves time" into any internet search engine, one can easily find merchandise emblazoned with the ironic quote.[5] The fact that nobody has ever gone to jail for taking someone else's text without crediting them is one indication that we as a society do not consider it a serious offense. Only in the most extreme and thoroughly documented examples have those who have claimed the work of others as their own faced civil lawsuits from their victims with monetary penalties when found guilty. Professors can lose their jobs, but they always seem to find another academic position as the sin is quickly forgotten.[6] Intellectual property right infringement is so low on anyone's list of serious crimes that it hardly seems to warrant mention in an academic article and certainly not in an entire book. Robinson is famed and still deeply admired for the volume of his publication record even though questions about how much he actually wrote himself have been raised since the time *Olynthus VIII* appeared.[7] Such questions do not seem to have hurt his reputation, however. Many are ready to forgive Robinson as they see what he did more as an indiscretion than a crime.

Choosing to acknowledge that there is a story here has a benefit: it turns Robinson from a myth back into a man. Before anyone took a close look at Robinson's publication record, he appeared to have been a prolific genius. The number of articles and books on which Robinson's name is listed as the author is staggering; it even appears heroic. It is not just the quantity, but much of his work had new and innovative ideas and interpretations of archaeological evidence, making him appear quite ingenious. He set a standard of scholarly output that is superhuman and one which few could ever hope to match much less surpass. To now know the truth, that he had unacknowledged aid with his publications, makes him not so different from any other excavation director. Robinson did write a great deal and did have good ideas, but Ellingson also introduced innovation into the study of terracotta figurines. Not all the concepts and text he published under his own name were his own. His reputation can return to a more human level.

For those who still think plagiarism is not an offense worth discussing to this extent, or that plagiarizers are more colorful rogues than harmful crooks as they are sometimes portrayed,[8] it is worth shifting the point of view away from the perpetrator and toward his victim. Robinson did not just copy Ellingson's words, he stole them from her, monopolizing them. Once published under his name, Ellingson could no longer claim her work as her own. For an MA or PhD scholar to be unable to commit her signature research to print meant her chances of obtaining an academic position were hobbled. Times were becoming increasingly difficult for women in academia in the 1930s and so she may have never actually realized her dream of being an archaeology professor even if she had published her thesis and dissertation. While we cannot be certain what she wanted, without these publications Ellingson could not have a career like that which Robinson and others enjoyed. Whether the option remained for her to return to Mount Calgary College after she completed her PhD and make a career as a junior college professor is unknown; the fact that she left that life in 1938 after pursuing it for six years suggests that it no longer interested her. She went back to Johns Hopkins in search of something more. We will never know what might have been, but to write Ellingson off by dismissing Robinson as committing an insignificant offense continues to put the powerful male professor ahead of the powerless female graduate student. His nefarious deeds limited her career options. To excuse Robinson is to participate in his victimization of Ellingson.

Ellingson as Symbol

Ultimately, the significance of Mary Ellingson lies in what she has come to mean to so many readers. She has become a fully visible proxy for so many invisible archaeologists and researchers in other fields, and she has become a symbol for how diverse voices strengthen our pursuit of knowledge. More than that, however, she has become an inspiration for how to live a full life despite adversity and the pleasure we can get by embracing the parts of archaeological field work that rarely make it into the final publications.

Simply because her photo album and letters provide such a rich source of documentation about her and her friends, unlike other unseen archaeologists of earlier generations, they and particularly *she* must stand in for the rest. Ellingson, Weinberg, and Freeman had to carve their own niches circumscribed by gender expectations and by a society and economy that limited their career prospects more severely than they had for the previous, or would for the subsequent, generations. These women made their way on the margins of academia but nonetheless made contributions to the field, all three overcoming the challenges of sexism and, for Weinberg in addition, of antisemitism. Because we can trace the stories of Ellingson, Weinberg, and Freeman, they are worth telling as they represent the unknown tales of many other women and others in archaeology and the sciences who left less evidence behind but who nonetheless participated in their fields in similar and meaningful ways despite the obstacles obstructing their paths.

This kind of representation matters for the history of classical archaeology, which, especially with relation to fieldwork, tends to be dominated by men. Repopulating that history with women and people from other diverse backgrounds shows those interested in entering the field today individuals who look like themselves and alerts them to how far we have come. When I was an undergraduate forty years ago, about half of my classmates were female, now women make up the vast majority of the undergraduate archeology majors at the University of Evansville. By the next generation, men will no longer dominate the field. All archaeology students, male and female, deserve to read about the women and other nontraditional archaeologists who came before them, people who gave future generations a base from which to work their way further into the field and higher up into positions of leadership. The new generation of budding archaeologists, as well as scientists and other scholars, should understand how the intellectual culture and expected gender roles in the field of archaeology have changed dramatically over the last decades. Sharing that truth with the current generation will allow them to appreciate the extraordinary pressures under which women and other outsiders in all fields worked in the past and which make any of their accomplishments all the more impressive. Seeing people in the history of archaeology who reflect their own identities should help the new generation feel welcomed to the field.[9]

Ellingson brought her own unique perspective to the material she was studying, leading her to interpretations others had not considered, an example of the benefits of diverse voices. It is perhaps a backhanded compliment to say that she made Robinson a better archaeologist because he recognized her ideas were innovative and so chose to claim them as his own, still much of what was praised in the reviews of *Olynthus VII* and *XIV* came from her, not him. Ellingson was one of the first archaeologists to consider the presences of children in the past, which helped her see some of the terracotta figurines she wrote about as toys rather than religious offerings. Robinson had little interest in descriptive statistics, nonetheless he used her numeric tables to support some of her interpretations that he had presented as his own. Ellingson brought her lived experience to the understanding of what she was finding, an experience so different from Robinson's and that of the other male excavation directors of their day. Classical archaeology, and indeed all disciplines, are richer for having insights from those whose identity allows them to approach the material from a point of view the majority might not share. This was true in the years before World War II and remains true today.

Finally, many readers have contacted to me to say they see a little of their own experience in Ellingson's, a realization that can be quite validating and even inspiring. Some of these people have commented on the way Ellingson embraced fieldwork and travel in Europe with enthusiasm and good humor or her clear respect for, and interest in, the local Greek and Vlach cultures. The moment she finally demanded recognition for her work, even if it was only by typing a few words on a form, is an act of defiance that has resonated with many, even offered strength when a reader faced long odds. Among the people I have heard from who have been moved and inspired by Ellingson's words, one young archaeologist stands out.

When I was preparing the initial manuscript for this book, I knew I would need to turn the photo album and letters over to the University of Evansville Archives. These valuable records could not be left on a storage shelf outside

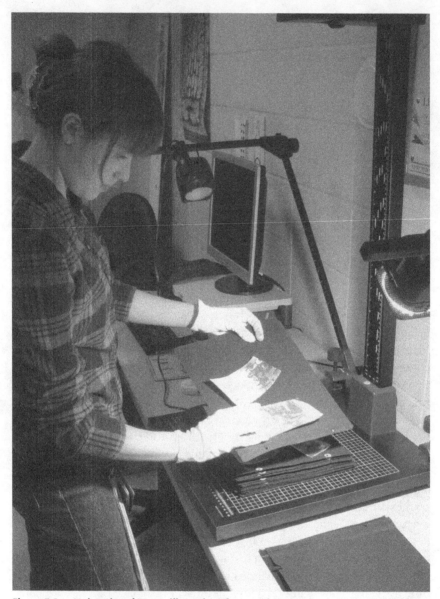

Figure E.2. University of Evansville archaeology student Stephanie Marcotte digitizing Mary Ellingson's photo album.
Photo by the author

my office. As preparation for depositing them with the archives, however, I wanted to properly document everything, transcribe the letters, and scan or photograph everything, a task so enormous I could not do it alone. Several students volunteered to help, but the most enthusiastic was a University of Evansville archaeology major, Stephanie Marcotte (figure E.2). Besides me, she is the person who came to know the collection the best. Marcotte used her work with Ellingson's letters and photographs as the basis for a project for the university's honors program, a project that was very well received. Ellingson's resiliency and adaptability impressed Marcotte as she was facing her own challenges. In addition to seeking to enter a male-dominated field, Marcotte had a chronic, wasting disorder. She refused to let it define her, however, drawing on Ellingson's example to find the determination she needed to pursue her career dreams. Marcotte excavated at Tin City and spent a summer at an Israeli excavation. At times her physical challenges made the work difficult, but she insisted on doing the same tasks as everyone else on the crew at both sites. Determined to experience life to the fullest as Ellingson had, she enjoyed learning about the cultures of Israel and traveling in the region, even journeying to Jordan to visit the UNESCO World Heritage site of Petra. She had a friend take a picture of her riding a camel in front of Treasury at the site. Marcotte passed away just a few months after figure E.2 was taken. At the time of her death, she was studying abroad in England and had just returned from a trip to Ireland. When she was participating in the Tin City project and a fellow student suggested we take a class photo, Marcotte insisted everyone arrange themselves around the Ellingson tree. She told her classmates about Ellingson, her accomplishments, the challenges she faced, and her love of discovering people and places. She hoped when her classmates passed the tree, they would remember for what Ellingson stood and draw strength to accomplish their goals. Hopefully, this book can serve a similar purpose.

Notes

1. Interview by the author with Andrea O. Kendrick on September 3, 2022.
2. Greg Britton, editorial director of Johns Hopkins University Press, personal communication, June 22, 2022.
3. Britton, personal communication, December 16, 2022.
4. Thomas Mallon, *Stolen Words: Forays into the Origins and Ravages of Plagiarism* (New York: Ticknor and Fields, 1989), xi.
5. The quote "plagiarism saves time" is often attributed to Stephen Hawking. Despite an extensive search, I can find no source in which Hawking made such a

statement. My guess is that someone chose to associate it with him to elevate the prestige of the phrase. I did, however, find these words as part of a longer quote by Stewart Home: "To conclude, plagiarism saves time and effort, improves results, and shows considerable initiative on the part of the plagiarist." When shortened to "plagiarism saves time," it has been turned into satire, but Home was trying to encourage plagiarism with all sincerity. He wanted artists to challenge the capitalist system by reusing the work of others, which he did not believe should or could be owned or commodified. Home was railing against the capitalist system and made a point of not seeking a copyright on his words, offering them to anyone to use as they saw fit. See Stewart Home, "Auto-Plagiarism," in *Plagiarism: Art as Commodity and Strategies for Its Negation*, edited by Stewart Home (Aporia Press, 1987), 5–6. One must wonder how he feels about seeing people advancing a capitalist agenda by putting his words on t-shirts and home decorations to sell.

6. For a discussion of punishment, or not, for plagiarism, see Colleen Flaherty, "Not-So-Cardinal Sin?" *Inside Higher Ed*, 2014, https://www.insidehighered.com/news/2014/07/28/why-does-academic-plagiarism-not-offend-much-public, accessed September 29, 2022.

7. See chapter 4.

8. Mallon, *Stolen Words*, xi–xii.

9. On the need to write about women of the past generation who can serve as role models for those of the present, see Lydia C. Carr, *Tessa Verney Wheeler: Women and Archaeology before World War II* (Oxford: Oxford University Press), 7.

APPENDIX I

~

An Unedited Letter

The preceding pages are filled with excerpts from Mary Ellingson's letters. Readers have expressed how much they have enjoyed perusing what she had to say, and some have asked for more, wanting to read the full text of a letter without the intervention of an editor. With that request as a catalyst, the purpose of this appendix is two-fold. The first is to offer the text of just one of Ellingson's letters from Olynthus in its entirety and without editing. Excerpts from this letter, dated April 21, 1931, and pictured in figure A.1, appear in an earlier chapter. The letter captures Ellingson's personality better than most. Her sense of humor, *joie de vivre*, and total embrace of her experience abroad shine through in her vivid description of participating in a Vlach wedding. Note as well how her eye as an archaeologist has developed; she is particularly interested in the role of material culture in the ceremony, describing how all participants use artifacts. To be as faithful as possible to what she wrote, I have transcribed the letter exactly. It is worth preserving her abbreviations and errors in spelling and punctuation as I think they serve to remind us she was writing this letter by hand while watching over dozens of men excavating on the hill at Olynthus. As for the ambiguous portions, of which there are several, I leave those to the reader to interpret.

The second purpose for publishing this letter in its entirety is that in it Ellingson offers an unprecedented and detailed description of a Vlach wedding. The Vlach ethnic identity is disappearing from modern Greece, and it is not clear that weddings like this are performed anymore. Future generations of Vlachs, as well as anthropologists and historians studying their culture, may find something useful for understanding Vlach society in the great detail

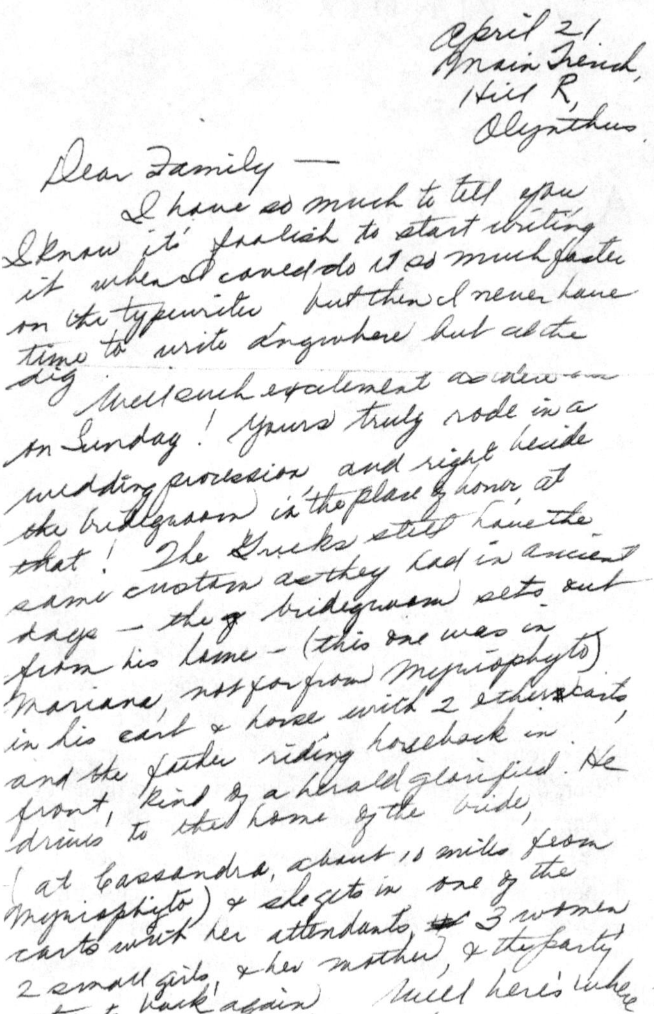

**Figure A.1.
First page of Mary Ross Ellingson's April 21, 1931, letter.**
Photo courtesy of the University of Evansville Archives

with which Ellingson describes the ceremony. Ellingson refers to the Vlachs as "Clefts," a term she later corrects to "Vlachs" in the undated newspaper clipping written by Thelma Atkinson.

With all that being said, it is best to allow Mary Ross Ellingson to have the last word.

The Vlach Wedding Letter

April 21
Main Trench,
Hill R,
Olynthus.

Dear Family—

I have so much to tell you. I know it's foolish to start writing it when I could do it so much faster on the typewriter, but then I never have time to write anywhere but at the dig.

Well such excitement as there was on Sunday! Yours truly rode in a wedding procession, and right beside the bridegroom in the place of honor, at that! The Greeks still have the same custom as they had in ancient days—the bridegroom sets out from his home—(this one was in Mariana, not far from Myriophyto) in his cart & horse with 2 other carts, and the father riding horseback in front, kind of a herald glorified. He drives to the home of the bride, (at Cassandra, about 10 miles from Myriophyto), & she gets in one of the carts with her attendants, 3 women, 2 small girls, & her mother, & the party starts back again. Well here's where I came in. It was Sunday, & I had been typing a letter for Davey, & the others had gone swimming (I wanted to go, but Davey's letter had to be rushed), so when I got thru, Davey & I walked over to the next village, Hagias Mamas, to look at some inscriptions on stone [see figure A.2]. We had the most exciting time—I wouldn't have missed it for worlds,—but more of that later, I must get back to the wedding, the big event.

We were walking along the road, when we heard the tramp of horses' feet, and the rhythmic song of the Clefts (spelling doubtful)[1] approaching. Turning around, we saw horses, carts, people, banners approaching at a great rate of speed [see figures 3.8 and A.3]. Much shouting and firing of guns and pistols. The party stopped when they got to us. The bridegroom rode in the first cart, a gay orange one with blue paintings on it. The marriage banner was waved aloft by one of the attendants. It was a long pole, with a cross-bar near the top. On the end of the pole, was stuck a big red rosy apple. On the two ends of the cross-bar, small green apples. And below was attached the banner—of fine white linen, a heavy lace edge, Greek script embroidered in gay colors, ribbons and lace hanging from various places. Other ribbons were attached at the edge of the banner, about 4 inches apart and a jingle-bell on the end of each one. The groom was very resplendent in a new tailored suit of navy blue, patent leather oxfords with brown insets (new) a loud, very loud, blue silk handkerchief in his pocket, on one lapel, a spray of purple flowers (known as βιολέττα[2]—violetta here), and on the left lapel a glorious Easter lily. The crowning touch—a straw sailor hat, bedecked with tinsel. The bride's costume was almost too complicated to describe. She had rows and rows and rows of frills and embroidery (very very beautiful), & a jacket, and some kind of queer hat of white linen & lace that looked like a cross between a Mother Hubbard cap & a boudoir cap. Her attendants are all very gorgeously dressed, too, but they wear dark handkerchiefs on their heads.

Well as I was saying, when they caught up to us, they stopped, & some got out, they passed the cognac around, and invited Davey & me to come along. Which we did, I being very anxious to ride in a bridal procession. The groom got out, if you please, & got in a car & drove to Myriophyto, & there awaited the procession. So we rode in his cart, me on the front seat, between the driver & one of the male attendants. Now I must explain about these carts. There is a board across the front, to sit on, but no place to put your feet or brace yourself. There isn't anything in the back to sit on except the sides of the cart. Well off we went, me feeling very tickled the while at this bit of local colour. Bump no. 1.—Mary slips back a little on the seat. Pistol shot, no. 1., horses lurch

Figure A.2. David Robinson making a squeeze of an ancient inscription reused as a block in the wall of a modern house.

Photo courtesy of the David M. Robinson Collection, Special Collections, University of Mississippi Libraries

Figure A.3. **Mary Ross Ellingson (to the left of the man standing in the forefront of the cart, the groom Athanasios) and David Robinson (on the groom's other side) ride in a wedding procession. Ellingson's delight in the situation is evident.**
Photo courtesy of the University of Evansville Archives

forward, Mary falls back into the cart, upon Davey & other members of the bridal party. After resuming my original place—on we go. Bump no.2.—Mary slips back a little. Pistol shot, no. 2.—horses lurch forward, & Mary, by dint of hard pulling on case, & a few friendly pushes from the back, retains seat. Bump no 3.—I have to have more room, but don't like to push the driver off the seat, because then we mightn't get there. I don't like to push the attendant off the seat, because that might complicate matters. Finally he fell off anyway, & I rode along in peace & comfort for a while, till he jumped on again. Oh I forgot to say that he told Dr. Robinson he would like to marry me, & thought I was very beautiful (this being my 3rd proposal during the course of the afternoon). Finally we arrive at Myriophyto, where the whole village, exclusive of our bunch, was out to greet us. Much firing of pistols, etc. I forgot to say, they sang the song of the Clefts (an old rogue song effect—something to do with marriage) all the way along. Andoni, the cook, was out to see it, too, & when he saw Davey & me sitting up in the front cart, as large as life, & twice as natural,—well his eyes just about popped. After recovering his first surprise, he made one dive for the house, & shrieked at the bunch—M'sieur Robinson . . . Mam'selle. . . Marriage! They didn't know what it was all about, & wondered if Davey & I were eloping, Mrs. R. being away in Saloniki for the week-end. They came running out in great awe & admiration. By this time, the bridegroom had taken his place beside me, & the marriage banner was back in the cart, we started off once more. Halfway thru the village, a lot of people had rope stretched across the road & a line of people behind it. That was all very well, just a playful gesture, as customary at weddings, but what did our 2 horses do, but rear up & take to the fields. Finally order was restored. More pistol shots—& the horses were well away. Well, this time I was in a fix. I couldn't shove the driver off, because then we couldn't get there. And as for shoving the bridegroom off—well—. However I finally acquired the knack of staying on the seat, and outside of the fact that the man who was holding the marriage banner kept biffing me on the head, all went smoothly. Finally, we arrived at Mariana [see figure A.4]. (The bunch had hired a truck & followed us.) (I forgot to say that some of the villagers thought I was the bride, & thru rice etc. at me.) We stopped at the threshold of the town, while the groom's father approached from the house! (Alex had taken a lot of pictures meanwhile). Then the groom descended, & followed by the marriage banner entered the house for a few last words (or more probably drinks). Then the bride, who had remained behind some distance, approached. In front of the house, she took a plate of things that look like skinny jelly beans, & thru them over her back. (I managed to get one in the scramble.) Then she entered the house (us tripping after.) We were shown to an upper room, where we sat & waited. Finally they passed around a tray, with about 10 tiny glasses on it, with cognac, & a plate of loucoumi (Turkish delight). Everybody took a sip, & then put the glass back for the next fellow, & took a piece of loucoumi. The groom follows the man who was passing it, & kept filling the glasses. Finally they decided to have the wedding downstairs instead. Thereupon we went downstairs, in a small low-ceilinged stuffy room. There was kind of a wooden altar effect in the middle of the room, & on it a huge Bible, covered with wine velvet & brass. Leaning against the mantle piece were 2 white candles tied with orange blossoms & white ribbon. The priest started things going by lighting 2 candles which 2 small children held for him while he read out of the Bible in a sing song voice. The bride & groom, Eleutheria & Athanasios were their names, stood side by side. Her mother held her arms around her all the time clasping her hands. All during the ceremony she kept her eyes shut. I forgot to say that 2 rings lay on top of the Bible. The priest lifted his censor, & swung it around so that the room was filled with smoke & incense. He took the rings & waved 'em around, touching different parts of the bride's & groom's face & then finally, put them on. Then he put on an extra robe from under the altar all embroidered in gold. Then the chief singer sang some marriage hymns in mournful tones. Then the priest lit another pair of candles, the 2 on the mantelpiece, & put the others out. Then he took a long pink shawl effect with ribbons & lace hanging on it, & put it around the bride & groom. Then he took a glass of cognac, blessed it, gave the groom a swallow, then the bride—his hand shaking terribly the while—he is a very old man, & feeble then gave the rest of it to the best man, who stood behind the 2 during the ceremony. More sing-song, then the priest asks ἄξιος- axios? (I think it means—who is worthy? Or something like that.) Then somebody lifts the best man off the ground 3 times, why, I do not know. More sing-song. Then a box is produced from somewhere & from it are taken two wreaths of orange-blossoms. The priest makes all manner of mystic passes with them, putting them first, on one head & then on the other, finally leaving one on the head of the each, & tying them with a long string. Two small sprays of orange blossom are stuck somewhere, I just forget where. Then the priest kisses the pair, and then kind of pulls them around the altar 3 times the mother of the bride & 2 attendants having to support her as she is just about dead by this time. (her eyes still closed). Then the final blessing by the priest. Then the relations come up, kiss the bride & groom, & put some money on a

Figure A.4. View of the village of Mariana that J. Walter Graham took about a month before the wedding described in this letter. Graham gave Ellingson a copy of the photo. The largest house in the center of the town belonged to the family of Athanasios, the groom, and is where Ellingson attended the Vlach wedding. The ruins to the right are the remains of a Byzantine-era tower. This view is what Ellingson would have taken in from her unsteady perch on the cart seat as the wedding party approached Mariana.
Photo courtesy of the University of Evansville Archives

brass plate for the priest—They are married! (I forgot to say the marriage banner hung outside the house all this while).

Before all this excitement started, Davey & I had been looking at some inscriptions. One was in the yard of a priest, & when we come along he asked us in, & of course I had to see the inside of the house so we went in. It was just a small affair, with very low roof & dirt floor—but I never saw such a clean house in my life. The priest's daughter I guess it was, was lying down on some rugs in one corner, suffering from the rheumatic. Then her husband got us something to drink. He passed us a tray with 3 tiny glasses on it, each with something different in. The one I chose was chipero[3]—something like uzo only more concentrated, & just about knocks you out, but leaves the nicest taste in your mouth. We all clinked our glasses together & said Χριστός Ἀνέστη—Christ is risen (This saying goes on for 40 days after Easter)

Oh yes, I forgot to say that the priest's daughter wanted me to marry her eldest son. And on the way over to the village, the village school master, just a young chap, walked quite a way with us. And he told Davey (all these people spoke Gk. & I couldn't understand a word of it) that he would make me an awfully good husband. He had a house of his own, & he could cook. There now, how's that for one afternoon?

No other news of note just now.

Had a letter from Helen, & she says she is arriving in Athens June 4. As things are now, I can't be there, so I don't know what to do. I'll just hope she comes later. Davey wants us all to stay later than June 1. If she is still in Edm[onton]. when you get this Mother will you please tell her about it; if she would like to come up to the excavation, the railway fare is $7, & I could meet her at the train in Saloniki. If she doesn't want to, I'll come down to Athens, regardless of Davey because I am working hard now. I wrote Helen a letter to the boat, one to her home, telling her I'd meet the Byron, Athens June 4. If she doesn't change her mind and come later, I'll cable her to the boat, and she can cable back what she wants to do. I can be in Athens then, I suppose, because I am keeping my inventory up to date. I told Davey the other day that Helen was coming to meet me June 4, and he said that *some* of us would have to plan to stay, so I don't think he'd mind a bit if I left before the others.

If anybody (I mean the girls) complains that I haven't written them, please tell them that I am awfully busy—I really don't have a minute except on Sundays, and then I like to rest in the morning and have church, and in the afternoon we usually go someplace and during the week it keeps me hopping to get my report and inventory done after we come back from the dig.

One thing, we have lots of clean clothes here and don't need to economize on washing. And another thing, Andoni has been making us the most wonderful lunches lately.

Heaps o' love,
Mary

Notes

1. The proper term is Vlach.
2. The proper modern Greek spelling is βιολέτα.
3. The proper transliteration is *tsipouro*. Since Ellingson was writing these foreign words after having only heard them, it is not surprising she would make some mistakes.

APPENDIX II

~

Feminism, Classical Archaeology, and Mary Ellingson

Some university professors who teach courses devoted to the history of archaeology or the history of women in science have found this book to be a good case study that touches on themes they develop over the course of a semester. To make it more useful to their pedagogical purposes, some have asked for one additional section that briefly and specifically examines the changing influences of the feminist movement on the development of archaeology and classical archaeology over time. This is an enormous subject, but one made manageable using Ellingson as an example. Her life straddles most major changes in both archaeology and feminism while it also makes sweeping historical events relatable, illustrating their impact on one person's situation. Below are my thoughts, which are certainly not the only possible way to interpret these events and their effect on Ellingson's story. I hope these reflections offer fodder for lively class discussions.

First-Wave Feminism

Historians of feminism in North America and the United Kingdom have settled on the metaphor of waves to best describe the various phases of the movement. The imagery emerged in the late 1960s, and historian Sara Evans codified it with her 2003 book *Tidal Wave: How Women Changed America at Century's End.*[1] Despite the inadequacies of the wave metaphor, even historians dissatisfied with it agree the notion provides such a simple and powerful frame for structuring an understanding of how feminist goals and methods progressed that we are stuck with it.[2] According to this metaphor, the first feminist wave emerged around the middle of the nineteenth century as a variety of groups worked in tandem to achieve suffrage as the first step toward advancing their own more specific political and social agendas.[3] The wave culminated in the years around 1920 as women in the United States, Canada, and the United Kingdom won the universal right to vote.

The origins of archaeology as a discipline distinct from classics or art history dates to the same time as the beginning of the first feminist wave. As nascent archaeologists sought to establish what would become the accepted practices and traditions, women seeking to break free of the gender confines imposed by Victorian society found a place for themselves in the study of the past and helped shape what it would become. The first women in archaeology emerged from a generation who had more expanded opportunities to advance their educations than their mothers and grandmothers as the western United States drew American men from the east coast to pursue their fortunes and careers. The United Kingdom witnessed a similar phenomenon as a vast global empire beckoned men to leave England. Society needed more educated people to fill some of the posts these men left vacant, which meant universities had to accept more female applicants.[4] Some of archaeology's roots lay in the same phenomenon. As the excitement of archaeological discoveries and field work were publicized, women were able to get the educational grounding they needed to participate in the new discipline. Rebellious and nonconformist women saw an opportunity to establish an identity not tied to their gender since when they were in the field, what they could do often mattered more than any other part of their identity; they were archaeologists first. While much depends on the tone an excavation director sets, archaeological field work did, and still does, provide some degree of escape from the normal conventions of society; behaviors that might be deemed unacceptable in polite society or the halls of academe are tolerated in the field. Some Victorian female archaeologists chose to wear clothing that gave them either a degendered or even a masculine appearance while participating in excavations.[5] Others engaged in behaviors that shocked even their fellow male archaeologists, men used to looser social norms in the field. Margaret Murray describes hearing a noise she feared was from a vandal one night while working at the site of Abydos in Egypt. She and two of her colleagues, Hilda Petrie and Lina Eckenstein, rushed into the desert to investigate for themselves, a male excavator volunteering to join them to protect them from the dangers he imagined lurking in the shadows. The alarm turned out to be false, so the trio joined hands and danced in wild abandon across the moonlit dunes. Murray revels in describing the look on the face of their self-designated protector who, nevertheless, did not try to stop them.[6] Charging after criminals and dancing in the moonlight were hardly activities in which they could have engaged back in urbane society in England or the United States. In Greece, Athens could have its own restrictions. To escape the repressive reach of the men leading the American School of Classical Studies at Athens, Harriet Boyd Hawes had to go to Crete and Hetty Goldman and Alice Leslie Walker to the Greek site of Halae and eventually to Turkey, all far from Athens.[7] For the first female archaeologists, participation in archaeology complemented their feminist political activity. Many of these archaeological pioneers worked toward universal women's suffrage[8] while one, Gertrude Bell, was a founding member of the Women's Anti-Suffrage League.[9] Either way, all were clearly aware of the first feminist wave and their activities bound feminism and archaeology together.

Born in 1908, Ellingson came of age at the height of the first feminist wave with the legalization of the right to vote for most women in her native Canada, in the United States, and in the United Kingdom. While an undergraduate, her two main mentors, William Hardy Alexander and Geneva Misener, were both proud suffragists who continued to push a very liberal feminist agenda even after Canadian women could vote. They both urged Ellingson to seek a career in archaeology, teaching at a university as universities were the main employer of archaeologists, and Misener insisted any woman could work, marry, or do both if she chose. Her professors most likely made her aware of the archaeological work of women like Boyd Hawes, Goldman, Walker, and perhaps others, providing potential role models she could seek to emulate. When she went to graduate school at Johns Hopkins, she had only been there a few months before Robinson invited her to join the Olynthus project in Greece. As at other excavations, David Robinson allowed for some freedom from gender-based conventions once in the field. Ellingson, Gladys Weinberg, and Sarah Freeman directed scores of Greek workmen in the trenches, a task normally reserved for men, especially in a patriarchal society like Greece. Her female friends also appear in some of her photos dressed in male clothing (see figures 1.5, 1.10, 2.10, 3.3, and 3.16), having left gender expectations in Baltimore and Athens. For Ellingson, during her undergraduate and graduate school years the options must have seemed limitless and her gender not a major limiting factor.

Between the First and Second Waves

With victory in hand, the suffrage movement fragmented and ceased to have the kind of sway it held previously after the 1920s; the wave had spent itself and receded, according to the metaphor.[10] That is not to say all feminist political work ceased, instead activists focused on their own narrow goals and a backlash against the movement's initial gains slowed visible progress.[11] World events, namely the Depression and World War II, also pushed the concerns of women to the background. With the onset of the economic collapse, American universities and state legislatures adopted policies limiting access of women to employment in higher education as good jobs needed to be reserved for the family breadwinners, the men.[12]

Archaeology for American women working in Greece changed rapidly as a result of these events and a simultaneous evolution in the role of the American School of Classical Studies at Athens. In the late 1920s, the American School obtained the legal right to recommend projects for excavation permits to the Greek government. This allowed School officials to set certain standards they expected from excavators, the first step toward the professionalization of the field. By the early 1930s, School leaders were setting quotas on the number of women who could attend and banning non-Americans. As they required archaeologists to gain better training, they limited the opportunity for women to get that training.[13] Women, though, still participated in the archaeology of Greece. During the first fifteen years of the School's journal *Hesperia*, founded in 1932, women authored 22 percent of the articles. Still possibilities for them were severely constrained as most of these articles covered art historical topics and involved cataloging finds rather that documenting field work and writing broad syntheses.[14]

These rapid reversals after the gains of the 1920s limited Ellingson's career options in a way that must have felt jarring. She was still a graduate student at Johns Hopkins when the American School set the quota on the number of women and was between completing her master's thesis and doctoral dissertation when the School banned Canadians like her. By the time she completed her dissertation in 1939, she understood that she had to choose between marriage and a career and that a career looked like an increasingly unlikely dream. After she married and moved to Evansville, she did work as the curator of archaeology at the local museum, but it was a volunteer position and one she chose to relinquish once she had children. Prior to the rise of the next wave, Ellingson spent much of her time in the roles of wife, mother, and homemaker.

Second-Wave Feminism

According to the popular metaphor, after a hiatus of roughly forty years, the second wave of feminism began advancing in the 1960s only to be overtaken by the third wave in the mid-1990s. Second-wave feminists sought freedom from societal-based gender expectations and the right to self-actualization on their own terms. They wanted equal access to career opportunities, equal pay, and the right to control their own bodies. American second-wave feminists sought to unite the movement behind a grand goal similar to the fight for universal suffrage that drove the initial feminist wave. The focus was the Equal Rights Amendment, a change to the federal constitution that would outlaw gender-based discrimination. The amendment has not yet been ratified.

During the time of the second feminist wave, archaeology was going through its own period of turmoil and change, at first unrelated to what was happening in the wider world. The period between the 1960s and 1980s was the heyday of what has been dubbed "processualist" archaeological theory, an approach that required a hypothesis-testing process adopted from the hard sciences. Archaeologists stopped talking about artifacts and started talking about data. Processualists did not have much interest in studying gender roles in ancient cultures or gender discrimination among modern archaeologists as these topics seemed to grow from political motives, not objective science. For the most part, women felt welcomed to join the field, but often found themselves working in site labs rather than in the trenches.[15]

The second feminist wave impacted Ellingson much earlier, and more powerfully, than it did the field of archaeology. The timing of her interest in returning to academia from homemaking corresponded with the explosion in college enrollment as the baby boomer generation aged. Evansville College, like many universities and colleges at the time, needed more faculty. Having her PhD made Ellingson unusual in 1960s Evansville and more attractive for hiring as she added prestige to the institution. Whenever her name is mentioned in the campus newspaper or yearbook, editors were always careful to add her title, "Dr. Ellingson," an honor few other faculty at the time had. The college did not have an archaeology program, so Ellingson taught classical languages and the classical roots of English vocabulary, splitting her time between the Department of Foreign Languages and Department of English. She left no record of her thoughts on the effects of feminism roiling the social conditions of her day, but it seems highly likely she participated in informal conversations on the subject. An article published in the school's newspaper, the *Crescent*, on May 27, 1970, with the optimistic if grammatically questionable title "Women Liberation Nearing Reality," the author quotes extensively from an interview with Virginia Grabill, an English professor and friend of Ellingson, who was outspoken about her opinions on the evolving rights and responsibilities of women. Grabill believed strongly that women should receive the same pay as men for the same work. It is hard to imagine she and Ellingson never discussed these matters. Just three years after Grabill's interview, Ellingson claimed authorship of *Excavations at Olynthus VII* and the first chapter of *Olynthus XIV* for the first time. While it is only a supposition, it still feels like a strong one to claim it was the feminist second wave, manifest in statements like Grabill's that women should receive the same compensation for the same work, that led Ellingson to conclude she should receive the same recognition as the author of some of the Olynthus material as any other male contributor to the series. It may have been a fleeting thought, expressed only on a form, but one likely prompted by the discussions of the feminist movement taking place around her.

While it took some time after the beginning of the feminist second wave, eventually a shift in archaeological theoretical paradigms created the opportunity for discussions of a feminist archaeology and women in the field. It was more than a decade after Ellingson claimed her authorship that the first archaeological article with a feminist perspective appeared in print. In this 1984 article, Margaret Conkey and Janet Spector highlighted a male bias in archaeological interpretation and the lack of a theoretical framework for considering gender issues.[16] Books and articles followed defining a feminist archaeological theory by which to interpret the evidence of the past.[17] In the 1970s and 1980s an increasing number of women sought careers in archaeology, although they still faced structural forms of sexism.[18] Just a year after Conkey and Spector's landmark article, Joan Gero was the first archaeologist to publish a study documenting the numbers of female archaeologists publishing, participating in excavations, getting grants, and teaching at universities in comparison to men.[19] It may have taken some time, but the basic expectation for equity of second-wave feminists that influenced Ellingson slowly infiltrated archaeological theory and practice.

Just two years after Conkey and Spector's article calling attention to the feminist movement in archaeology, Ian Hodder published his landmark *Reading the Past* in which he challenged the objectivity of the processual archaeologists and established the "post-processualist" school of thought. While post-processualists still relied on science and hard data, they did not hesitate to point out the previously unacknowledged social and political assumptions undergirding archaeological research.[20] Post-processualist archaeology encouraged the feminist political movement within archaeology as second-wave feminist ideas fit very neatly with post-processual arguments about the invisible biases in archaeological interpretation. Hodder's book even contained a section entitled "Feminist Archaeology" in which he sought to identify and define how the movement was opening up new fields of inquiry.

Looking back from our current vantagepoint may make it seem as if the growing influence of the feminist movement on archaeology was inevitable. It was not. The level of resistance is difficult to overstate, and some subfields of archaeology proved more welcoming to new ideas than others. Originally, archaeology had been a comprehensive discipline. When the *American Journal of Archaeology* began publication in 1897, it was a source on all archaeological subjects. For much of the twentieth century, archaeologists specialized more and more, a trend that created divides in the field. *American Antiquity*, a journal for prehistoric archaeologists coming from an anthropological tradition, commenced publication in 1935. Editors at the *American Journal of Archaeology* gave up their general approach and began to focus on the archaeology of the Mediterranean basin. The division of classical and other text-focused archaeologists from anthropological archaeologists grew over the decades as practitioners implemented their own standards of excavation and research expectations. Conkey, Spector, and Gero came from anthropological archaeology, which proved somewhat more amenable to feminist theory than classical archaeology. Classical archaeologists demonstrated a particularly strong reluctance to apply feminist theory to draw conclusions about their data.[21] Many classical and some anthropological archaeologists viewed such endeavors with deep suspicion and subjected feminist interpretations to a great deal more scrutiny than other research, often treating perceived feminist archaeologists as naïve and politically motivated.[22] In an article from the mid-1990s voicing support for considering feminist approaches to the study of ancient physical remains, Tracey Cullen, concluded, "[t]he most successful of these studies offer an improved account of the past, expanding the scope of inquiry to include men *and* women."[23] The emphasis is Cullen's and it undercuts the point of her review. Regardless of her initial intent, she ends by arguing any approach to gender had to include the male viewpoint in addition to the female, an insistence that makes the then recent developments in feminist theory within archaeology appear flawed and wanting. Even the statements of a supporter of feminist approaches to Mediterranean archaeology in the 1990s were tentative and qualified. In terms of archaeological culture, some leaders in the field denied that women lacked equal access to participation. Classical archaeologist James Russell, then president of the Archaeological Institute of America which is the umbrella organization for those engaged in Mediterranean archaeology, wrote an article in 1993 reassuring readers that while other areas of scientific endeavor had limited the participation of women, archaeology had not. He lists examples of famed women archaeologists, all but one born in the nineteenth century, to show archaeology has always welcomed women. He continues, "Delicacy forbids me from mentioning the names of the current *grandes dames*, but I can assure you that we have no dearth of brilliant women in our discipline."[24] Russell provided cover for those who did not want to acknowledge that women faced systemic challenges while working in archaeology.

Part of this resistance to acknowledging and discussing feminist issues during the second wave came from the assumption that it was a political topic that indicated a partisan agenda, an agenda that bends data to fit predetermined interpretations.[25] In 1994, Lauren Talalay wrote in the popular magazine *Archaeology* about the motives her fellow archaeologists ascribed to any of their colleagues using certain vocabulary stating, "terms such as feminist and feminism are intended to be explicitly political and confrontational, connoting a challenge to the status quo."[26] She justified fears about the objectivity of anyone addressing issues that could be categorized as feminist. Although second-wave feminism did change the discipline, that change came slowly and at different rates in anthropological and classical archaeology.

Third-Wave Feminism

Historians date the transition from second- to third-wave feminism to the early to mid-1990s. Today they describe third-wave feminists as feeling entitled to live a life not limited by arcane concepts of race, binary gender, or sexual orientation; participants in the third wave want to define themselves, not be defined by others, and seek to empower everyone to rise above traditional roles and stereotypes, not just the cisgendered females who were the focus of the second wave. Technologically sophisticated, the members of the third wave are proficient at bypassing the traditional editors and peer-reviewers of print media to get their messages out via social media. Rejecting the need for syntheses and theory, the new third wavers stress action, even if that action is simply posting a comment online. The #MeToo movement specifically targets the exposing and ending of sexual harassment and is either an outgrowth of the third wave or is part of a fourth feminist wave; it is too early to say which way of viewing it is more appropriate.[27]

Since the 1990s, archaeological research on feminist and gendered issues has grown steadily and archaeologists have developed an interest in understanding views of race, sexual orientation, and nonbinary genders. In terms of studying and changing the culture of archaeological practice, three themes have emerged during the period of the third wave, the quest for representation in the history of archaeology, the search for hard data to support claims of sexism, and the demand for workspaces free of harassment.

Histories of various subfields of archaeology have tended to take the "great man" approach, focusing on the contributions of a single man while either ignoring or downplaying the contributions of individual women or of anyone else working with the "great man."[28] Since the beginning of the third wave, authors have been restoring women, and more recently people of color and those with non-binary sexual identities or orientations, to our history. There has been an increase in the number of biographies and autobiographical books and articles in which the experiences of one woman in the field are featured or obituaries that acknowledge the unique challenges a woman faced. These recent publications bring up issues traditionally ignored or glossed over such as the balancing of a career with being a mother and wife, discriminatory impediments to advancing a career, and sexual harassment.[29] Yet American classical archaeologists are notoriously uninterested in their own past.[30] It was not until 1998 that the first history written by an American, Stephen Dyson's *Ancient Marbles to American Shores*, was published, long after the history of other branches of archaeology had appeared.[31] Coming during the third wave, its author did not hesitate to mention a number of women who contributed to the field, a refreshing change from the earlier histories of other branches of archaeology that hardly mention women but also an approach that felt normalized by that time.

Generating data to prove discriminatory systems exist is another way the third wave has impacted archaeology. Gero was the first archaeologist to look at the numbers of female anthropological archaeologists publishing, participating in excavations, getting grants, and teaching at universities in comparison to men; others followed, providing statistical evidence to challenge assumptions about gender equity in the field.[32] Among classical archaeologists, the most comprehensive attempt to gather data comparing the opportunities for men and women in grant applications, publishing, and academic positions remains one conducted in 1996. The Archaeological Institute of America's Subcommittee on Women in Archaeology surveyed practicing archaeologists, both male and female, to gather data. While a final report on the survey does not appear to have ever been published, one of the people with access to the data, Cullen, included some of the topline numbers comparing the responses of women and men in several articles she wrote, which she supplemented with her access to published and unpublished information she gathered while working for the *American Journal of Archaeology*, the journal of the Archaeological Institute of America, and *Hesperia*, the journal of the American School. For instance, Cullen found that 45 percent of classical archaeologists are women, while women were the lead or sole authors of 38 percent of the articles submitted to the *American Journal of Archaeology*. Since the journal's acceptance rate for pieces written by women was identical to the submission rate, she concluded that the reason for the gender discrepancy was not sexism at the journal but rather broader societal impediments. Cullen reports that women made up 50 percent of the presenters at the annual conference of the Archaeological Institute of America while the percentage of women in the pool of speakers for the institute's lecture series, which sends archaeologists across North America, was only 26 percent, suggesting the institute is not completely free from structural bias.[33] Only 27 percent of the excavation projects supported by the American School have female directors.[34] More male than female archaeologists tend to have permanent, tenure-track academic appointments. Cullen reports 35 percent of male archaeologists are highly satisfied with their jobs compared to 25 percent of females.[35] In the last few years, surveys in anthropological archaeology have been more inclusive, seeking data on all archaeologists including those who do not identify as white, straight, or cisgendered.[36] All these data make dismissal of problems more difficult and identify specific problems that need to be addressed.

The third impact of the third wave on archaeology is happening in the area of sexual harassment and the use of the MeToo hashtag to make sure problems are no longer ignored. An incident at the annual meeting of the Society for American Archaeology in 2019 focused a harsh light on harassment in the field. An archaeologist who had recently been dismissed from his university position for repeated episodes of sexual harassment attended the conference, forcing his victims to skip sessions he attended and make sure they were never alone at any point. Eventually a journalist escorted the disgraced archaeologist from the conference.[37] Many criticized the inadequate response from the Society for American Archaeology leadership and critically evaluated the policies of other archaeological organizations like the Archaeological Institute of America. These professional groups have been slow to address the harassment and even assault at excavations and in the workplace despite studies showing it to be a matter that has affected all archaeologists.[38] In surveys, professional and academic archaeologists routinely rank sexual harassment as the most serious problem in the field today with women being three to four times more likely to be treated inappropriately than men.[39] The incident at the conference in 2019 has forced a reckoning at many archaeological organizations that would never had occurred had it not been publicized and a response been demanded by those active on social media.[40]

It is this last factor, social media, that has given third wavers power that their predecessors lacked as events at the conference prove. Third-wave feminism emerged alongside the advent of social media, upending the traditional routes of publishing. Now authors can reach vast audiences without needing to go through the filtering process required by peer reviewers and editors at journals and academic publishing houses. Print publications still earn more respect and trust than online-only publications, but the electronic format removes the gatekeepers, opening an audience for younger authors and those wishing to discuss topics their elders find uncomfortable or inappropriate. Social media proved essential in forcing a reckoning on sexual harassment at the Society for American Archaeology conference as the MeToo hashtag trended in real time while events at the conference unfolded.[41]

Ellingson died in 1993, still the third wave made it possible to share the arc of her career with a new generation. No archaeological journal had an interest in publishing an article about David Robinson's plagiarism or Ellingson's career challenges. It took a young editor, and someone whose college major had been both archaeology and gender and women's studies, to push for the initial publication of this book. Reviews in anthropological archaeology and classical studies journals followed and one from a journal devoted to Greek archaeology, but social media proved essential for sharing Ellingson's tale. One important online source was the website *TrowelBlazers*, a site set up by three professionals in the "digging" sciences, archaeology, geology, and paleontology, who vowed to show a new generation of women and people from underrepresented populations that they have predecessors in these fields and so can and should participate. In addition to a website, they post on a variety of social media platforms.[42] The TrowelBlazers added an entry about Mary Ellingson to their catalog of pioneering women in the field. They also posted a review of the book and did an episode of their podcast about it. From there, posts of Ellingson's picture and those relating her career were shared via other sites. A review of the book appeared in the archivist's blog from the American School in Athens.[43] An anonymous author added an article about Ellingson to Wikipedia. Someone edited the Wikipedia entry on David Robinson to mention his plagiarism. The Indiana State Library asked for a post for their Indiana history blog as they sought to celebrate less-well-known Hoosier historians and archaeologists.[44] The Archaeological Institute of America created an online site called *Archaeologists You Should Know*, to which students at the University of Evansville petitioned to add an article about Ellingson.[45] Without the habit of people supporting third-wave causes of posting to social media, the events in Ellingson's life and her relationship with the Olynthus project would have remained less amplified.

The discipline of archaeology and the feminist movement emerged and developed at the same moment in history, making the influence of the movement on the discipline inevitable. Relating that influence to archaeology by focusing on the experiences of Mary Ellingson moves the discussion from the abstract to the very real. During the first wave the women who became archaeologists were often nonconformists seeking to escape Victorian gender expectations. Participating in the politics of suffrage, whether for or against, came naturally to many of them. The suffrage movement expanded educational and employment opportunities for women like Ellingson. It also inspired a sense of possibility in her generation; if achieving the vote was possible, anything could be. The female archaeological pioneers also provided role models for the women like Ellingson who followed. The power of representation like that cannot be underestimated. The motto of the TrowelBlazers is "if you can see it, you can be it." Her Victorian predecessors allowed Ellingson to see it. The repressive response to the gains of the first wave in higher education and among American archaeologists, justified by economic challenges in the 1930s, limited Ellingson's career options in a reversal of the optimistic spirit of the 1920s. Nonetheless, by all accounts she enjoyed her roles of wife and mother. The second wave convinced her she had a right to let others know she had written some of the *Excavations at Olynthus* series. And long after her death, third-wave feminists used the power they have gained from social media to keep her memory alive. It is difficult to find a better case study than Ellingson's to show the interplay between the field of archaeology and the feminist movement.

Notes

1. Kathleen A. Laughlin, Julie Gallagher, Dorothy Sue Cobble, Eileen Boris, Premilla Nadasen, Stephanie Gilmore, and Leandra Zarnow, "Is It Time to Jump Ship? Historians Rethink the Waves Metaphor," *Feminist Formations* 22, no. 1 (2010): 90.

2. Nancy A. Hewitt, "Feminist Frequencies: Regenerating the Wave Metaphor," *Feminist Studies* 38, no. 3 (2012): 659; Laughlin et al. "Is It Time to Jump Ship? Historians Rethink the Waves Metaphor."

3. Sara Evans, *Tidal Wave: How Women Changed America at Century's End* (New York: The Free Press, 2003): 5.

4. Margaret C. Root, "Introduction: Women of the Field, Defining the Gendered Experience," in *Breaking Ground: Pioneering Women Archaeologists*, edited by Getzel M. Cohen and Martha S. Joukowsky (Ann Arbor: University of Michigan Press, 2004), 22–23.

5. Root, "Introduction," 20.

6. Margaret Murray, *My First Hundred Years* (London: William Kimber, 1963): 116; Root, "Introduction," 21–22.

7. See chapter 1.

8. Root, "Introduction," 19.

9. Janet Wallach, *Desert Queen, The Extraordinary Life of Gertrude Bell: Adventurer, Adviser to Kings, Ally of Lawrence of Arabia* (New York: Anchor Books, 2005): 82.

10. Evans, *Tidal Wave: How Women Changed America at Century's End*: 5.

11. Hewitt, "Feminist Frequencies: Regenerating the Wave Metaphor," 665. See also chapter 5.

12. See chapter 5.

13. See chapter 1.

14. Tracey Cullen, "Celebrating 75 Years of Hesperia," *Hesperia* 76, no. 1 (2007): 11.

15. For a vivid, firsthand account of what it was like for a woman seeking to become an archaeologist in the 1970s and 1980s, see Diane Z. Chase, "Archaeology, the Academy, and Women: Finding One's Own Path," *Heritage* 4 (2021): 1725–36. Chase discusses the women in the lab, men in the trenches phenomenon. For a more thorough and contemporary discussion of the phenomenon, see as well, Joan M. Gero, "Gender Bias in Archaeology: A Cross-Cultural Perspective," in *The Socio-Politics of Archaeology*, edited by J. M. Gero, D. M. Lacy, and M. L. Blakey (Amherst: Department of Anthropology, University of Massachusetts, 1983), 51–57.

16. Margaret W. Conkey and Janet D. Spector, "Archaeology and the Study of Gender," *Advances in Archaeological Method and Theory* 7 (1984): 1–38.

17. For a summary of some of the most significant works, see Margaret Conkey, "Has Feminism Changed Archaeology," *Signs* 28, no. 3 (2003): 867–80; Lauren E. Talalay, "Indiana Joans," *Archaeology* 47, no. 3 (1994): 60–61; Tracey Cullen, "Contributions to Feminism in Archaeology," *American Journal of Archaeology* 100, no. 2 (1996): 409–14.

18. For a contemporary examination of sexism, see Gero, "Gender Bias in Archaeology"; Chase's reflections on the time period are also instructive; see "Archaeology, the Academy, and Women: Finding One's Own Path."

19. Joan M. Gero, "Socio-Politics and the Woman-at-Home Ideology," *American Antiquity* 50, no. 2 (1985): 342–50.

20. For a good summary of these theoretical developments and their impact on classical archaeology, see Stephen L. Dyson, "From New to New Age Archaeology: Archaeological Theory and Classical Archaeology – A 1990s Perspective," *American Journal of Archaeology* 97, no. 2 (1993): 195–206.

21. Louise Zarmati, "Gendered Past: A Critical Bibliography of Gender in Archaeology," *American Journal of Archaeology*, 98 no. 4 (1994), 773; Cullen "Celebrating 75 Years of Hesperia": 8.

22. Michael Fotiadis, "What Is Archaeology's 'Mitigated Objectivism' Mitigated By? Comments on Wylie," *American Antiquity* 59, no. 3 (1994): 545–55; Margaret

Conkey, "Has Feminism Changed Archaeology," 873; Tracey Cullen, "Contributions to Feminism in Archaeology," 410; Talalay, "Indiana Joans," 62; Gero, "Socio-Politics and the Woman-at-Home Ideology," 343.

23. Tracey Cullen, "Contributions to Feminism in Archaeology," 414.

24. James Russell, "From the President: Heroines of Archaeology," *Archaeology* 46, no. 6 (1993): 6.

25. Michael Fotiadis, "What Is Archaeology's 'Mitigated Objectivism' Mitigated By? Comments on Wylie," 546; Margaret Conkey, "Has Feminism Changed Archaeology," 873.

26. Talalay, "Indiana Joans."

27. For a much more thorough discussion and definition of third-wave feminism and the #MeToo movement, see R. Claire Snyder, "What Is Third-Wave Feminism? A New Directions Essay," *Signs* 34, no. 1 (2008): 175–96 and Hewitt, "Feminist Frequencies: Regenerating the Wave Metaphor"; Lisa Hodgetts, Kisha Supernant, Natasha Lyons, and John R. Welch, "Broadening #MeToo: Tracking Dynamics in Canadian Archaeology through a Survey on Experiences within the Discipline," *Canadian Journal of Archaeology* 44, (2020): 22. https://canadianarchaeology.com/caa/publications/canadian-journal-archaeologyjournal-canadien-darcheologie/44/1/020-047, accessed September 30, 2022.

28. Root, "Introduction," 5–10.

29. Just a few examples include *Women in Archaeology*, edited by Cheryl Claassen (Philadelphia: University of Pennsylvania Press, 1994); Aileen Fox, *Aileen: A Pioneering Archaeologist* (Leominster, Herefordshire, UK: Gracewing, 2000); *Breaking Ground: Pioneering Women Archaeologists*, edited by Getzel M. Cohen and Martha S. Joukowsky (Ann Arbor: University of Michigan Press, 2004); Nicholas K. Rauh, "Elisabeth Lyding Will, 1924–2009," *American Journal of Archaeology* 114, no. 3 (2010): 547–48; Lydia C. Carr, *Tessa Verney Wheeler: Women and Archaeology before World War II* (Oxford: Oxford University Press, 2012); Chase, "Archaeology, the Academy, and Women: Finding One's Own Path," 1725–36; Alice Beck Kehoe, *Girl Archaeologist: Sisterhood in a Sexist Profession* (Lincoln: University of Nebraska Press, 2022).

30. Tracey Cullen, "Research and Publication in Classical Archaeology in the United States," in *Engendering Aphrodite: Women and Society in Ancient Cyprus*, edited by Diane Bolger and Nancy Serwint (Boston, American Schools of Oriental Research, 2002): 434–36.

31. Root, "Introduction," 30; Cullen, "Research and Publication in Classical Archaeology in the United States," 434.

32. Gero, "Socio-Politics and the Woman-at-Home Ideology." Other examples include Lisa Hodgetts et al., "Broadening #MeToo"; Megan Goulding, Kristal Buckley, and Gabrielle Brennan, "The Role of Gender in Archaeological Career Structures: A Victorian Case Study," in *Women in Archaeology, A Feminist Critique*, edited by Hilary du Cros and Laurajane Smith (Canberra: The Australian National University, 1993), 222–31; Marilyn Truscott and Laurajane Smith, "Some Descriptive Statistics

of Permanent Employment in Australian Archaeology," in *Women in Archaeology, A Feminist Critique*, edited by Hilary du Cros and Laurajane Smith (Canberra: The Australian National University, 1993), 217–21; Stephanie Moser, "On Disciplinary Culture: Archaeology as Fieldwork and Its Gendered Associations," *Journal of Archaeological Method and Theory* 14, no. 3 (2007): 235–63; Joann K. Bowman and Sean Ulm, "Grants, Gender and Glass Ceilings? An Analysis of ARC-Funded Archaeology Projects," *Australian Archaeology* 68 (2009): 31–36; Dana N. Bardolph, "A Critical Evaluation of Recent Gendered Publishing Trends in American Archaeology," *American Antiquity* 79, no. 3 (2014): 522–40; Laura E. Heath-Stout, "Guest Editorial Introduction: Gender, Equity, and the Peer Review Process at the Journal of Field Archaeology," *Journal of Field Archaeology* 45, no. 3 (2020): 135–39.

33. Cullen, "Research and Publication in Classical Archaeology in the United States," 435.

34. Tracey Cullen, "A Profile of Aegean Prehistorians, 1984–2003," in *Prehistorians Round the Pond: Reflections on Aegean Prehistory as a Discipline*, edited by John F. Cherry, Despina Margomenou, and Lauren E. Talalay (Ann Arbor, MI: Kelsey Museum of Archaeology, 2005): 58.

35. Cullen, "A Profile of Aegean Prehistorians, 1984–2003," 53.

36. For example, Lisa Hodgetts et al., "Broadening #MeToo"; Laura E. Heath-Stout, "Who Writes about Archaeology? An Intersectional Study of Authorship in Archaeological Journals," *American Antiquity* 85 no. 3 (2020): 407–26.

37. For a discussion of events at the Society for American Archaeology conference, see Lizzie Wade, "#MeToo Controversy Erupts at Archaeology Meeting," *Science* 364, no. 6437 (April 15, 2019): 219–20.

38. Heath-Stout, "Guest Editorial Introduction," 135.

39. Lisa Hodgetts et al., "Broadening #MeToo," 24; Maureen Meyers, "Task Force Stage 2 and Principle No. 9 of the SAA Principles of Archaeological Ethics Safe Educational and Workplace Environment," *The SAA Archaeological Record* 21, no. 2 (2021): 41–44; Maureen S. Meyers, Elizabeth T. Horton, Edmond A. Boudreaux, Stephen B. Carmody, Alice P. Wright, and Victoria G. Dekle, "The Context and Consequences of Sexual Harassment in Southeastern Archaeology," *Advances in Archaeological Practice* 6 (2018): 275–87; Amber VanDerwarker, Kaitlin Brown, Toni Gonzalez, and Hugh Radde, "The UCSB Gender Equity Project: Taking Stock of Mentorship, Equity, and Harassment in California Archaeology through Qualitative Survey Data," *California Archaeology* 10 (2018): 131–58.

40. Lisa Hodgetts et al., "Broadening #MeToo," 21.

41. Wade, "#MeToo Controversy Erupts at Archaeology Meeting."

42. Brenna Hassett, Tori Herridge, Suzanne Pilaar Birch, and Rebecca Wragg Sykes, *TrowelBlazers*, https://trowelblazers.com/, accessed July 14, 2022.

43. Natalia Vogeikoff-Brogan, "Tales of Olynthus: Spoken and Unspoken." *From the Archivist's Notebook* (October 1, 2015): https://nataliavogeikoff.com/2015/10/01/tales-of-olynthus-spoken-and-unspoken/, accessed June 30, 2022.

44. Alan Kaiser, "The Long-Suppressed Story of One Woman's Discoveries and the Man Who Stole Credit for Them" *Indiana History Blog* (2017): https://blog.history.in.gov/tag/mary-ellingson/, accessed July 14, 2022.

45. Jennie Ebeling, Al Reem Al-Alawi, Suad Alharrasi, Wajd Alzakwani, Lauren Bray, Abigail Ecklund, Avy Henrikson, and Katcha Papesh, "Mary Ross Ellingson (1908–1993): Canadian Archaeologist Known for Her Work with Greek Terracotta Figurines," *Archaeologists You Should Know* (2021): https://www.archaeological.org/archaeologists-you-should-know-ellingson/, accessed July 14, 2022.

~

References

Agard, Walter R. "Review of *Excavations at Olynthus, Part VII: The Terra-Cottas Found in 1931* by David M. Robinson." *Classical Journal* 30, no. 3 (1934): 173–74.

The Alberta Women's Memory Project. "Profiles of Alberta Women: Geneva Misener," May 10, 2022. Accessed June 29, 2022. http://awmp.athabascau.ca/profiles/gmisener/.

Albright, Frank P. "Red Figured Vases of Olynthus Found in 1934." MA thesis, Johns Hopkins University, 1936.

———. "Funeral Customs of the Greeks." PhD diss., Johns Hopkins University, 1940.

Alexander, John A. "Potidaea." PhD diss., Johns Hopkins University, 1939.

———. *Potidaea.* Athens: University of Georgia Press, 1963.

Allen, Susan H. "The Archaeology of the AIA: An Introduction." In *Excavating Our Past: Perspectives on the History of the Archaeological Institute of America*, edited by Susan H. Allen, Colloquia and Conference Papers 5, 1–28. Boston: Archaeological Institute of America, 2002.

———. *Classical Spies: American Archaeologists with the OS in World War II Greece.* Ann Arbor: University of Michigan Press, 2011.

"Allies Bomb Salonika Bases." *New York Times*, October 28, 1943, 3.

Allsebrook, Mary. *Born to Rebel: The Life of Harriet Boyd Hawes.* Oxford: Oxbow Books, 1992.

American Association of University Professors. "Academic Freedom and Tenure." *Bulletin of the American Association of University of Professors* 26, no. 1 (1940): 49–54.

Andres, Lesley, and Maria Adamuti-Trache. "You've Come a Long Way, Baby? Persistent Gender Inequality in University Enrolment and Completion in Canada, 1979–2004." *Canadian Public Policy / Analyse de Politiques* 33 no. 1 (2007): 93–116.

Archaeological Institute of America. "Seventy-Second General Meeting of the Archaeological Institute of America." *American Journal of Archaeology* 75, no. 2 (1971): 194–217.

———. "Archaeological Institute of America Award for Distinguished Service Gladys Davidson Weinberg." *American Journal of Archaeology* 90, no. 2 (1986): 173.

———. "Saul S. Weinberg." *American Journal of Archaeology* 90, no. 2 (1986): 174.

Bardolph, Dana N. "A Critical Evaluation of Recent Gendered Publishing Trends in American Archaeology." *American Antiquity* 79, no. 3 (2014): 522–40.

Bathurst, William H. *Roman Antiquities at Lydney Park, Gloucestershire.* London: Longmans, Green, 1879. Accessed August 12, 2010. https://archive.org/details/romanantiquitie00bathgoog.

Blegen, Carl W. "Review of *Excavations at Olynthus, Part II: Architecture and Sculpture: Houses and Other Buildings* by David M. Robinson." *American Journal of Archaeology* 36, no. 3 (1932): 368–69.

Bolger, Diane L. "Ladies of the Expedition: Harriet Boyd Hawes and Edith Hall at Work in Mediterranean Archaeology." In *Women in Archaeology*, edited by Cheryl Claassen, 41–50. Philadelphia: University of Pennsylvania Press, 1994.

Bowman, Joann K., and Sean Ulm. "Grants, Gender and Glass Ceilings? An Analysis of ARC-Funded Archaeology Projects." *Australian Archaeology* 68 (2009): 31–36.

Brown, David. *Aircraft Carriers.* New York: Arco Publishing, 1977.

Brown, Shelby. "Feminist Research in Archaeology: What Does It Mean? Why Is It Taking So Long?" In *Feminist Theory and the Classics*, edited by Nancy Sorkin Rabinowitz and Amy Richlin, 238–70. New York: Routledge, 1993.

Cahill, Nicholas. *Household and City Organization at Olynthus.* New Haven, CT: Yale University Press, 2002.

Carr, Lydia C. *Tessa Verney Wheeler: Women and Archaeology before World War II.* Oxford: Oxford University Press, 2012.

Chamberlain, Mariam K. *Women in Academe: Progress and Prospects.* New York: Russell Sage Foundation, 1988.

Chamonard, Joseph. *Exploration archéologique de Délos. Fascicule viii. Le Quartier du Théâtre.* Paris: E. de Boccard, 1924.

———. *Exploration archéologique de Délos. Fascicule xiv. Les mosaïques de la Maison des Masques.* Paris: E. de Boccard, 1933.

Chase, Diane Z. "Archaeology, the Academy, and Women: Finding One's Own Path." *Heritage* 4 (2021): 1725–36.

Chiswick, Barry R., Nicholas Larsen, and Paul Pieper. "The Production of PhDs in the United States and Canada." *IZA Discussion Paper Series* no. 5367 (2010). Accessed July 22, 2022. https://www.iza.org/publications/dp/5367.

City of Edmonton Development. *Edmonton Population, Historical*, 2008. Accessed June 29, 2022. http://webdocs.edmonton.ca/InfraPlan/demographic/Edmonton%20Population%20Historical.pdf.

Clement, Jr., Paul Augustus. *Thessalian Cults*. PhD diss., Johns Hopkins University, 1930.

———. "Review of *Excavations at Olynthus, Part VIII: The Hellenic House, a Study of the Houses Found at Olynthus with a Detailed Account of Those Excavated in 1931 and 1934* by David M. Robinson and J. Walter Graham." *L'Antiquité Classique* 8 (1939): 474–77.

Clogg, Richard. *A Short History of Modern Greece*. New York: Cambridge University Press, 1979.

Cohen, Getzel M., and Martha S. Joukowsky (Eds.). *Breaking Ground: Pioneering Women Archaeologists*. Ann Arbor: University of Michigan Press, 2004.

Conkey, Margaret W. "Has Feminism Changed Archaeology." *Signs* 28, no. 3 (2003): 867–80.

Conkey, Margaret W., and Janet D. Spector. "Archaeology and the Study of Gender." *Advances in Archaeological Method and Theory* 7 (1984): 1–38.

Cook, R. M. "Review of *Excavations at Olynthus, Part XIV: Terracottas, Lamps and Coins Found in 1934 and 1938* by D. M. Robinson." *Classical Review* 5, no. 3/4 (1955): 326–27.

Cookingham, Mary E. "Combining Marriage, Motherhood, and Jobs before World War II: Women College Graduates, Classes of 1905–1935." *Journal of Family History* 9, no. 2 (1984): 178–95.

Couch, Hebert N. "Sources for the Study of Sardis." MA thesis, Johns Hopkins University, 1926.

———. "Treasuries of the Greeks and Romans." PhD diss., Johns Hopkins University, 1927.

———. *Treasuries of the Greeks and Romans*. Menasha, WI: George Banta, 1929.

Craft, John R. "The City Drainage at Olynthus." MA thesis, Johns Hopkins University, 1939.

———. "The Civic Water Supply of Ancient Greece." PhD diss., Johns Hopkins University, 1940.

Cullen, Tracey. "Contributions to Feminism in Archaeology." Review of *Women in Prehistory* by Margaret Ehrenberg; *Engendering Archaeology: Women and Prehistory* by Joan M. Gero and Margaret Conkey; *The Archaeology of Gender: Proceedings of the 22nd Annual Chacmool Conference* by Dale Waide and Noreen D. Willows; *Exploring Gender through Archaeology: Selected Papers from the 1991 Boone Conference* by Cheryl Claassen; *Women in Archaeology* by Cheryl Claassen; *Equity Issues for Women in Archaeology* by Margaret C. Nelson, Sara M. Nelson, and Alison Wylie; *Women in Ancient Societies: "An Illusion of the Night"* by Léonie J. Archer, Susan Fischler, and Maria Wyke. *American Journal of Archaeology* 100, no. 2 (1996): 409–14.

———. "Research and Publication in Classical Archaeology in the United States." In *Engendering Aphrodite: Women and Society in Ancient Cyprus*, edited by Diane Bolger and Nancy Serwint, 434–36. Boston, American Schools of Oriental Research, 2002.

———. "A Profile of Aegean Prehistorians, 1984–2003." In *Prehistorians Round the Pond: Reflections on Aegean Prehistory as a Discipline*, edited by John F. Cherry, Despina Margomenou, and Lauren E. Talalay, 43–72. Ann Arbor, MI: Kelsey Museum of Archaeology, 2005.

———. "Celebrating 75 Years of Hesperia." *Hesperia* 76, no. 1 (2007): 1–20.

Davidson, Gladys R. "Miscellaneous Finds from Corinth, 1896–1933." PhD diss., Johns Hopkins University, 1935.

de Miroschedji, Pierre. "Obituary for Gladys Davidson Weinberg." *Israel Exploration Journal* 52, no. 2 (2002): 97–98.

Des Jardins, Julie. *The Madame Curie Complex: The Hidden History of Women in Science*. New York: Feminist Press of the City University of New York, 2010.

Dessy, Raymond. *Exile from Olynthus. Women in Archaeology.com. Mentoring and Networking in Greece, 1927–1928*, 2005. Accessed August 13, 2010. http://scholar.lib.vt.edu/faculty_archives/dessy/T_HOME-PAGE.htm.

Dincauze, Dena F. "Exploring Career Styles in Archaeology." In *Rediscovering Our Past: Essays on the History of American Archaeology*, edited by Jonathan E. Reyman, 131–36. Aldershot: Avebury, 1992.

"Dr. Arthur Parsons." *New York Times*, October 1, 1948, 26.

"Dr. Robinson Dies; Archaeologist, 77." *New York Times*, January 3, 1958, 21.

Dohan, Edith H. "Review of *Excavations at Olynthus, Part IV: The Terra-cottas of Olynthus, Found in 1928* by David M. Robinson." *American Journal of Archaeology* 36, no. 2 (1932): 207–8.

Dow, Sterling. "Review of *Excavations at Olynthus, Part XIV* by David M. Robinson." *The American Historical Review* 58, no. 3 (1953): 586–87.

Dyson, Stephen L. "From New to New Age Archaeology: Archaeological Theory and Classical Archaeology – A 1990s Perspective." *American Journal of Archaeology* 97, no. 2 (1993): 195–206.

———. *Ancient Marbles to American Shores: Classical Archaeology in the United States*. Philadelphia: University of Pennsylvania Press, 1998.

Ebeling, Jennie, Al Reem Al-Alawi, Suad Alharrasi, Wajd Alzakwani, Lauren Bray, Abigail Ecklund, Avy Henrikson, and Katcha Papesh. "Mary Ross Ellingson (1908–1993): Canadian Archaeologist Known for Her Work with Greek Terracotta Figurines." *Archaeologists You Should Know* (2021). Accessed July 14, 2022. https://www.archaeological.org/archaeologists-you-should-know-ellingson/.

"Edmonton Girl Finds Interest in Archaeology." *The Albertan*, September 18, 1931.

Elderkin, George Wicker. *Antioch-on-the-Orontes I*. Princeton, NJ: Princeton University Press, 1934.

———. "Review of *Excavations at Olynthus, Part VII: The Terra-Cottas Found in 1931* by David M. Robinson." *American Journal of Archaeology* 38, no. 3 (1934): 497.

Evans, Sara. *Tidal Wave: How Women Changed America at Century's End*. New York: The Free Press, 2003.

"Excavations in Old Greece Are Recounted." *Evansville Courier and Press*, March 3, 1940.

Fishman, Aleisa. "Gladys Davidson Weinberg 1909–2002." In *Jewish Women in America: An Historical Encyclopedia*, edited by E. Paula Hyman and Debora D. Moore, 1462. New York: Routledge, 1997.

Flaherty, Colleen. "Not-So-Cardinal Sin?" *Inside Higher Ed*, 2014. Accessed September 29, 2022. https://www.insidehighered.com/news/2014/07/28/why-does-academic-plagiarism-not-offend-much-public.

Fotiadis, Michael. "What Is Archaeology's 'Mitigated Objectivism' Mitigated By? Comments on Wylie." *American Antiquity* 59, no. 3 (1994): 545–55.

Fotou, Vasso, and Ann Brown. "Harriet Boyd Hawes, 1871–1945." In *Breaking Ground: Pioneering Women Archaeologists*, edited by Getzel M. Cohen and Martha S. Joukowsky, 198–273. Ann Arbor: University of Michigan Press, 2004.

"Four College Girls Join Olynthus Quest." *New York Times*, February 15, 1931, 33.

Fox, Aileen. *Aileen: A Pioneering Archaeologist*. Leominster, Herefordshire, UK: Gracewing, 2000.

Freeman, Sarah E. "The Excavation of a Roman Temple at Corinth." PhD diss., Johns Hopkins University, 1934.

———. "Temple E at Corinth." In *Corinth, Results of Excavations Conducted by the American School of Classical Studies at Athens* I.2: *Architecture*, edited by Richard Stillwell, Robert L. Scranton, and Sarah E. Freeman, 166–236. Princeton, NJ: American School of Classical Studies at Athens, 1941.

Freidenreich, Harriet Pass. "Joining the Faculty Club: Jewish Women Academics in the United States." *Nashim: A Journal of Jewish Women's Studies and Gender Issues* 13 (2007): 68–101.

"G. E. Mylonas, 89, Archeologist Who Led Greek Excavations, Dies." *New York Times*, May 2, 1988, D14.

Gaca, Kathy L. "Alan Kaiser, *Archaeology, Sexism, and Scandal: The Long-Suppressed Story of One Woman's Discoveries and the Man Who Stole Credit for Them*." *Byrn Mawr Classical Review*, February 2, 2015. Accessed July 23, 2022. http:// http://www.bmcreview.org/2015/02/20150203.html.

Gero, Joan M. "Gender Bias in Archaeology: A Cross-Cultural Perspective." In *The Socio-Politics of Archaeology*, edited by J. M. Gero, D. M. Lacy, and M. L. Blakey, 51–57. Amherst: Department of Anthropology, University of Massachusetts, 1983.

———. "Socio-Politics and the Woman-at-Home Ideology." *American Antiquity* 50, no. 2 (1985): 342–50.

Goldman, Hetty. "Excavations of the Fogg Museum at Colophon." Paper presented at the fourteenth annual meeting of the Archaeological Institute of America, Washington, DC, December 29, 1922. *American Journal of Archaeology* 27 (1923): 67–68.

Goulding, Megan, Kristal Buckley, and Gabrielle Brennan. "The Role of Gender in Archaeological Career Structures: A Victorian Case Study." In *Women in Archaeology, A Feminist Critique*, edited by Hilary du Cros and Laurajane Smith, 222–31. Canberra: The Australian National University, 1993.

Graham, J. Walter. "Domestic Architecture in Classical Greece." PhD diss., Johns Hopkins University, 1933.

———. "Lamps from Olynthus, 1931." In *Excavations at Olynthus V: Mosaics, Vases, and Lamps of Olynthus Found in 1928 and 1931*, edited by David M. Robinson, 265–84. Baltimore, MD: Johns Hopkins University Press, 1933.

———. "Review of *Excavations at Olynthus XII: Domestic and Public Architecture* by D. M. Robinson." *American Historical Review* 53, no. 1 (1947): 145–46.

Gude, Mabel. "A History of Olynthus." PhD diss., Johns Hopkins University, 1930.

———. *A History of Olynthus, with a Prosopographia and Testimonia. Johns Hopkins University Studies in Archaeology* 17. Baltimore, MD: Johns Hopkins University Press, 1933.

Haagsma, Margriet. "Historiography and Theory." *Journal of Greek Archaeology* 5 (2020): 630–40.

Hanfmann, George M. A. *Metal Objects from Olynthus*. PhD diss., Johns Hopkins University, 1935.

———. *The David Moore Robinson Bequest of Classical Art and Antiquities*. Boston: Harvard University Press, 1961.

Hassett, Brenna, Tori Herridge, Suzanne Pilaar Birch, and Rebecca Wragg Sykes. *TrowelBlazers*. Accessed July 14, 2022. https://trowelblazers.com/.

Heath-Stout, Laura E. "Guest Editorial Introduction: Gender, Equity, and the Peer Review Process at the Journal of Field Archaeology." *Journal of Field Archaeology* 45, no. 3 (2020): 135–39.

———. "Who Writes about Archaeology? An Intersectional Study of Authorship in Archaeological Journals." *American Antiquity* 85 no. 3 (2020): 407–26.

Herbert, Sharon C. "Saul S. Weinberg, 1911–1992." *American Journal of Archaeology* 97, no. 3 (1993): 567–59.

Hewitt, Nancy A. "Feminist Frequencies: Regenerating the Wave Metaphor." *Feminist Studies* 38, no. 3 (2012): 658–80.

Higgins, Reynold A. "Review of *Excavations at Olynthus, Part XIV: Terracottas, Lamps and Coins Found in 1934 and 1938* by D. M. Robinson." *Antiquaries Journal* 35 (1955): 97.

———. "Review of *Excavations at Olynthus, Part XIV: Terracottas, Lamps and Coins Found in 1934 and 1938* by D. M. Robinson." *Journal of Hellenic Studies* 75 (1955): 180–81.

Hill, Ida Thallon, and Lida Shaw King. *Corinth, Results of Excavations Conducted by the American School of Classical Studies at Athens IV, Part I: Decorated Architectural Terracottas*. Princeton, NJ: American School of Classical Studies at Athens, 1929.

Hills, E. C. "The Degree of Doctor of Philosophy." *Bulletin of the American Association of University Professors* 12, no. 3 (1929): 163–85.

Hodgetts, Lisa, Kisha Supernant, Natasha Lyons, and John R. Welch. "Broadening #MeToo: Tracking Dynamics in Canadian Archaeology through a Survey on Experiences within the Discipline." *Canadian Journal of Archaeology* 44, (2020): 20–47. Accessed September 30, 2022. https://canadianarchaeology.com/caa/publications/canadian-journal-archaeologyjournal-canadien-darcheologie/44/1/020-047.

Hollenshead, Carol S., Stacey A. Wenzel, Barbara B. Lazarus, and Indira Nair. "The Graduate Experience in the Sciences and Engineering: Rethinking a Gendered Institution." In *The Equity Equation: Fostering the Advancement of Women in the Sciences, Mathematics, and Engineering*, edited by Cinda-Sue Davis, Angela B. Ginorio, Carol S. Hollenshead, Barbara B. Lazarus, and Paula M. Rayman, 122–62. San Francisco: Jossey-Bass, 1996.

Home, Stewart. "Auto-Plagiarism." In *Plagiarism: Art as Commodity and Strategies for Its Negation*, edited by Stewart Home, 5–6. London: Aporia Press, 1987.

Hornig, Lilli S. "Affirmative Action through Affirmative Attitudes." In *Women in Academia: Evolving Policies toward Equal Opportunities*, edited by Elga Wasserman, Arie Y. Lewin, and Linda H. Bleiweis, 8–19. New York: Praeger Publishers, 1975.

Iakovidis, Spyros. "George Emmanuel Mylonas, 1898–1988." *American Journal of Archaeology* 93 (1989): 235–37.

"In Memoriam: Sarah Elizabeth Freeman 1907–1986." *Ákoue*, Spring 1986, 12.

Irwin-Williams, Cynthia. "Women in the Field: The Role of Women in Archaeology before 1960." In *Women of Science: Righting the Record*, edited by G. Kass-Simon and Patricia Farnes, 1–41. Bloomington: University of Indiana Press, 1990.

"Italians Raid Salonika." *New York Times*, January 27, 1941, 2.

Johnson, Franklin P. "Review of *Excavations at Olynthus, Part II: Architecture and Sculpture: Houses and Other Buildings* by David M. Robinson." *Art Bulletin* 12, no. 4 (1930): 421–22.

———. "Review of *Excavations at Olynthus, Part III: The Coins Found at Olynthus in 1928* by David M. Robinson and *Excavations at Olynthus, Part IV: The Terra-cottas of Olynthus, Found in 1928* by David M. Robinson." *Classical Philology* 26, no. 3 (1931): 339–40.

Kaiser, Alan. "The Long-Suppressed Story of One Woman's Discoveries and the Man Who Stole Credit for Them." *Indiana History Blog* (2017). Accessed July 14, 2022. https://blog.history.in.gov/tag/mary-ellingson/.

Kalman, Jason. "Dark Places around the University: The Johns Hopkins University Admissions Quota and the Jewish Community, 1945–1951." *Hebrew Union College Annual* 81 (2010): 233–79.

Kehoe, Alice Beck. *Girl Archaeologist: Sisterhood in a Sexist Profession*. Lincoln: University of Nebraska Press, 2022.

Kelley, Jane H. "Being and Becoming." In *Rediscovering Our Past: Essays on the History of American Archaeology*, edited by Jonathan E. Reyman, 81–90. Aldershot: Avebury, 1992.

Klinger, George. *We Face the Future Unafraid: A Narrative History of the University of Evansville*. Evansville, IN: University of Evansville Press, 2003.

Kourelis, Kostis. "Byzantium and the Avant-Garde: Excavations at Corinth 1920s–1930s." *Hesperia* 76, no. 2 (2007): 391–442.

———. *Peschke: Colors of Greece*. Lancaster, PA: Franklin and Marshall College, 2012.

———. "Flights of Archaeology: Peschke's Acrocorinth." *Hesperia* 86, no. 4 (2017): 723–82.

Lamb, Winifred. "Review of *Excavations at Olynthus, Part II: Architecture and Sculpture* by David M. Robinson." *Journal of Hellenic Studies* 51 (1931): 114–15.

Laughlin, Kathleen A., Julie Gallagher, Dorothy Sue Cobble, Eileen Boris, Premilla Nadasen, Stephanie Gilmore, and Leandra Zarnow. "Is It Time to Jump Ship? Historians Rethink the Waves Metaphor." *Feminist Formations* 22, no. 1 (2010): 76–135.

Lay, Eleanor B. "Terra-cottas Found at Olynthus in 1934." PhD diss., Johns Hopkins University, 1936.

Levine, David O. *The American College and the Culture of Aspiration, 1915–1940*. Ithaca, NY: Cornell University Press, 1986.

Levine, Mary Ann. "Creating Their Own Niches: Career Styles among Women in Americanist Archaeology between the Wars." In *Women in Archaeology*, edited by Cheryl Claassen, 9–40. Philadelphia: University of Pennsylvania Press, 1994.

———. "Presenting the Past: A Review of Research on Women in Archaeology." In *Equity Issues for Women in Archaeology*, edited by Margaret C. Nelson, Sarah M. Nelson, and Alison Wylie, 23–36. Archaeological Papers of the American Anthropological Association Number 5. Arlington, VA: American Anthropological Association, 1994.

Lord, Louis E. *A History of the American School of Classical Studies at Athens 1882–1942*. Cambridge, MA: Harvard University Press, 1947.

Lynn, C. D., M. E. Howells, M. J. Stein. "Family and the Field: Expectations of a Field-Based Research Career Affect Researcher Family Planning Decisions." *PLoS ONE* 13 no. 9 (2018). Accessed August 20, 2022. https://doi.org/10.1371/journal.pone.0203500.

Mallon, Thomas. *Stolen Words: Forays into the Origins and Ravages of Plagiarism*. New York: Ticknor and Fields, 1989.

"Man Convicted of Murdering Retired Professor." AP News Archive, July 7, 1987. Accessed November 21, 2013. http://www.apnewsarchive.com/1987/Man-Convicted-of-Murdering-Retired-Professor/id-7498088409c4759742230947017034d8.

McDonald, William A. *The Political Meeting Places of the Greeks*. PhD diss., Johns Hopkins University, 1940.

———. *The Political Meeting Places of the Greeks*. Johns Hopkins University Studies in Archaeology 34. Baltimore, MD: Johns Hopkins University Press, 1943.

———. "Review of *Excavations at Olynthus, Part XIV: Terracottas, Lamps and Coins Found in 1934 and 1938* by David M. Robinson." *Classical Journal* 50, no. 2 (1954): 94–95.

McDonald, William A., and George R. Rapp Jr., editors. *The Minnesota Messenia Expedition: Reconstructing a Bronze Age Regional Environment.* Minneapolis: University of Minnesota Press, 1972.

McGehee, Mary W. "Replicas of Scenes on Attic Red-figured Vases." MA thesis, Johns Hopkins University, 1926.

———. "Replica Scenes of Attic Red-figured Vases." PhD diss., Johns Hopkins University, 1932.

McGrayne, Sharon Bertsch. *Nobel Prize Women in Science. Their Lives, Struggles, and Momentous Discoveries.* New York: Brick Lane Press, 1993.

McMahon, Philip. "Review of *Excavations at Olynthus, Part III: The Coins Found at Olynthus in 1928* by David M. Robinson." *Parnassus* 3, no. 8 (1931): 34.

Medwid, Linda M. *The Makers of Classical Archaeology.* New York: Humanity Books, 2000.

Mellink, Machteld J., and Kathleen M. Quinn. "Hetty Goldman 1881–1972." In *Breaking Ground: Pioneering Women Archaeologists*, edited by Getzel M. Cohen and Martha S. Joukowsky, 298–350. Ann Arbor: University of Michigan Press, 2004.

Meredith, Christina B. "The Finger Rings Found at Olynthus in 1931 and 1934." MA thesis, Johns Hopkins University, 1937.

Merlin, Alfred. "Review of *Excavations at Olynthus, Part II: Architecture and Sculpture: Houses and Other Buildings* by David M. Robinson." *Revue Historique* 165, no. 2 (1930): 348–50.

Meritt, Lucy Shoe. *History of the American School of Classical Studies at Athens 1939–1980.* Princeton, NJ: American School of Classical Studies at Athens, 1984.

Meyers, Maureen. "Task Force Stage 2 and Principle No. 9 of the SAA Principles of Archaeological Ethics Safe Educational and Workplace Environment." *The SAA Archaeological Record* 21, no. 2 (2021): 41–44.

Meyers, Maureen S., Elizabeth T. Horton, Edmond A. Boudreaux, Stephen B. Carmody, Alice P. Wright, and Victoria G. Dekle. "The Context and Consequences of Sexual Harassment in Southeastern Archaeology." *Advances in Archaeological Practice* 6 (2018): 275–87.

"Miss Annie C. Hare Is Married in London to Dr. J. Walter Graham, Archaeologist." *New York Times*, July 26, 1934, 16.

"Mrs. Robinson's Rites Tomorrow." *Baltimore Evening Sun*, May 16, 1960.

Mitten, David G. "George Maxim Anossov Hanfmann, 1911–1986." *American Journal of Archaeology* 91, no. 2 (1987): 259–66.

Moholy-Hagy, Hattula. "Archaeology in a Gilded Age: The University of Pennsylvania Museum's Tikal Project: 1956–1970." *Codex* 29 (2021): 3–18.

Moser, Stephanie. "On Disciplinary Culture: Archaeology as Fieldwork and Its Gendered Associations." *Journal of Archaeological Method and Theory* 14, no. 3 (2007): 235–63.

Morgan, Julia B. *Women at the Johns Hopkins University: A History.* Baltimore, MD: Johns Hopkins University Press, 1986.

Müller, Valentin. *Frühe plastik in Griechenland und Vorderasien; ihre typenbildung von der neolithischen bis in die griechisch-archaische zeit (rund 3000 bis 600 v. Chr.)*. Augsburg: B. Filser, 1929.

———. "Review of *Excavations at Olynthus* by David M. Robinson." *Classical Philology* 31, no. 1 (1936): 92–93.

Murray, Margaret. *My First Hundred Years*. London: William Kimber, 1963.

Mylonas, George E. *Excavations at Olynthus I: The Neolithic Settlement. Johns Hopkins University Studies in Archaeology* 6. Baltimore, MD: Johns Hopkins University Press, 1929.

———. "Biographical Sketch." In *Studies Presented to David Moore Robinson on His Seventieth Birthday*, Vol. 1, edited by Geroge Mylonas, vii–x. St. Louis, MO: Washington University, 1951.

Mylonas, George E., and Doris Raymond (Eds.). *Studies Presented to David Moore Robinson on His Seventieth Birthday*, Vol. 2. St. Louis, MO: Washington University, 1953.

Myrdal, Alva, and Viola Klein. *Women's Two Roles: Home and Work*, second ed. London: Routledge and Kegan Paul, 1968.

Nickolaidou, Marianna. "Reviews of Books: Kaiser (A.) Archaeology, Sexism and Scandal: The Long-Suppressed Story of One Woman's Discoveries and the Man Who Stole Credit for Them." *Journal of Hellenic Studies* 137 (2017): 282–83.

Nixon, Lucia. "Gender Bias in Archaeology." In *Women in Ancient Societies: An Illusion of Night*, edited by Léonie J. Archer, Susan Fischler, and Maria Wyke, 1–23. New York: Routledge, 1994.

Obituary for Saul Weinberg. *Israel Exploration Journal* 43, no. 2/3 (1993): 198–99.

Pace, C. Robert. *They Went to College: A Study of 951 Former University Students*. Minneapolis: University of Minnesota Press, 1941.

Palmer-Sikelianos, Eva. *Upward Panic. The Autobiography of Eva Palmer-Sikelianos*. Translated by John P. Anton. Philadelphia: Harwood Academic Publishers, 1993.

Parsons, Arthur W. "The Long Walls to the Gulf." In *Corinth, Results of Excavations Conducted by the American School of Classical Studies at Athens III.2: The Defenses of Acrocorinth and the Lower Town*, edited by Rhys Carpenter and Antoine Bon, 84–127. Princeton, NJ: American School of Classical Studies at Athens, 1936.

———. "Klepsydra and the Paved Court of the Python." PhD diss., Johns Hopkins University, 1942.

———. "Klepsydra and the Paved Court of the Python." *Hesperia* 12, no. 3 (1943): 191–267.

Perrot, Paul N. "Gladys Davidson Weinberg—A Tribute." *Journal of Glass Studies* 24 (1982): 8–9.

———. "Gladys Davidson Weinberg (1909–2002)." *Journal of Glass Studies* 44 (2002): 211–15.

"Pioneer Residents of Edmonton to Mark 67th Wedding Day." *Edmonton Bulletin*, December 31, 1940.

Pitard, Wayne T. "Alexander the Great: How Grad Student Alexander Schulz Became a Key Figure in the Museum's History." *Spurlock Museum Magazine* (Fall, 2012): 6–8.

Rauh, Nicholas K. "Elisabeth Lyding Will, 1924–2009." *American Journal of Archaeology* 114, no. 3 (2010): 547–48.

Reyman, Jonathan E. "Women in American Archaeology: Some Historical Notes and Comments." In *Rediscovering Our Past: Essays on the History of American Archaeology*, edited by Jonathan E. Reyman, 69–80. Aldershot: Avebury, 1992.

Robinson, David M. "Greek and Latin Inscriptions from Asia Minor." *Transactions and Proceedings of the American Philological Association* 57 (1926): 195–237.

———. "The *Res Gestae Divi Augusti* as Recorded on the Monumentum Antiochenum." *American Journal of Philology* 47, no. 1 (1926): 1–54.

———. "Foreword to *Excavations at Olynthus I. The Neolithic Settlement* by George Mylonas." *Johns Hopkins University Studies in Archaeology* 6, vii–x. Baltimore, MD: Johns Hopkins University Press, 1929.

———. "Mosaics from Olynthus." *American Journal of Archaeology* 36, no. 1 (1932): 16–24.

———. *Excavations at Olynthus V: Mosaics, Vases, and Lamps of Olynthus Found in 1928 and 1931.* Baltimore, MD: Johns Hopkins University Press, 1933.

———. *Excavations at Olynthus VII: The Terra-Cottas of Olynthus Found in 1931.* Baltimore, MD: Johns Hopkins University Press, 1933.

———. "The Third Campaign at Olynthus." *American Journal of Archaeology* 39, no. 2 (1935): 210–47.

———. "Prähistorische und Griechische Häuser." In *Realencyclopädia der Classischen Altertumswissenschaft*, Supplementband 7, edited by August Pauly and Georg Wissowa, 224–78. Stuttgart: E. B. Metzler, 1938.

———. *Excavations at Olynthus X: Metal and Minor Miscellaneous Finds, an Original Contribution to Greek Life. Johns Hopkins University Studies in Archaeology* 31. Baltimore, MD: Johns Hopkins University Press, 1941.

———. *Excavations at Olynthus XI: Necrolynthia, a Study of Greek Burial Customs and Anthropology. Johns Hopkins University Studies in Archaeology* 32. Baltimore, MD: Johns Hopkins University Press, 1942.

———. *Excavations at Olynthus XIII: Vases Found in 1934 and 1938. Johns Hopkins University Studies in Archaeology* 38. Baltimore, MD: Johns Hopkins University Press, 1950.

———. *Excavations at Olynthus XIV: Terracottas, Lamps, and Coins found in 1934 and 1938.* Baltimore, MD: Johns Hopkins University Press, 1952.

Robinson, David M., and Paul A. Clement. *Excavations at Olynthus IX: The Chalcidic Mint and the Excavation Coins Found in 1928–1934. Johns Hopkins University Studies in Archaeology* 26. Baltimore, MD: Johns Hopkins University Press, 1938.

Robinson, David M., and J. Walter Graham. *Excavations at Olynthus VIII: The Hellenic House; a Study of the Houses Found at Olynthus with a Detailed Account of those*

Excavated in 1931 and 1934. Johns Hopkins University Studies in Archaeology 25. Baltimore, MD: Johns Hopkins University Press, 1938.

Robinson, David M., and George E. Mylonas. "The Fourth Campaign at Olynthus." *American Journal of Archaeology* 43, no. 1 (1939): 48–77.

Root, Margaret C. "Introduction: Women of the Field, Defining the Gendered Experience." In *Breaking Ground: Pioneering Women Archaeologists,* edited by Getzel M. Cohen and Martha S. Joukowsky, 1–33. Ann Arbor: University of Michigan Press, 2004.

Ross, Helen M. M. "The Terra Cotta Industry at Olynthus." MA thesis, Johns Hopkins University, 1932.

———. "The Terra-cotta Figurines of Macedonia and Thrace." PhD diss., Johns Hopkins University, 1939.

Rossiter, Margaret W. *Women Scientists in America: Struggles and Strategies to 1940.* Baltimore, MD: Johns Hopkins University Press, 1982.

Russell, James. "From the President: Heroines of Archaeology." *Archaeology* 46, no. 6 (1993): 6.

Schulz, Alexander H. G. "The Burials and Burial Customs of Prehistoric Greece." MA thesis, Johns Hopkins University, 1935.

Scranton, Robert. "Review of *Excavations at Olynthus, Part XIV: Terracottas, Lamps, and Coins Found in 1934 and 1938* by David M. Robinson." *Classical Philology* 49, no. 2 (1954): 143–44.

Shaw, Joseph W. "James Walter Graham 1906–1991." *American Journal of Archaeology* 96, no. 2 (1992): 325–26.

Shea, John. *Macedonia and Greece: The Struggle to Define a New Balkan Nation.* Jefferson, NC: McFarland, 1997.

Shoe, Lucy T. "Review of *Excavations at Olynthus, Part VIII: The Hellenic House, a Study of the Houses Found at Olynthus with a Detailed Account of Those Excavated in 1931 and 1934* by David M. Robinson and J. Walter Graham." *American Journal of Archaeology* 43, no. 4 (1939): 707–8.

Sicherman, Barbara. "College and Careers: Historical Perspectives on the Lives and Work Patterns of Women College Graduates." In *Women and Higher Education in American History,* edited by John M. Faragher and Florence Howe, 130–64. New York: W. W. Norton, 1988.

Snyder, R. Claire. "What Is Third-Wave Feminism? A New Directions Essay." *Signs* 34, no. 1 (2008): 175–96.

Snyder, Thomas D. (Ed.). *120 Years of American Education: A Statistical Portrait.* National Center for Educational Statistics, U.S. Department of Education, Office of Educational Research and Improvement, 1993. Accessed January 22, 2014. http://nces.ed.gov/pubs93/93442.pdf.

Special Collections, Milton S. Eisenhower Library, Johns Hopkins University. N.d. "Freeman (Sarah Elizabeth) 1906–1986, Papers 1944–1969, MS. Gar30." Accessed August 1, 2013. http://old.library.jhu.edu/collections/specialcollections/manuscripts/msregisters/msgar30freeman.pdf.

Spiegel, Max B. "The Garrett Collection: Coins, Medals, and Archives at the American Numismatic Society." *American Numismatic Society Magazine* 5, no. 3 (2006). Accessed November 21, 2013. http://ansmagazine.com/Winter06/Garrett.

Statistics Canada. *Education in Canada, Catalogue no. 81-229-XPB.* Ottawa: Minister of Industry, 1996. Accessed July 2, 2022. https://www150.statcan.gc.ca/n1/en/pub/81-229-x/81-229-x1996000-eng.pdf?st=wFCaCExd.

Stebbins, Eunice B. "The Letters of Augustus Preserved in Greek Inscriptions and in the Greek Writers." MA thesis, Johns Hopkins University, 1926.

———. "The Dolphin in the Literature and Art of Greece and Rome, Including Pre-Hellenic Civilizations." PhD diss., Johns Hopkins University, 1927.

———. *The Dolphin in the Literature and Art of Greece and Rome, Including Pre-Hellenic Civilizations.* Menasha, WI: George Banta, 1929.

Stillwell, Richard "Mary Hamilton Swindler (1884–1967)." *American Journal of Archaeology* 71, no. 2 (1967): 115.

Stillwell, Richard, Robert L. Scranton, and Sarah E. Freeman, editor. *Corinth, Results of Excavations Conducted by the American School of Classical Studies at Athens* I.2: *Architecture.* Princeton, NJ: American School of Classical Studies at Athens, 1941.

"Student Rebuilds Ancient Bathtub." *Baltimore Sun,* November 24, 1935.

"Students to Assist in Greek Excavation." *Baltimore Evening Sun,* February 14, 1931.

Sullivan, Lynne P. "Madeline D. Kneberg Lewis: Leading Lady of Tennessee Archaeology." In *Grit-Tempered: Early Women Archaeologists in the Southeastern United States,* edited by Nancy M. White, Lynne P. Sullivan, and Rochelle A. Marrinan, 57–91. Gainesville: University Press of Florida, 1999.

Talalay, Lauren E. "Indiana Joans." *Archaeology* 47, no. 3 (1994): 60–63.

Thompson, Homer. "In Memoriam: J. Walter Graham 1906–1991." *Ákoue* Fall (1991): 15.

Touchton, Judith G., and Lynn Davis. *Fact Book on Women in Higher Education.* New York: Macmillan, 1991.

Truscott, Marilyn, and Laurajane Smith. "Some Descriptive Statistics of Permanent Employment in Australian Archaeology." In *Women in Archaeology, A Feminist Critique,* edited by Hilary du Cros and Laurajane Smith, 217–21. Canberra: The Australian National University, 1993.

University of Mississippi, "Biographical Sketch of David Moore Robinson" (2000). Accessed September 19, 2022. https://classics.olemiss.edu/wp-content/uploads/sites/159/2011/01/Robinson_biography.pdf.

VanDerwarker, Amber, Kaitlin Brown, Toni Gonzalez, and Hugh Radde. "The UCSB Gender Equity Project: Taking Stock of Mentorship, Equity, and Harassment in California Archaeology through Qualitative Survey Data." *California Archaeology* 10 (2018):131–58.

Vogeikoff-Brogan, Natalia. "Ida Thallon Hill (1875–1954)." *Breaking Ground: Women in Old World Archaeology* (n.d.). Accessed February 2, 2014. http://www.brown.edu/Research/Breaking_Ground/bios/Hill_Ida%20Thallon.pdf.

————. "The Modern Greek Exam, 'Professor Blank's' Method, and Other Stories from the 1930s." *From the Archivist's Notebook*, October 1, 2013. Accessed December 3, 2013. https://nataliavogeikoff.com/2013/10/01/the-modern-greek-exam-professor-blanks-method-and-other-stories-from-the-1930s/.

————. "Tales of Olynthus: Spoken and Unspoken." *From the Archivist's Notebook*, October 1, 2015. Accessed June 30, 2022. https://nataliavogeikoff.com/2015/10/01/tales-of-olynthus-spoken-and-unspoken/.

Wace, Alan. "Review of *Excavations at Olynthus, Part II: Architecture and Sculpture: Houses and Other Buildings* by David M. Robinson." *Classical Review* 45, no. 2 (1931): 87.

Wade, Lizzie. "#MeToo Controversy Erupts at Archaeology Meeting." *Science* 364, no. 6437 (April 15, 2019): 219–20.

Wallach, Janet. *Desert Queen, The Extraordinary Life of Gertrude Bell: Adventurer, Adviser to Kings, Ally of Lawrence of Arabia*. New York: Anchor Books, 2005.

Weinberg, Gladys D. *Corinth, Results of Excavations Conducted by the American School of Classical Studies at Athens XII. The Minor Objects*. Princeton, NJ: American School of Classical Studies at Athens, 1952.

Weinberg, Saul S. "The Prehistoric House of the Mainland of Greece." PhD diss., Johns Hopkins University, 1936.

West, Jennifer K. "Observations on Selected Papers of David Moore Robinson from the University of Mississippi Archives." MA thesis, University of Mississippi, 1995.

White, Nancy M. "Women in Southeastern U.S. Archaeology." In *Grit-Tempered: Early Women Archaeologists in the Southeastern United States*, edited by Nancy M. White, Lynne P. Sullivan, and Rochelle A. Marrinan, 1–24. Gainesville: University Press of Florida, 1999.

Wichmann, Anna. "The Vlachs: The Proud Greeks Who Speak a Romance Language," *The Greek Reporter*, December 21, 2021. Accessed October 4, 2022, https://greekreporter.com/2021/12/21/vlachs-greece/.

Wiegand, Theodor, and Hans Schrader. *Priene: Ergebnisse der Ausgrabungen und Untersuchungen in den Jahren 1895–1898*. Berlin: G. Reimer, 1904.

Wilson, Lillian M. *The Roman Toga. Johns Hopkins University Studies in Archaeology* 1. Baltimore, MD: Johns Hopkins University Press, 1924.

————. "A Study of the Roman Toga." PhD diss., Johns Hopkins University, 1924.

————. "The Loom Weights." In *Excavations at Olynthus II Architecture and Sculpture: House and Other Buildings*, edited by D. M. Robinson, 118–28. *Johns Hopkins University Studies in Archaeology* 9. Baltimore, MD: Johns Hopkins University Press, 1930.

Winnifrith, Tom J. *The Vlachs: The History of a Balkan People*. New York: St. Martin's Press, 1987.

"Wins Degree." *Edmonton Bulletin*, June 12, 1939.

Wisenthal, M. "Section W: Education." In *Historical Statistics of Canada*, edited by F. H. Leacy. Ottawa, Statistics Canada, 1983. Accessed July 1, 2022. https://www150.statcan.gc.ca/n1/pub/11-516-x/sectionw/4147445-eng.htm.

Wood, R. C. "Review of *Excavations at Olynthus, Part XIV: Terracottas, Lamps and Coins Found in 1934 and 1938* by D. M. Robinson." *American Journal of Archaeology* 57, no. 3 (1953): 227–28.

Woodhouse, Chase Going. "Women." *American Journal of Sociology* 37, no. 6 (1932): 956–62.

Wycherley, Richard E. "Review of *Excavations at Olynthus, Part X: Metal and Minor Miscellaneous Finds: An Original Contribution to Greek Life* by David M. Robinson"; "*Excavations at Olynthus, Part XI: Necrolynthia: A Study in Greek Burial Customs and Anthropology* by David M. Robinson." *Journal of Hellenic Studies* 62 (1942): 103–4.

———. "Review of *Excavations at Olynthus XII: Domestic and Public Architecture* by D. M. Robinson." *Journal of Hellenic Studies* 66 (1946): 134–35.

———. *How the Greeks Built Cities*. London: Macmillan, 1949.

Zarmati, Louise. "Gendered Past: A Critical Bibliography of Gender in Archaeology by Elisabeth A. Bacus, Alex W. Barker, Jeffrey D. Bonevich, Sandra L. Dunavan, J. Benjamin Fitzhugh, Debra L. Gold, Nurit S. Goldman-Finn, William Griffin, and Karen M. Mudar." *American Journal of Archaeology*, 98 no. 4 (1994): 773–74.

~

Author's Note on the Locations of the Mary Ross Ellingson and David Moore Robinson Papers

Mary Ross Ellingson's papers and photographs are in two locations: with her daughter, Barbara Petersen, and in the Archives of the University of Evansville. The University Archives have placed all her photographs in one box, her thesis and dissertation in another, and all remaining letters and documents in a third box, making them easy to find. With the help of undergraduate interns and work-study students, the archives have scanned and transcribed nearly all the material, making specific photos and documents available electronically upon request. Some of her photos are available for viewing at https://faculty.evansville.edu/ak58/Ellingson/.

Primary materials about David M. Robinson are spread across three institutions and two continents. Robinson left his materials to the final institution at which he worked where they now reside in the David M. Robinson Collection, Special Collections, University of Mississippi Libraries. The specific archival box numbers are listed in the notes throughout this book. Since my visit to the Robinson Collection the archivists have done further processing of his material; as a result some of the material has been moved to new boxes rendering some of the references in the endnotes obsolete. While Robinson did not intentionally leave any primary documents or photographs to Johns Hopkins University Sheridan Libraries University Archives nor the American School of Classical Studies in Athens, numerous letters and documents by and about him are retained by these two institutions. Anyone interested in viewing or referencing the material from either library should feel free to contact the archivists; they know the material well and are always happy to help.

Index

Page references for figures are italicized.

#MeToo movement in archaeology, 252, 254–5

Acadia University, 30
Alexander, William Hardy, 15–9, 30, 148, 151, 153, 184, 186, 247
American Association of University Professors, 135, Committee W, 29
American Association of University Women, 135
American School of Classical Studies at Athens, 27, 36, 40, 41–3, 46, 64–5, 121–3, 141, 142, 144, 150, 152, 153, 178, 213, 227–8, 247, 253–4, 255, 277; early history, 26–27; fellowship program, 26, 30, 41–2, 132–3, 151, 184, 203, 248; oversight of excavators and permits, 26, 38, 39, 42–3, 116, 173, 248
anti-nepotism policies, 136
Antioch in Psidia excavation, 5, 37, 43
antisemitism, 22, 41–42, 142, 205, 207, 228, 230

Archaeological Institute of America, 37, 116, 201, 211, 214, 251, 253–4, 255, Gold Medal for Distinguished Archaeological Achievement, 6, 121, 143
Aristotle, 69
Athens, Agora excavation, 26, 28, 64–5, 115, 121, 153, 188, 213–4
Axtell, Ann, 179

Beck Kehoe, Alice, 137, 144, 179
Bennett College, 43–4
biologists, 177–8
Boston University, 281
botanists, 138, 179
Boyd Hawes, Harriet, 27–8, 140, 247
Brown, Shelby, 183

Cahill, Nicholas, 113
Capps, Edward, 41–3, 132
chemists, 133, 152
children, effect on career, 137–40, 153–5, 156, 248

279

~

About the Author

Alan Kaiser is a professor of archaeology at the University of Evansville and chair of the university's Department of Archaeology. He holds a BA in anthropology and history from the University of Minnesota, a PhD in archaeology from Boston University, and is certified by the Register of Professional Archaeologists. Having worked on archaeological projects in Greece, Italy, Spain, the United Kingdom, Israel, Rhode Island, Indiana, and on the Caribbean island of Nevis, Kaiser has a variety of field experience. His published works include scholarly and popular articles as well as two books aimed at a scholarly audience, *The Urban Dialogue: An Analysis of the Use of Space in the Roman City of Empúries, Spain* (2000) and *Roman Urban Street Networks* (2011). He is the recipient of the University of Evansville Arts and Sciences Dean's Teaching Award and the Sadelle and Sydney Berger Award for Scholarship.